THE HAUNTED SOUTH

JOAN FORMAN

JARROLD COLOUR PUBLICATIONS, NORWICH

First published in Great Britain by Robert Hale Ltd. 1978
First published by Jarrold Colour Publications 1989

Copyright © Joan Forman 1978

Printed in Great Britain by Jarrold Printing, Norwich. 1/89

ISBN 0-7117-0359-0

Contents

	page
Acknowledgements	4
About the author	5
Introduction	7
Kent	9
Sussex	47
Hampshire	88
Wiltshire	124
Surrey and Middlesex	152
Berkshire	184
Bibliography	209
Index	211

Acknowledgements

My thanks are due to the many people who wrote, telephoned and talked to me on the subject of the South's hauntings, and particularly to those who unhesitatingly allowed me to enter their homes and property in connection with my investigations, and patiently answered my many questions.

Particular gratitude is due to those people who took considerable trouble to verify details or undertake additional research on my behalf. Of these Mrs Sheila White and Mrs Rosemary Stevens, both of Hampshire and Mr Robert Armstrong of Sussex were exceptionally helpful, as also were my old friends, Irene and Gerald Young, formerly of Sussex. Thanks must also be given to a number of kind persons who lent me printed material.

A book of this nature can hardly be undertaken without the assistance of the media, and I should wish to thank warmly the various editors who allowed me space to appeal for case-histories, and the producer and presenter of the radio programme which gave me air space for a similar purpose.

Most of those interviewed had no objection to the use of proper names and places—for this my thanks. Where anonymity was desired, however, pseudonyms have been used and indicated by an asterisk.

Lastly, my thanks to Mrs Jill Little who typed my usual illegible manuscript as though it were written in copperplate. And to friends and relatives who, while kindly offering hospitality, were heartlessly repaid by having to listen to recitals of hauntings into the wee, sma' hours. I hope they have forgiven me.

Picture credits Britain On View Photographic Library (BTA/ETB), pp. 22, 28, 31, 138, 153, 170; Mr and Mrs F. Stevens, p. 38; Mr McKinnon, p. 59; Colonel L. Sheppard, p. 91; Hants County Magazine, p. 95; Mrs R. Stevens, p. 99; Mr David White, p. 117; The Wiltshire Gazette and Herald, p. 147; Reverend A. Millard, p. 191; Mrs E. M. Maidment, p. 199.

About the author

Joan Forman began writing professionally in the 1960s, following a successful career in educational administration. She was for several years writer/editor of 'The Poetry Page' feature in *John o'London's* and *Time & Tide*, and has contributed literary journalism to *The Times, The Sunday Times, The Daily Telegraph* and many other publications in this country and in Canada. Her work has also included poetry, drama, history, natural history and parapsychology. She is a regular broadcaster and also lectures for the Eastern Arts Association. Her knowledge of parapsychology is highly respected and she is a member of The Society for Psychical Research. Her work in this field has led to considerable television involvement, and many of her books have received wide media coverage. Her study of the nature of time, *The Mask of Time*, published in 1978, resulted in two television series based on its contents.

The present book and its companion volume, *Haunted East Anglia*, reflect her interest in the paranormal, as do *Haunted Royal Homes* (1987) and *Royal Hauntings* (1987). Her most recent work, *The Golden Shore: A Survey of the Evidence for Death Survival*, forms the important concluding work in her parapsychology series.

Joan Forman has recently completed a social history of working lives in Edwardian England (*Yesterday's England*) and *Loro's Kingdom*, a novel with a wildlife background which reflects her interest in and love of the countryside. She lives in Norfolk.

Introduction

Having written one book on the supernatural and another which acknowledges its existence, I shall have no need to declare in this volume my allegiance. In answer to the incredulous reader who would ask "Do you believe in ghosts?" I must say, "No, I do not believe in them, any more than I believe in the moon. Both seem to exist, and what *is* must be accepted."

The difficulty with a statement of this kind is that in general people only believe what they have themselves experienced, or what they know beyond doubt to have been experienced by others. In the case of hauntings and general supernatural occurrences, a considerable proportion of the population has never encountered anything of the kind, and in all probability never will, therefore they do not believe in its existence.

This does not invalidate the experiences of the many who have had paranormal encounters and will probably continue to have them. The discrepancy between the first group and the second does not mean that Group 1 is composed entirely of the sane, the rational, the ungullible, and Group 2 made up of the unbalanced, hysterical and credulous. All it signifies is that there appear to be two types of mentality in the human structure—one which is geared to an apprehension outside its five senses, and the other which is not. Science, rather than contradicting this proposition as in the past, seems likely now to become its staunch friend.

This change in attitude is spreading, for whereas the subject of hauntings was, until about ten years ago, regarded as good only for party conversation, for Hallowe'en and Christmas entertainment, it is now listened to with interest and an open-minded curiosity. No longer does the raising of the subject produce immediate ridicule or a half-afraid cold-shouldering.

I suspect the latter attitude to have arisen not so much from a feeling of intellectual superiority on the part of the sceptics as a reaction to the breach of a taboo. The supernatural has always been associated with an area of human experience which does not seem to be subject to the laws of science. And science and the rationalistic view of the cosmos with which it is associated, has come over the last hundred and fifty years to represent safety and stability in a changing world.

During the past twenty years (and particularly the last ten) the place of science itself has altered. It is no longer the major touchstone of our beliefs, but has come to be recognized as possibly only one aspect of a much larger truth.

This shift in perspective has allowed old ideas and knowledge to come to the surface. More important, it has allowed reconsideration of many questions not concerned with material living. Do we survive death? Do ghosts exist? Is reincarnation likely? These have become respectable areas for investigation—though a little suspect still in the most conservative quarters—and seen now not to contradict the great god Science, but perhaps even to support him.

Neither need the paranormal contradict the precepts of religion. Indeed, it would seem in some subtle way to be an essential part of them, sharing in the mystery which is at the heart of all religious belief.

There remains the need to test, examine and prove, to defeat the credulousness in human nature, and to apply to that end the disciplines and knowledge given us by science. Unfortunately, the supernatural will not function to order, and to test a haunting under laboratory conditions is hardly possible. One does not say "Today I will arrange to see a ghost under test conditions"; the nature of the phenomenon is that it is involuntary, unheralded. However, there are other, allied areas, where this does not apply—or does so to a lesser extent. Any reader interested in current experimental work on the paranormal will find the American, Canadian and Russian researches of value.

In the meantime, we may speculate and examine on our own account. Speculations, while never as comforting as certainties, may often lead one near the truth of a matter. Perhaps all roads arrive eventually at Rome.

Kent

If there is one county above all others which has a special place in English affections it is perhaps Kent. I suspect this is because it is a microcosm of the whole country, containing a little of everything which can be seen elsewhere. There are fine rolling hills, compact woods, fertile valleys, picturesque villages, delectable small towns and one beautiful city. Its lanes, moreover, ramble and its roads roll in the best Chesterton manner, and in spring the entire countryside is irresponsibly set alight. Not by spontaneous combustion but by pink, white, cream and red blossom, which runs wild-fire up and down the hedges, over orchards and woodland, until to walk or drive there is to be overwhelmed, half suffocated. The spring burns itself out from within, turning the little corner county into a dazzling conflagration. Flowers are everywhere; the primroses thick as cream along the hedge-banks, violets and wild hyacinth blueing the woodlands, apple and pear flowing rosily silver through the orchards.

Here and there dark conical hats protrude through the flames; the oast-houses which in autumn will reek with the dry, sweet-sour scent of the hops. A smell never to be forgotten as long as one has the use of one's memory and one's senses.

Kent is a ravishment to those senses, and one cannot help casting a glance backward to the time before the motor-car, when travel was difficult and private acres were safe from invasion. What a paradise Kent must have been then! All beauty, and seclusion, too; greenery without plastic bags, hedgerows without detergent packets, orchards without Coke bottles. Thoughts such as these floated through my mind, as I drove out of Sussex and into the green garden, along the middle route through Lamberhurst and Goudhurst and beyond.

As well as being a voyage of discovery (what and who haunts Kent?), it was also for me a journey into the past. I had not seen the county for twenty years. I had lived in it for a twelve-month and then left it, and this was the first return. How changed would I find the once familiar places?

There seemed little sign of alteration as I slid into Goudhurst. The pubs were still there though I had confused their names in my memory. The church still stood, and nobody had drained the village pond or turned it into an adventure playground. The only adventuring was being done by a pair of ducks, casually up-ended, their beaks in the alluvia, searching for food.

The Haffenden Guest House was still there, too, where I had once spent the night before an interview for a job in a nearby school. It had been June then, I remembered, with the old house supported by the strong scent of honeysuckle, epitome of early summer. Strange how the recollection of flowers dominated one's memory of this county.

I intended later to return via Goudhurst in order to visit the school where I had once worked, but before this sentimental excursion would be completed, there was much talking, listening and recording to do. Accordingly I made for the centre of the Weald, a good point from which to work outwards, and settled on and in Biddenden.

Many of the Kentish village names end in '-den', Biddenden, Tenterden, Bethersden, Marden, Benenden, Shottenden, and half a hundred others. 'Den' was once 'dene' or 'dean', a clearing in the forest, so the modern names give some indication of the kind of terrain in which our ancestors lived. The Romans found Kent heavily afforested, with the occupied areas small glades where the tribal units had settled.

What of Biddenden itself? Its dominant mnemonic is the tale of the Biddenden Maids, Siamese twins born in A.D. 1100, who lived to the age of thirty-four, joined at hips and shoulders. A charity still exists in their names—the revenue from 18 acres of land, to be spent on bread and cheese and beer for the poor of the parish. An Easter gift which must once have had considerable significance.

It would be fitting if the Maids haunted their village, but unfortunately for symmetry they do not. There are rumours that one or two old houses (and Biddenden has many) run to hauntings of the footsteps and doors variety, but I could find no verification of the rumours. The village was one of those in which the Huguenot weavers settled, bringing with them their manual skills and their spiritual dedication and refinement. One such premises in the High Street is now a tea shop, rich with the fragrance of home-baked buns and cakes and the sweet breath of a huge log fire in the inglenook. Of actual ghosts, however, authenticated sightings and soundings, there was no evidence, though much speculation.

I decided to enquire into the current happenings at Pluckley, a Weald village long noted for the number and variety of its ghosts.

Noted? Famous, more likely, for Pluckley has featured in a television programme and more than one book. However, after talking with some of the village's inhabitants I came to the conclusion that the Red Lady, the Screaming Man, the Watercress Woman and their companions no longer walk, if they ever had. However, the legendary coach and horses—in this case a coach and pair—which is said occasionally to thunder down the main street has been seen in comparatively recent times, once by a racing driver, once by a local farmer. Why phantom coaches should be so readily perpetuated after their material life is finished is difficult to say. Where there is truth in the stories, it seems usually to be associated with some violent accident in which the coach was wrecked or its occupants killed. The method of perpetuation is possibly through the passengers' heightened state of emotion in the seconds before the crash, such emotion having registered on a part of the surrounding area. I hope to throw some light into this dark statement shortly. Sufficient for the moment to say that I believe all hauntings to work by a similar process, which involves the use of energy in order that it shall operate at all.

A local man, Mr Cowles, told me two authentic stories of ghosts in the district as a counterweight to the highly-coloured standard tourist fodder which has become associated with Pluckley.

A man, his wife, son and a step-daughter, took a small cottage outside the village, and were not there long before each of them in turn saw the figure of a young girl, dressed in the costume of the late 1890s. The apparition appeared to be of a girl about the same age as the step-daughter, for whom on at least one occasion she was mistaken. The curious factor here is that apparently the members of the family saw the ghost independently, and did not confide in each other about their experiences. It was not until the young step-daughter was dying of tuberculosis that she told her mother what she had seen. After the girl's death the family seems to have left the district, so further details are unfortunately unobtainable.

Mr Cowles's second story concerned a well-known writer (whose name he preferred not to give me) who lived in a small house on the outskirts of the village. The man's wife had died, and his aunt now lived with him and acted as housekeeper.

On one occasion, a collector for the R.S.P.C.A. called at the cottage with (one assumes) her collecting-box, and on leaving she casually said goodbye to the elderly lady seated in an armchair in the sitting-room. This somewhat surprised the cottage's inhabitants as the armchair was empty at the time.

If they had not known about the female ghost, they were in no doubt at all about the male haunter of the house. It seems that the writer-occupant on a particular afternoon was about to enter his bedroom, when he heard the sound of footsteps within. He attempted to open the door but it appeared to be locked from the inside. Convinced now that someone had broken into his premises and was burgling his room, he found the nearest weapon he could lay hands on (a cricket bat) and shouted to the burglar to come out. There was no reply. He therefore struggled again with the door, finally forcing it open and half-falling into the room. He fell in good earnest a few moments afterwards, for he was forcibly flung on to the bed, by whom or what he had no idea, for the room was empty.

Not surprisingly the occupants did not remain long in the house and left Pluckley altogether. Some time afterwards, the writer himself returned briefly to the village and during his visit called in at the local stores. He must have related his nasty experience, for he was at once told that a teenage daughter of a previous occupant of his cottage had had a similar encounter, though her attacker had gone so far as to tie her in a blanket. Villagers take these things calmly. A local man who overheard this conversation commented, "Oh, that would be Billy Bandon*, the Poor Law man. He finally went potty." A laconic comment covering who knows what areas of misery.

Lacking further information, one can only assume that the unfortunate Billy had been so distraught before his death that he had carried his unquietness through the experience and beyond it. Or alternatively—and more likely—that his distress during his lifetime had been great enough to remain in the place where it had been most strongly concentrated, his own bedroom. The later interlopers merely got in the way, interfering unwittingly with the record of past proceedings.

Apart from recording individual vicissitudes, hauntings often register pieces of history, usually through presenting details of an action which belongs recognizably to the historical record of an area. Occasionally the record is so dramatic and heightened that the story takes on the quality of legend.

One tale of this nature is that of a highwayman who earned his living from the coaches which regularly cross Hothfield Common *en route* for London. Although gentlemen of the road were plentiful enough in the seventeenth and eighteenth centuries, this particular man had built himself an interesting reputation. Not only did he not rob the local Kentish folk, confining his attentions to the long-distance coach passengers, he had a genius for disappearing after a robbery. It was as though he melted into the landscape. His raids were executed with speed and efficiency and his withdrawal no less so. The coaches' rattling as they bowled along the post road, announced their coming well ahead of time, and when Robert the Highwayman descended upon them like the wrath of God, there was no argument about whether or not you stood and delivered. All did. And perhaps afterwards a few brave spirits might give chase to the elusive robber, though always unsuccessfully. Robert the Wizard, as he became known, had vanished into the nearby forest as though the very trees knew him and offered a refuge. The fact was that Robert thoroughly knew the forest and was able to go to earth and remain there until coffers needed replenishing.

In due time the Wizard over-reached himself, was caught and gibbeted on the triangle of green land marking Westwell crossroads; this according to the official view of such matters, should have been the end of him. I would have assumed this to be the case had I not received a letter from a local woman, Mrs C. M. Nicholls of Hothfield.

The Nicholls family occupy a council house in Hothfield on a fairly new estate. The house was new when they moved into it, and in fact they had watched the estate being built. One night in October 1974 Mrs Nicholls awoke abruptly, not knowing at first what had awakened her. As soon as she was fully conscious, she knew that a figure was standing on her side of the bed, near its foot. She saw the apparition quite clearly; it appeared to be wearing brown check trousers and a type of cloak. Let Mrs Nicholls herself continue: "As my eyes travelled upwards, I was horrified to see he had no head. I was shouting by this time and without taking my eyes off him, shaking my husband to wake up and look."

Her husband did wake up, but in fact could see nothing and was convinced his wife had dreamed the whole episode. This was little comfort to the lady, who was, not surprisingly, frightened. She enquired locally regarding cases of sudden death which might account for the manifestation, and although there was one instance of suicide, its subject's description did not appear to fit the ghost.

Mrs Nicholls saw the apparition just once more, and on this occasion a white mist appeared where the head should have been. She did not mention the second visitation to her family in view of their reception of the first.

Some weeks after the second encounter, an article in a local paper regarding the history of Westwell and Hothfield told the story of Robert the Wizard. Mrs Nicholls is now certain that the apparition she saw is that of the highwayman. The council estate in which she lives is very near to his old place of work, Hothfield Common. Who knows how many times he walked, rode or hid on the piece of land which is now occupied by the Nicholls's house? The pattern of a lifetime lingers in the area in which it was laid down; as does intense emotion experienced in that area. These are the photographic images, the tape-recordings of the past, which we in the present receive with such astonishment and dismay.

Not far from Hothfield lies the village of Great Chart and from one of its inhabitants, Mrs Dorothea Percy*, I heard the story of her own house which appears to possess at least one ghost, if not two. The Percies have lived in their present home for about twenty years, and the manifestations they experienced mainly took place in the earlier part of this period.

According to my correspondent, there have always been certain doors in the house which the occupants disliked having shut, rooms in which the children could not bear to remain alone. A neighbour, longer resident in the village than the Percies, told them of a "little, old white-bearded gentleman who had appeared to two strangers at separate times, sitting on their bed and 'talking' quite peacefully in the middle of the night".

However, the presence apprehended by Mrs Percy was of a very different sort, "an evil restless presence, which made me paralysed with fear". The last experience she had of this was a truly terrifying encounter about five years ago. The percipient was lying face downwards in bed, when she felt her spine gripped as though someone were trying to drag her out. She shouted to her husband, who heard her but did nothing, either thinking she was in the throes of a nightmare (to which she is subject) or fearing that to answer her might increase the terror of whatever experience she was undergoing. The subject is quite certain that on this occasion she was not having a bad dream but was on the contrary very wide awake. For a few minutes she was totally unable to move and in her own words "felt quite desperate. But somehow I managed to collect my thoughts and project some sort of love on the subject until it gradually faded away."

A highly unpleasant encounter, but with what or whom? The Percies apparently know of nothing in the history of the house to account for these repercussions. It is perhaps significant that since Mrs Percy's 'projection' towards the haunter—in itself a kind of exorcism, I think—she has had no similar experiences in the building and the evil presence now seems to be absent from the premises.

This percipient tells another story of a Kentish farmhouse at Appledore, in which her family lived for some time. She states that they had lived there for a fair period without noticing anything untoward, until one particular week when for no apparent reason she became intensely depressed and aware of a presence in the house. She thought it seemed to be of a man who was deeply unhappy. In addition to the sensation of presence, she also experienced a series of strangely sinister coincidences. Twice during the week instances of suicide were told her, and on one night when she was taking a bath, she found herself actually contemplating the act on her own account. Shocked, she hurriedly retired to bed, but on picking up her bedside book found herself reading about yet another suicide. As she reached the climax of the story, her bedside lamp fell to the floor and went out. By this time quite unnerved, she was not encouraged when she heard the dog from a nearby farm howling on her own front lawn outside the house.

Some days after these events, she began to learn a little of the house's history. A few years before the Percies' occupation of it, a doctor had lived there. In course of time his marriage failed, his wife apparently deserting him for another man. In his despair and wretchedness, he went to the small room which he used as a surgery, took an overdose of sleeping tablets, then telephoned his partner to tell him what he had done. The very room in which he had died was used by the Percies—when they could bear to stay in it—as a study. However, throughout their occupancy of the house they had found this particular room uncomfortable and unpleasant.

The week in which Dorothea Percy experienced her oppressive thoughts and hints of self-destruction was the exact anniversary of the doctor's suicide. He had died in the identical week in July thirteen years previously.

Inevitably one asks why and how such things can occur. Why should there be such an identity of date, with an exact repetition in the house of the feelings which must have been generated there originally? There is unfortunately no sure answer. It is possible that similarities of temperature and light conditions at that particular time of the year could cause a reproduction of the violent emotions which had been recorded on the first occasion. But *the exact week*? To think that coincidence of temperature and light should occur on the actual anniversary of the doctor's death and be precise enough to precipitate a repetition of the emotions involved, is to stretch credulity to its limits. Yet there must be an explanation, since Mrs Percy was unaware of the house's history at the time she experienced these strange reminders. I am convinced there is a law of some kind governing the operation of these anniversary-type hauntings. It may well be similar to that affecting coincidence, the operation of which also often exceeds the bounds of credibility.

It is this presentation of information which we have been conditioned to regard as incredible which causes such distress to witnesses of apparitions. The senses perceive that which they are unaccustomed to perceive and are unwilling to accept. The mind, indoctrinated by rational beliefs of what does and does not happen according to the material laws of the cosmos, reacts violently to the irrationality of hauntings. Such things cannot happen, but apparently they do, and if we are to dismiss these experiences as hallucinations, we must so define that term that it includes optical, aural and tangible manifestations of the many varying types which appear to occur. Personally I do not believe that the term 'hallucination' can be made to stretch so far.

Consider the following, for instance. At Kemsley near Sittingbourne is a large paper mill belonging to the nationally known firm of Bowaters. As is usual in modern establishments of this kind, the mill has its own shower rooms for the use of employees, and it was in one of these that three of the men perceived an apparition. There were two separate occurrences, one four weeks before the other. The subject of the first was a Mr Gordon May of Bobbing, near Sittingbourne. He was in the shower room and just beginning to dress when he saw a blurred figure directly in front of him. To quote his own words, "I picked up my clothes and ran like hell."

On the second occasion, two of the men were showering in the same room as that in which the first manifestation had taken place. They felt a sensation of marked chill, then saw in the corner of the room the apparition of a human figure. On this occasion there was no waiting to put on clothes; the men fled naked from the shower room. After these incidents apparently the room was locked and boarded up and has not been in use since. Mr Colin Baker of Sittingbourne, who works in Kemsley Mill, sent me this account. Although certain aspects of it are vague—for instance, why was the second manifestation regarded at once as an apparition rather than being thought to be a living human? Had the account of Gordon May predisposed the two men to expect something to occur in that particular room? But if it had, why was there a lapse of four weeks before they saw the second ghostly figure? Mr Baker himself had not had an opportunity to examine the area as by the time he took employment with the firm the room had already been closed up.

This same correspondent told me of reports concerning the road from Maidstone to Chatham. Over a period of years, drivers travelling that road after 11.00 p.m. have reported picking up a girl hitch-hiker. Apparently the girl has sometimes said that she wanted a lift into Rochester, sometimes that she had been involved in a car accident. Invariably she has travelled in the back seat of the car which picked her up, but has mysteriously disappeared before her destination was reached.

The latest incident occurred in 1974. A motorist, Maurice Goodenough of Mooring Road, Rochester, rushed into Rochester Police Station in an agitated state, saying he had hit a young girl on Bluebell Hill. He had hurriedly wrapped her in a tartan rug and left her by the roadside while he went to get help. When the police returned with the man, they found only the crumpled rug on the grass verge. Of the girl there was no sign, neither was there any mark on Maurice Goodenough's car.

There is, as you may imagine, a factual story preceding the extraordinary series of incidents reported over the years. One miserable night of wind and rain in November 1965, saw a party of four girls driving towards a public house where they had arranged to meet a young man. The man was the fiancé of one of the girls, and the other three, including twenty-two-year-old Judith Lingham, were to be bridesmaids at their marriage on the Saturday of that week. On the Thursday the girls had spent the afternoon trying on their dresses for the wedding, and had left happily in the evening for the rendezvous at the inn. The young man waited in vain, however. At a sharp bend on Bluebell Hill, their car skidded off the road. Three of the girls were killed, the fourth seriously injured.

According to descriptions of the apparition, it is Judith Lingham who haunts the fatal stretch of roadway, and since reports of the phantom hitch-hiker's behaviour vary, it would seem that this is one of the hauntings where free will rather than a laid-down repetitive pattern operates. This, in my view, lends particular interest to the case, for it suggests that whatever survives at this spot is a conscious, thinking, decision-making entity. I use the word 'survives' advisedly, for the activities of this apparition do make a case for death-survival.

There are numerous reports of ghostly hitch-hikers throughout

Britain, but these often fall into a pattern. A hitcher is picked up, usually at the same place by every vehicle which encounters the apparition, and generally vanishes at another given spot; or as a variant, will disappear immediately on being set down at its destination. By contrast, the Bluebell Hill ghost sometimes would say she wished to go into Rochester, sometimes that she had been involved in a car accident. On a least one occasion (when Maurice Goodenough's car was involved) she was actually 'struck' by the vehicle, and—most curious of all—her body picked up by the car's driver, wrapped in a rug and laid at the side of the road. Insubstantial, non-material bodies can hardly be lifted up and wrapped in a car rug. Did the 'body' on this occasion have weight and substance, then, as though it were in the flesh and alive? If not, what kind of an illusion was perpetrated that could convince Goodenough, a working bricklayer and presumably a practical man, that he had hit a living person?

The remaining possibility is that Mr Goodenough actually drove into a living girl, who after being left on the road's edge, was well enough to get up and leave it before he returned with the police. In which circumstances why was no trace of her found? If she were injured enough to be incapable of standing after the car struck her, then she would almost certainly have needed medical attention later, but it is not reported that any doctor attended a girl involved in such an accident.

Insufficient evidence is available in this case to make it possible to come to a conclusion. All that can be said is that some mystery appears to attach to Bluebell Hill near Rochester.

Perhaps it is the element of mystery which so attracts us as we plod through our prosaic twentieth-century lives. There appears to be some aspect of human nature which needs mystery, which requires the certainty of hidden and unattainable knowledge to parallel material living. Throughout Man's history this secret elusive quality has been omnipresent in his religion, hinting at some other life, some better world, some finer values than those with which he must make do in his three score and ten years as a clay creature. During the last half century that mysterious certainty has been eroded as religion has been discarded, leaving untouched and unassuaged the essential basic hunger for it. Now the sole substitute to which mankind may turn for the lost mystery is its sapling and distant echo, the supernatural. It is not the real thing, not the heart of the matter, but it is assuredly better than nothing; better perhaps than the fake mysteries of the thriller, the whodunnit, the horror movie, though these no doubt have their place as entertainment.

So man seeks his lost mystery wherever he thinks he can catch its echo, and perhaps will continue to do so until he finds his old God or gods again. The urge to seek the mystery is in itself perhaps a sign of hope that shortly he will stumble upon it once more. In the meantime we have its faint reflection, the paranormal.

Mrs Phyllis Hudson of Broadstairs told me of strange happenings in the apartment house in which she lives. Once a Victorian family home, the building is now converted into flats with a restaurant occupying the ground floor. These are Dickensian houses, for it was in Broadstairs that Dickens found Bleak House and here that he wrote *Barnaby Rudge*.

The particular building in which my correspondent lives appears to have more than one ghost, though that which Mrs Hudson has seen most often is of a child, a girl of eight or nine years old, who wears a pinafore with stiffly frilled lace over the shoulders and a pair of side-buttoning boots. The girl's long hair hangs down in plaits over her shoulders. The apparition appears on the stairs as though it had come from the flat above, walks to the bottom of the flight then disappears.

Other residents in the apartments have heard tapping sounds for which they are unable to account, and one or two have seen an opaque, misty shape but are unable to tell whether it represents a male or female figure. Among percipients of this shapeless apparition is the caretaker of the block, who I am assured does not drink anything stronger than tea. From what has been reported, it seems likely that although this particular house is over two hundred years old, the chief echoes of its former life are Victorian. There is no evidence as to the reason for the hauntings or the identity of the apparitions.

An unusual pair of manifestations is reported by Mrs M. Burkett-Delgado of Deal. This lady's own vivid description of her first experience is worth quoting. "About three years ago, I went out of the lounge at my bungalow at the above address shutting the door, went along the hall—I do not need to put the hall light on as the street lamp almost opposite provides sufficient light just to walk along to the dining-room door. I opened the door, the room was in darkness but before I was able to raise my hand to put on the light switch just inside the door, I saw a large disc, about fourteen inches in diameter suspended over the nearest dining-room chair to the door. It was a beautiful light golden colour, but I was so shocked and I was alone in the bungalow that from automatic reaction to the shock, I dashed on the light and it was gone. I cursed myself afterwards that I was not able to take a longer look at it. There are no possible lights that could shine into this room, I went into the garden, there was no moon and nothing in the way of lightning. I have always hoped to see this again when of course I would not be so shocked, but no luck. On the anniversary of the day on which I saw it and at roughly the same time I went again into the dark dining-room, but there was nothing."

The subject of this encounter asked if I were able to explain what she had seen, and although one cannot say with certainty, from previous similar cases reported one may perhaps conclude that discs of this nature are concentrations of energy, possibly directed by some intelligence. In *Haunted East Anglia* (Jarrold, 1985) I have recounted the sighting of a similar disc at Oundle (described by its percipient as 'a ball of light') which moved across a floor, travelled up a wall and along a mantelpiece, where it finally came to rest. It then proceeded to resolve itself into a human face wearing a particularly malevolent expression.

Had the Deal subject waited a while before switching on the electric light she might have witnessed a similar change. However, since she seems to have felt that the manifestation was benevolent, presumably had a face materialized she would have had better luck with its expression than did the Oundle subject.

If one is correct in thinking that all hauntings occur by the use of energy, it is reasonable to suppose that some form of energy manifestation (electricity?) may be responsible for these shining discs. It may be one form which it is possible for human energy to use after death. The fact that such lights (and lights in various forms are often reported as a part of hauntings) seem sometimes though not always to precede actual materialization, suggests that this is a simpler form of manifestation than the more specific one requiring a true physical likeness to a particular individual. It may be that a complete materialization of a human likeness demands a higher concentration of energy to operate. These are guesses, but there is evidence available that something of this nature does occur.

The second of Mrs Burkett-Delgado's experiences is equally unusual. Having had a garden shed demolished to make room for a new garage, this lady moved some of its contents into her house until such time as the garage should be erected. In an enamel pail in her bedroom, therefore, were temporarily stored light switches, a cable and other small items.

Several times when lying awake at night, she heard movements within the pail as though something were stirring inside it. Suspecting a mouse or rat, she would examine the pail in the morning but was never able to find a sign of rodent droppings. On one occasion the noise was so loud that she got up from bed, took the pail to the front door, being careful not to take her eyes from it as she did so, and then shook out most of the contents. Absolutely nothing unusual was found to account for the disturbance. The subject describes herself as a matter-of-fact person who dislikes mysteries. Her letter to me certainly did not suggest that she is given either to exaggeration or wild flights of imagination.

One factor may be significant: the bungalow in which these events took place was erected in 1931 on land formerly the property of the See of Canterbury. One wonders what activities took place in this area in times past.

As far as logical explanations for the noises in the bucket are concerned, failing small rodents, the only other possibility for a natural inhabitant of the pail is a monster spider. I remember once in adolescence having a disturbed night when a roll of cartridge paper propped in a corner of my bedroom emitted persistent scrabbling noises. When the sheet was unrolled (though not, I hasten to add, by me) a huge tree spider was revealed. The sounds had been caused by the patter of eight little feet moving up and down the roll! Yet it is probable that Mrs Burkett-Delgado would have noticed a large spider in the pail since she was specifically looking for a noise-producer.

The alternative is that the pail itself was responsible for producing the noise, i.e., that it was 'broadcasting' sounds registered by its own structure at some time in the past. There is no credible explanation possible of this odd event, nor is one likely to come to light.

Since my visit to Kent was so early in the year, I did not hope to see the onrush of blossom which is its glory. However, there was much beauty in these early spring days, and although flurries of rain followed me persistently from place to place, they merely enhanced the clear lines and colours of the Rowland Hilder landscapes. Yellow-green sallows edged the streams—ex-pussy willows; scatterings of blackthorn blossom powdered the tops of hedges, spatterings of primroses dusted the banks beneath them. There were lambs in the fields, young woolly bundles which didn't seem much inclined to frolic. Are lambs, like everything else, grown serious-minded these days? They peered up occasionally at a thrush's egg sky, but there was no gambolling, no rushing about from hillock to hillock. Lambs, like policemen and the postal service, are not what they used to be.

I drove into Penshurst in search of the ghost of Sir Philip Sidney, the sixteenth-century poet and courtier who is said to haunt his old home, Penshurst Place. I found instead a story concerning Penshurst vicarage. A familiar enough tale, it is of a love affair between the daughter of a some-time vicar of the parish (the precise period of the story is not known) who fell in love with a man considered unsuitable by her father. The couple were forbidden to marry and met clandestinely. Local legend avers that the man's ghost walks across the lane to the vicarage as once his physical self did in real life. There was little to suggest that an apparition had been seen in recent times.

Sir Philip Sidney owned Penshurst Place, Kent, and is said (though not by the present inhabitants) to haunt there. A more certain ghost, a woman in Elizabethan dress, has been seen descending a flight of stone steps in the garden.

When I moved on to the great house of the Sidneys I found it not yet open for the season and therefore barred to visitors no matter what the purpose of their visit. An employee of the owner assured me that there was no ghost whatever at Penshurst Place. And as for looking at the house, the staff were much too busy getting the place ready for the public at Easter to cope with a single sightseer. I had therefore to be content with viewing this delicious house from afar—from the flight of steps just inside the entrance, to be precise. I was presently joined by a young American making his first ever visit to England on a ten-day working trip. We stood at the top of the steps and looked at one of the loveliest buildings in England, feeling like Moses viewing Canaan. We were shortly joined by a gardener who shooed us away from the entrance and out into the roadway as though we were strayed chickens. Although I explained that I had spoken to an official of the house and had been given permission to look at the exterior, the shooer was not convinced. The American was philosophical. "I guess we came on the wrong day," he said.

I thought of Philip Sidney, he of the grace and the courtesy, who wrote:

> Who is it that, this dark night,
>   Underneath thy window plaineth?
> It is one who from thy sight
>   Being, ah, exiled, disdaineth
> Every other vulgar light.

Would he have let us in, I wonder, shown us his house and left us to find whatever it was we were seeking of knowledge and ancient beauty?

The sun shone blithely on Penshurst as I left it. It was a quiet village that day, waiting for the showers of tourists which would descend at Easter.

An East Worthing woman was luckier than the American and I at Penshurst, however. She, visiting the great house with relatives on one of its open days, was walking up a flight of stone steps when she had the sensation that some other person was descending them. She glanced to one side and saw the figure of a woman wearing Elizabethan costume (ruff and farthingale were unmistakable) almost beside her. Astonished, she drew her companions' attention, but they could see no one on the steps apart from their own small party. Was the wish mother to the thought, I wonder? The percipient's relatives thought so on that occasion, but perhaps they could only recognize the tangible.

Often interference with the structure of a house said to be haunted will abolish the ghost permanently. That is, if major alterations take place, such as the removal of walls, doors etc. I know of one house in Huntingdonshire where the replacement of the old roof by a new completely removed its ghosts. Prior to the renovation, the place had appeared to contain a complete recording of earlier inhabitants—a troop of Roundhead cavalry. After the renovation neither sight nor sound of the soldiers was heard again. The phenomenon also appears to work in reverse. Occasionally basic alterations to an unhaunted house will cause manifestations to begin. How and why do such things occur? Perhaps we can pause a moment to examine one of the theories regarding the operation of hauntings.

Since human beings generate electricity in their brains (as also in other organs of the body), electric currents are given out by such activity in the form of an electromagnetic field which can actually be measured and photographed in its situation around the body. In times of particularly strong emotion, this electrical activity appears to be intensified. It is now thought that in certain circumstances—though investigations are not yet so far advanced that it is possible to suggest what these are—the patterns of such 'given out' electricity can be absorbed by part of the material surroundings, operating much in the way of a tape-recorder or a sensitive film, and the recording thus obtained can later reproduce exactly the circumstances in which it took place. By this means it should therefore be possible to 'tune in' to happenings which originally involved heightened emotional states in the original participants, such as violent fights, murder, suicide; or on a different level, states involving grief, love, remorse or fear. The exact method of recording is not yet understood, neither is the mechanism by which reproduction of the original action takes place. The latter appears to need the presence of outside energy in some form or another. It also, if it is to be experienced by witnesses, seems to need the presence of at least one individual whose mental processes operate in a certain manner. On the latter, I hope to say more during the course of this book.

An example of interference with physical surroundings actually promoting a haunting is that of The White Horse public house at Chilham. In 1956, the then licensees opened up a fireplace in one of the rooms, and discovered an ancient inglenook, dated about 1460 behind the modern façade. Almost immediately afterwards they began to be aware of a grey-haired man, wearing a long black gown, who appeared in front of the fireplace. He would stand with his back to the fire, and would be noticed by members of the staff out of their eye-corners. Two features of the haunting were constant: the figure always appeared at precisely 10.10 a.m., and immediately on being spoken to, disappeared.

This haunting was reported to a trade paper, *The Whitbread News*, in May 1967, by the wife of the licensee, Mrs Veronica Sampson. Nothing certain was known of the ghost's identity, but Mrs Sampson put forward a possible explanation. The inn is next door to a church and was originally ecclesiastical property. The church itself contains a list of incumbents from 1293 to 1961. From 1655 to 1662 the vicar was one Sampson Hievar, who was deprived of his living for a reason unspecified. Could he be the fireside ghost perhaps? Mrs Sampson noted also the identity of his name with her own, implying that this might have been instrumental in producing the manifestation.

Tempting though it is to think so, I am more inclined to the opinion that the opening up of the fireplace is responsible for the punctual ghost. If it were indeed the old inglenook which had registered the presence of the cleric in life, recording his physical shape and appearance as he stood before it, it would have been unable to project that image while bricked up. However, once remove the impeding façade, the recorder (that is, the inglenook) would be free to play, to project its record of the earlier occupant of the room. In a manner similar to this perhaps most hauntings do work. There are certain outstanding exceptions to which I hope to refer later.

Not far from Chilham lies Godmersham where Jane Austen used to visit when her brother was in residence there. Edward Austen, bequeathed Godmersham Park by an uncle, changed his name to Knight, and it is likely that Jane based the character of Mr Knightley in *Emma* upon that of her brother Edward. However, it is not with the Park that the next story is concerned but with the remains of a thirteenth-century priory, a chantry of Canterbury, now known as Court Lodge Farm.

Several years ago, the then vicar of Godmersham, Canon Graham Brade-Birks, discovered a carved figure over an upper window of the farmhouse. It is of a seated archbishop, his staff in his left hand while his right is raised in benediction. Probably hidden at the Dissolution of the Monasteries this, one of the oldest known sculptures of Thomas à Becket, is thought to have been carved no later than the year 1200. The statue had therefore been lost for centuries, and even when discovered had survived in an outer porch for a hundred years without being recognized for what it was.

My informant in this case, Mr Ralph Dawson of Barham, visited the place shortly after the end of World War II and found it then in a pretty dilapidated state, since it had been only recently occupied by troops. The open front door bore jovial legends such as "Ghosts! Beware!" and "Danger! Do not enter! Haunted!" and in case anyone should be in doubt, a further one which read "The Risk is Yours. Keep out!"

The Dawsons, however, went in. They found immediately ahead of them a staircase which rose to a first floor landing. The stairs were minus most of their banisters, but this did not deter the visitors from going up. On the landing they discovered a series of doors which led to communicating rooms, and no matter from which room they emerged they always found themselves back on the landing facing the staircase.

Having completed their upstairs exploration they were about to descend, when they heard the sound of footsteps approaching across the gravelled drive beyond the front door. Not just one pair of feet but a number. The sound was accompanied by that of several voices, suggesting a group of three or four persons, male and female. The listeners could not make out what was said. Unwilling to be caught trespassing, they decided to conceal their embarrassed presence behind one of the landing doors in the hope that whoever was below would stay there and not climb to the upper regions.

The Dawsons were out of luck. The new arrivals appeared to enter the front door, banging it behind them, and cross the hall. Barely had the trespassers time to hide themselves in the hope of slipping out of one door while the newcomers were entering another, when they heard the noise of approaching voices and feet mounting the stairs. Although the sound of speech grew appreciably louder, at no time were they able to distinguish any spoken words. The clatter of feet upon the stairs would anyway have made precise listening difficult.

After a while, Mr and Mrs Dawson hurried down and made a search for the visitors but found no trace whatever, though it would have been impossible for anyone to have left the house without being either seen or heard. The area surrounding the house was also completely deserted. They were apparently the only living beings on the premises.

Court Lodge farmhouse eventually became so dilapidated that the building was demolished, thus losing to posterity not only the ghostly echoes of the stair-climbers but also the thirteenth-century priory to which they belonged. Godmersham has retained the prehistoric barrow, however, known as Juliberry's Grave. Juliberry of the intriguing name, seems to have been a certain Julii Laberius, one of

Caesar's generals slain in an early fight against the native Britons. Tradition states that he was incorporated into a tomb which antedated him by at least 2,000 years. Roman remains have certainly been found in the area.

In 1939 the Mr and Mrs Dawson whose experience I have just related lived in Canterbury, immediately opposite the Archbishop's Palace. In the war's early days the gates into the precincts of the cathedral were still left unlocked, and frequently the Dawsons would take a stroll past the cathedral late in the evening before retiring to bed.

On one particular night with the moon almost full, they went as usual through the Green Court, past the deanery and into the Dark Entry. Now this is the area supposedly haunted by the ghost of Nell Cook, a servant of a cathedral canon who, discovering that her employer was emotionally involved with his niece, is said to have murdered both in a fit of jealousy. However, it was no ghost of Nell that the Dawsons encountered. They were about to go out past the ruins of the old infirmary when they stopped short, neither of them speaking. Let Ralph Dawson continue the story: "We stayed silent, neither saying a thing. Every item seemed clean cut and sharply edged—the trees almost like black silhouettes. The diamond-panes of the Crypt windows glittered as bright as real diamonds. My wife and I held this silence almost stiffly for a minute or more. Then the tension ceased. We turned to each other, both aware of something but not knowing what the still face of the other was hiding. Then I said, 'You say something first and then I'll have my say'. We had both heard the same thing. Unaccompanied chanting coming from the locked up and empty cathedral crypt."

Mrs Phyllis Dawson's recollection included one additional feature; in her memory of the incident, a silvery light had seemed to be present, the very leaves appearing to be made of silver.

There seems little doubt that what the couple experienced on this occasion was a time-slip, an identification with a moment in the past history of the spot on which they were standing, when the cathedral crypt must have echoed to the sound of plainsong chanting. The crypt of Canterbury was the site of Thomas à Becket's tomb for fifty years before the latter was translated into its magnificent shrine and chapel in the cathedral proper; as such it must have resounded often to the hymns of monks and pilgrims. If it is an echo of this nature which the Dawsons heard, then the original incident must have occurred in the thirteenth century. They were 'hearing' sounds which had been silent these seven hundred years. The occurrence, interestingly enough,

The sound of medieval plainsong chanting has been heard from the locked crypt of Canterbury Cathedral.

bears one of the classic marks of a 'time' experience—the silvery quality of the light present throughout. In this case it may have been a result of moonlight, but nevertheless, 'silveriness' applied to light conditions is often a term used concerning cases of time-dislocation.

As for Nell Cook, when I visited Canterbury I was told by a cathedral employee that the shadowy grey form of a woman is often seen moving through the Dark Entry. The figure is believed to be of a nun rather than of the canon's servant, however. I met no one who had actually encountered it.

Canterbury is an enchanting city—old, mellow, beautiful, accommodating as well as it can the rude upthrust of contemporary living. Motor traffic surges through streets built for the occasional horse and cart, tourists jostle and crowd, their eyes glazed with too much looking, motor coaches honk like despairing geese, fighting their way foot by foot through to the city's heart. Yet in that heart, the cathedral precincts, all is serene, green, timeless.

Whatever changes have occurred since the days when Becket took his last walk to the great church must surely be recompensed by the exterior and interior beauty of the building. True, Lincoln and Durham are better set above their cities, Winchester has a more imposing approach, Salisbury is more intimate, but none can boast Canterbury's length of history, nor its close association with the fortunes of England. It was here that Augustine founded what was to become the main centre of Christianity in the land and of the entire Anglican Communion throughout the world. The later succession of archbishops stud the history books with resounding names—Dunstan, Lanfranc, Anselm, Becket, and so on into modern times. But without doubt the archbishop whose name most generally conjures Canterbury Cathedral is Thomas à Becket who was murdered within it. The site of the martyrdom can still be seen (though altered somewhat since Becket's day) and it takes little imagination to evoke the scene as it must have been; the stubborn, strong, inflexible priest awaiting his death as the four knights raged to get at him. Awaiting it? How? Impatiently, I think. De Tracey, De Moreville, FitzUrse and Le Breton tore into the building shouting for the man who had dared to challenge the King. Becket's friends scattered and hid in the shadows, bent on saving their skins and their souls. Only two remained with him, William, a monk, and Edward Grim, a clerk. Perhaps Becket was undismayed by the general desertion. There was, after all, a good precedent for it in Church history.

The knights attempted to drag him out, away from consecrated ground, so that they should not add the sin of sacrilege to that of murder. Yet being a tall, strong man as well as an obstinate priest, the archbishop did not budge. They had no choice but to cut him down, and this they did, aiming at the head. They did not cease their hacking until his brains lay spilled upon the pavement.

Now this small enclosure—not quite chapel, not quite sanctuary—is a minor place of pilgrimage. One tries vainly to recreate the scene, but it can scarcely be done with half a hundred people streaming through and over it. It would have been easier for the true Canterbury pilgrims, those who visited the shrine of St Thomas for centuries after his death. Then there was some focal point for attention, for the shrine itself was a world's wonder, being overlaid with gold plate and covered with jewelled rings and precious stones—pearls, rubies, emeralds.

Within this splendour lay Becket's remains. He conferred greater benefit on Canterbury by his death than ever he had by his life, for the foundation grew rich on the fame of his relics and drew pilgrims from the length and breadth of Europe. In time this wealth came to line the bottomless pocket of the Crown. In 1538, twenty-six cartloads of treasure were confiscated for Henry VIII, and the bones of the martyr mysteriously vanished from their resting-place.

With such saturation of an historic area by high drama, one would have expected it to be St Thomas's spirit which would walk here, but there is no record that it has ever done so. Perhaps such lingerings only occur where violent death is unexpected, unlooked for and unwanted. What evidence remains to us suggests that Becket was prepared for the manner of his death, not finding martyrdom unwelcome. It is true that hauntings frequently seem to occur where death of the individual has been violent, but this presupposes that the dead one was wrenched from life against his will. If you go willingly to your destruction, courting it no matter how violent, presumably there is no wrench, no being torn loose from the body—rather a gentle relinquishing leaving no shadow, no shock.

One shadow, though, is said to lie upon Canterbury's flagstones occasionally; that of Simon of Sudbury, the archbishop who was murdered by a mob on Tower Hill and bereft of his head. Even now, apparently, the skeleton in his tomb is headless. Those who believe that Simon's ghost haunts the cathedral say he comes to seek the missing skull which was buried in Suffolk centuries ago.

The cathedral's soaring grandeur makes thoughts of hauntings irrelevant. If the 'living' part of a human being—its energy or spirit—must remain on earth when it might have hoped to move on, perhaps no better environment could be found for it than this majestic building.

Canterbury is not all cathedral, nor are its echoes purely attached to the Church. A short way from the precincts, the River Stour runs sedately through the town, and on its banks stands the Old Weaver's House, its gables overhanging the stream. The inside, darkly panelled, is a shop now but one of the assistants, Mrs Kathy Hastings, has an interest in the faint echoes of history which are still detectable in Canterbury. Within the Weaver's House itself the presence of a ghost is suspected. A grey figure of a woman has been seen going up the stairs, and twice encountered on the landing by a cleaner. The latter is apparently not given to hysterical imaginings but is "a down-to-earth elderly soul". Mrs Hastings found her testimony particularly convincing on this account. It is thought the 'grey lady' may belong to

The medieval painting known as 'Beckett's Ghost' on a pillar in the crypt of Canterbury Cathedral, though it is more likely to represent Christ, a saint, or a king appropriately crowned and garbed.

the period when the house was the property of weavers, but there is no proof that this is so.

Mrs Hastings also told me of the ghost of a former mayor of Canterbury who is said to have been seen riding through the city streets on his bicycle on several occasions after his death. Several local persons are reported to have seen the apparition.

A more interesting tale attaches to Howfield Manor, Chartham, which lies just a mile or two from Canterbury. This is old monastic land, and it is not surprising to find that the ghost is of a monk. (When one considers England's ghosts, one understands how large a part the monastic system played in the lives of our medieval ancestors.) The word-of-mouth legend states that a disastrous fire occurred at this monastery, and that a particular monk died in trying to save another from the flames. Not surprisingly, it is he who has been seen around the manor. Though how any observer can be certain the ghost is of the saver rather than the saved I do not know. However, legend usually prefers romantic to prosaic explanations of these matters, and failing any detailed knowledge of the original event the romantic version will have to serve. On many occasions, the sound of chanting voices had been heard in the vicinity of Howfield Manor. The monks at their devotions no doubt; this would appear the most likely explanation since the inflexible pattern of monastic life must have bitten deeply into its environment over the centuries. These, the 'pattern-hauntings' which are records of actual living patterns, are perhaps the commonest type of manifestation and the most innocuous. They merely reproduce events which took place with clockwork regularity day after day, year after year, presumably generating the same emotional responses time after time from the human beings concerned in them.

A phenomenon of a different nature took place in Chartham in December 1975. A young married couple living in a cottage in the village began to experience so-called poltergeist disturbances. The facts as reported at the time are that the young woman alleged she had been thrown to the floor in an upstairs room by something or someone unseen. She was also certain that occasionally a hand touched her face. Apparently the disturbances grew severe enough for the Bishop of Dover to be called in to exorcize the property. It is not known if this were successful for shortly afterwards the man gave up his employment and the couple moved into Canterbury to live; some time afterwards according to reports, they divorced. The house has been occupied since, but there has apparently been no complaint of supernatural disturbance by subsequent occupants.

The known facts here do not suggest a haunting. If they are an example of poltergeistery (and the typically violent movement of objects associated with this kind of manifestation seems to be absent), then it may be that the energy involved to operate the manifestation stemmed from the woman concerned. Poltergeist phenomena are also known as Recurrent Spontaneous Psychokinesis (R.S.P.K.)—the involuntary movement of objects repeated over a time span. This type of activity seems usually to be associated with adolescents, particularly where an atmosphere of emotional tension exists in the home. It is, if you care to put it so, a kind of uncontrolled, involuntary protest against emotional distress, the subject apparently projecting unconsciously enough energy to cause the movement of objects around him. However, in view of the absence of true psychokinesis in the Chartham case, the explanation may lie elsewhere than in R.S.P.K.

A well-documented haunting is that of Cleve Court in Minster. A mellow old house with its roots in the fifteenth century though with Elizabethan and Georgian additions, the property was bought in 1920 by Lord Carson, formerly the barrister, Sir Edward Carson. During the Carsons' occupation, several persons heard sounds of footsteps or of furniture being moved during the night, and at least three children at different times saw the figure of a 'grey lady'. Most of the manifestations took place in the older portion of the building, which had in earlier times been the servants' quarters. Indeed one old servant wrote from an address in West Hampstead to Lady Carson following national publicity on the subject of the Cleve Court ghost. It appears that as a girl she had worked at the house in the early years of the century, and on one occasion at about 7.00 a.m. was preparing a bedroom for a day nursery to be used by incoming guests. Hearing footsteps approaching along the corridor she raised her eyes and saw a woman "in an old-fashioned dress" coming towards her. The woman apparently waved her hand and walked on, but according to other members of the staff no person of this description was in the house at the time.

The figure was also seen by Lady Carson herself on one occasion. Having got up from her bed one night in order to let out the family spaniel, she had descended the stairs into the hall when the dog dashed past her in evident terror, attempting to return the way it had come. At that point Lady Carson switched on the hall lights and saw a woman coming down the stairs, wearing a dress with a full skirt and a lighter fichu; both garments appeared to be of a soft grey colour.

Although initially the percipient thought that what she saw was a flesh-and-blood figure, the noiselessness of its movement convinced her that she was seeing an apparition, and she was then considerably afraid.

Alexander Mackenzie, a respected member of the Society for Psychical Research, refers, in his book *The Unexplained,* to the story of a female owner of Cleve Court who made a marriage of convenience. Local verbal tradition stated that the husband treated his wife unkindly, frequently locking her in her room while he roistered with friends and other women. The wife, who had greatly wanted children, was childless, and it is said to be the figure of this unhappy lady which walked the house, appearing generally only to children.

There is no means of checking the accuracy of the original story, though in the 1920s there was certainly one bedroom at Cleve possessing an old-fashioned bolt which could only be opened from the outside.

Lady Carson died in 1966, but her daughter-in-law has confirmed to me the story of the sighting as given by Alexander Mackenzie. Mrs Carson also states that after the house was divided into four separate units following the death of her mother-in-law, nothing more was seen or heard of the ghost. Such a cessation following extensive material alterations is not unusual in haunted houses, as we have seen.

One further point of interest arises from the Cleve Court story. The ghost is again the very familiar one of a 'grey lady'. Indeed the colour grey is so often used to describe visual manifestations that I think one must conclude that it applies not so much to the colour of the apparition's costume as to the whole form itself. This suggests that in general such materializations have no or very little colour—rarely black, white or coloured, in fact; merely an indeterminate overall grey.

If when 'seeing a ghost' we are actually witnessing the rebroadcast of an image absorbed by the surroundings years ago, then it would seem that the process records the original encompassed shape and textural detail only, and that only rarely are gradations of colour registered. I hope some interested scientist will eventually provide an explanation for this phenomenon.

I first heard the story of Cleve Court from Mrs Anne Chesshyre, who had a fascinating story of her own to relate. During the summer of 1929 this correspondent's parents returned from China and the family stayed with her mother's cousin at a manor house near Canterbury.

The young Anne was given two ponies to look after, one belonging to the house and the other, more valuable, a borrowed animal. She took her duties seriously, regularly exercising the ponies, cleaning their tackle and seeing that they were securely shut into their field each night.

On one occasion she came back from her afternoon ride, accompanied by an old spaniel, Dashie, and after turning the ponies into their paddock returned to the stable to clean down the tack before dressing for dinner. She had been industriously rubbing away for about twenty minutes when she heard the drumming of hooves coming along the grass track from the ponies' field and in to the cobbled stable yard. As the gallopers approached, the spaniel Dashie rushed into the yard, furiously barking.

Anne's one desire was to catch the horses before the dog should further stampede them. The thought of the valuable borrowed pony and what might happen to it (and her for her failure to secure the field gate) speeded her exit. She snatched her bicycle and fled down the main drive to the front gate, but could see no sign of the horses. Assuming they had escaped down the rear drive—which led to a grassy common stretching for several miles beyond—she hopelessly cycled to the ponies' field to see how they could have escaped.

It was a relief to the girl to find she was not responsible for the disaster. The field gate was as firmly shut as she had left it. She searched then for a gap in the hedge but found none; and indeed her next discovery was even more mystifying. The ponies were still in the field, quietly grazing.

Less puzzled than relieved, Anne returned to the stable to finish the tack-polishing. So did the spaniel, Dashie. However, when a few minutes later, the wild galloping once more split the silence, only the girl went out to see. The dog cowered in a corner of the stable whimpering, his hair bristling.

Again it did not occur to the subject of this experience that anything untoward was happening. She had shut both front and back drive gates after her first investigation so knew the ponies could not have escaped on to the road this time. In fact on her second emergence from the stable she was met by complete silence. Nevertheless she checked as before and once again found the ponies peacefully grazing in their own pasture.

Over dinner, to mitigate Anne's disgrace in being late, her mother remarked that she had heard the ponies galloping round the house the previous night and wondered if her daughter had left their gate open—although she could not, she said, see any hoof-marks in the flower beds and assumed the gardener must have caught the animals in time to prevent damage.

At that point their hostess interposed. "I expect you heard the Manor House ghost." Years earlier, apparently, during a dance at the house, carriages had been waiting to put down their occupants at the front door when one pair of horses bolted. They tore wildly round the house again and again until at last the vehicle turned over, throwing out and killing its occupants. At intervals since then at approximately the same time of year the incident is repeated, though at no time has the carriage ever been seen.

This is a fascinatingly detailed and vivid story. Not the least interesting part is its note of absolute conviction. The sound was at once assumed by the mother (once) and by the daughter (twice) to be that of living horses galloping. Neither percipient was aware of the ghost story until the house's owner spoke of it at dinner—*after* their individual experiences had occurred.

There appears to have been no distortion at all of sound, so that the reproduction tallied exactly with the actual noise of drubbing hooves. A parallel can be found in the experience of a Miss Cobern near the prehistoric white horse above Alton Priors, Wiltshire. It is worth noting that in cases of speech reproduction in hauntings, there is invariably some distortion, and in only a few cases can the words spoken be clearly identified or mistaken for actual living heard speech. As with the 'greyness' of apparitions, it seems likely that a physical explanation (i.e., in the realm of physical science) may account for this oddity.

An unusual account of a limping ghost was sent to me by a Chatham man, Mr J. C. Horsewood, and although its lack of date and place detail denies its usefulness as evidence, I include it here for interest purposes.

In the early hours of a single morning (thought by the subject to be around the year 1950) this apparition was seen twice, once by Mr Horsewood in his own bedroom, and on the second occasion by a sentry in a nearby barracks. The season was summer, the approximate time between 1.00 and 2.00 a.m., when Mr Horsewood was sitting up in bed, wide awake and apparently unable to sleep. He suddenly became aware of the "ghostly figure of a man with his back to the window". The apparition, he thought, looked directly at him, then limped towards him and began to walk up and down the bedroom, passing close to the left side of the bed. The figure appeared to be rehearsing a speech of some kind, for Mr Horsewood could hear muttered words repeated though he was unable to make sense of them. They sounded to him to be in a foreign language possibly German, "the letters *t* and *d* being much in evidence as *det* and *detter* and *detra*".

At this point the percipient took from under his pillow a copy of the New Testament which he always kept there, and began to read aloud the seventeenth chapter of St John's gospel which incorporates the great prayer of Jesus. The ghost disappeared immediately, vanishing, according to Mr Horsewood, through the open window.

About an hour later this same limping apparition appeared in front of a sentry on duty at the barracks. The living man assumed he was being attacked and put a bullet through the ghost, whereupon it vanished. The unlucky sentry was later interviewed by his Commanding Officer, and unfortunately I have no record of the C.O.'s assessment of the situation. Was the sentry charged with damaging Government property, or hospitalized for psychiatric treatment, I wonder? No more appears to have been heard of the limping ghost and there is no clue to its identity. If its 'det, detter detra' cannot be identified with any known language, perhaps what we have here is a stuttering ghost.

A much stronger and more tightly structured case was reported to me by a Mr and Mrs Stevens, licensees of The Chequers Inn at Smarden. The Chequers is an old and pleasant pub situated on a corner facing Smarden's twisting main street. Smarden itself is a thing of beauty, its buildings mellowed and gracious, so to round the corner and come upon the magnificent timbered inn is no surprise. Inside the beams are low, the furniture dark, the copper gleaming. I would have been surprised had there not been a ghost story attached to the place.

Jennie and Frank Stevens had been in occupation of The Chequers barely a month when a series of extraordinary events began to happen. At the time they kept a dog, an Afghan bitch, which had always been in the best of health. However, one night between 11.00 and 12.00 p.m. the animal began to tear around the lounge of the pub apparently half-demented, tongue lolling, saliva dripping from her jaws, and in a state of great distress. The owners were concerned at this unusual behaviour and eventually took the dog upstairs to their own bedroom.

The ghost of a Napoleonic soldier haunts the interior of the Chequers Inn, Smarden, Kent, and is particularly active in spring.

The next night the animal was again left in the lounge and to the dismay of her owners the performance was repeated. The following day a local veterinary surgeon was called in. After taking various tests he pronounced the bitch fine and healthy.

Some time later Mrs Stevens's mother stayed with the couple, bringing with her her dachsund, a rather elderly deaf dog. Both dog and owner slept in a small bedroom on the first floor, and the woman was awakened by the barking of the dog some time during the night. The animal had its hackles up and was staring intently at what appeared to be a blank wall. The incident was particularly puzzling since the dog's deafness made it difficult to awaken once asleep.

On another occasion Jennie and Frank Stevens were due to attend an evening function, and Mrs Stevens, having pressed her evening dress hung it up until she was ready to wear it. As the garment had a scooped neckline, she bent the ends of the coat-hanger upward to retain it securely, then hung it on the beading of the wardrobe. Later when she came upstairs she found the dress on the floor by the wardrobe. Thinking it had simply fallen from its perch, she felt in the folds for the coat-hanger. It was not to be found. Some minutes later she discovered it—at the farther end of the bedroom. No one had been in the room since she had placed the evening dress there earlier.

At a later date a pop group playing in the neighbourhood stayed one night at the inn. When Jennie and Frank Stevens arose from bed the next morning they were surprised to find a pair of jeans lying beside the bed. The garment did not belong to either husband or wife. The person to whom it did belong—one of the young men—was busily searching his own bedroom for it. None of the three had any idea how such a migration could have taken place.

However, this continual movement of objects around the building appears typical of this particular manifestation. A miscellaneous selection of objects has moved around the premises over a long period of time. Knives, spoons, forks, plates, appear which do not belong to the house, and implements which do belong mysteriously vanish to reappear elsewhere. While I was actually in the building a young employee reported that a plate which had unaccountably found its way into the hotel's stock a week earlier had now as abruptly gone again.

On one cold and rainy day before leaving the house, Mrs Stevens carefully shut and fastened all the front windows, which are of the lattice type. When she and her husband returned home after a lapse of some hours, Jennie Stevens found two of the upper windows standing open. Although she questioned members of the staff, no one had touched the windows since she had left them.

Perhaps the most disconcerting incidents occurred when two young couples were resident for two nights in the hotel. On the first night one of the girls awoke to see the bedroom door open and the figure of a small dark man (unknown to her) standing there.

On the night following, the girl of the second pair awoke to the sensation of something or someone touching her back. She awakened her husband and although at first he thought she had been dreaming, he later found the mark of an inverted cross upon her skin at the point where she had felt the touch. Thoroughly unnerved, the couple sat up in their room for the rest of the night and left early the next day. They have not stayed at the pub since.

With such a long and detailed history of haunting, there was almost certain to be a story to which the happenings related, and this I eventually learned. During the Napoleonic Wars a young French prisoner had been lodged in the inn. For some reason, about which local verbal tradition is uncertain, the man was murdered in the place, and it is his spirit which is thought to haunt it. One noteworthy point is that the manifestations only seem to occur in the months of April and May; which suggests an anniversary haunting.

One further detail of interest, is that the veterinary surgeon who attended the Stevenses' Afghan bitch, on his second inspection of the animal suggested that it might be hallucinating. He was not at that time aware of any story of a ghost connected with the building, but when told of it appeared to think this a possible explanation of the dog's behaviour.

I was shown the two bedrooms which are said to be the worst affected. The smaller struck me as being possibly the less active area; the larger had the unmistakable feeling of an active haunting— a sensation of tension which affected one's own body; as though some form of electricity were operating in the vicinity. I had the impression of a fierce and furious frustration, but the landlady denied that anything of the kind could be present. She thought of the ghost as a friendly, comfortable entity. Not quite the terms I would have used about it myself, but then I wasn't living with it. Both the affected rooms were extremely cold, the double room being so atmospheric that I should not have cared to spend the night in it.

The various members of the staff to whom I spoke verified the details of the incidents related. Almost all had had some strange experience within the walls of The Chequers. It is, as I said, a beautiful old place, part fourteenth-, part fifteenth-century. It would have been standing when the last of the Plantagenets reigned and would have seen the advent of the Tudors.

But the last, the very last, of the Plantagenets never did reign. He sleeps under a slab of Kentish marble in the church at Eastwell, a tired old man who lived the life of a simple country labourer and died as he had lived, in obscurity.

There is a charming story related by Arthur Mee in his book *Kent* and no doubt well known to Kentish people, that Sir Thomas Moyle who built Eastwell House in the first Elizabeth's reign, noticed an old white-bearded man known to his fellow workmen as Richard. Perhaps the gentleman would have remarked the labourer not at all, had not the latter been in the habit of slipping away by himself to read a book in his leisure moments. Reading was a rare accomplishment in 1545, and among the poor almost unheard of. Sir Thomas, his curiosity aroused by this phenomenon, made friends with the old fellow and eventually was told his story.

Richard had been brought up and taught by a scholar (presumably a monk or other cleric), and occasionally a gentleman would call to see him, to question him and enquire about his well-being. It was this man who paid for his board and tuition, although the boy apparently never knew his identity.

When he was in his early teens, this same gentleman called and without announcing their destination, took young Richard away on a visit. They must have ridden long and hard, for eventually they reached the camp of a great army and man and boy were ushered into the presence of a nobleman in magnificent armour.

The latter placed his hands on the lad's shoulders, gazing seriously at him and said, "Richard, I am your father. If I succeed in tomorrow's battle I shall provide for you as befits your birth and blood. If I am defeated and killed, then we shall not meet again."

The astounded boy asked who it was who spoke to him so, what was the name of this man of majesty who stood before him.

"Today I am the King of England," he replied, "But if the Earl of Richmond wins the field tomorrow he will destroy every Plantagenet still living. Therefore if I am defeated tell no one of your name and lineage."

The name of the battlefield was Bosworth; that of the King, Richard of Gloucester, Richard Plantagenet, Richard III. His judgement of the situation proved true, for his successor hunted out and removed all known blood relatives of the late king. The boy in Kent kept his secret to himself. He was, he said, a poor orphan, a common working man; and so he remained, his life inviolate.

Sir Thomas Moyle, greatly moved, had a little house built for him in his own park, and here the last of the Plantagenets spent his autumn years, cared and provided for and safe against betrayal as his father had never been.

Whether or not the story is true the intervening centuries will not tell us, but word-of-mouth, the oral tradition, is almost as old as the human race and not to be despised as a source of information. The story is that Richard III's last surviving son, his bastard son, lived and died in Kent and still lies in Eastwell church.

The gentle romanticism of this Gothic echo stayed with me for some time as I took the Goudhurst road, then gradually the old spell faded and the contemporary landscape reasserted itself. It was a bad weather time still, cold and windy with rain like a slap in the face. The first blossom was beginning now, the vivid wooing pink of the almond, the sandy pink of the prunus, flattering the country gardens. Careless handfuls of primroses strewed the hedgesides, and in the villages the dark foliage of wintered evergreens was lit by brilliant shafts of daffodils, sharp stars of forsythia.

I noticed a swan upended in a nearby river, industriously dredging for his living. Rooks black-armoured, battled through the wind with wisps of straw in their beaks; and a thrush sang late into the rainy dark as I came back into Goudhurst village.

I spent the evening with friends I had not seen for twenty years, and as we filled in the pieces of a quarter-lifetime's history I remembered the school nearby in which I had worked and lived for a year. Remembered not as though it were yesterday, but as though that twelve months had occurred in another life and for a different woman; as in a sense it had, for in such a span our very cells had changed three times, our bodies passed through three successive cycles. Whatever we were then was a memory and a residue rather than an actuality.

The school, too, had changed, corridors had collapsed into classrooms, classrooms spread comfortably into nearby cloakrooms. The library had thankfully removed into a new building, and the music rooms, Victorian, dark and forbidding in my day, had sought fresh woods and a more congenial atmosphere. Yet much of the building was as it had always been, including the part with the ghost. For of course there was a ghost, or something at least which did not belong to the now and here.

My sole encounter with it—and one was enough—was at the beginning of the only summer vacation I ever spent in the place. Most of the staff had departed for far-flung and no doubt exotic holidays, and I found myself working and sleeping alone in the oldest part of the building for about three days until I, too, should leave.

This particular section of the house retained its Victorian structure, and was notable for a series of linking corridors both upstairs and down off which rooms sprang. My study bedroom was a largish room looking on to the garden; a pleasant enough place, though hot in summer and cold in winter.

On the second of my three nights (the first had passed without event, and the solitariness and silence had not worried me), I awoke at about 3.30 a.m. It was that time of a summer's night when dawn was about to break, when the cracks were appearing in effect without making any appreciable difference to the darkness.

I came awake abruptly, from full sleep to full awareness at once.

And the awareness announced that something was crouched on the floor of my bedroom to the left of the bed. I did not need to turn my head to know where it was. Indeed, I could not have turned had I wanted to for I was paralysed by fear. Even the fear was not normal, for it was a kind of thick terror, like a blanket in which I was rolled. All I could do in that petrified state was to turn my eyes toward the creature on the floor.

It was about two feet in length, I suppose, the size of a large cat or a small corgi. It resembled neither of these. It had a pair of huge nocturnal eyes like those of a lemur, and these were the clearest feature of the apparition. I noticed them particularly because they were unwaveringly fixed on me. I think it was the most revolting gaze I have ever had to endure, for what emanated from the thing was an atmosphere of extreme malevolence and obscenity. With all its exudation of evil it was at the same time mocking. It stared at me for what seemed half an hour (although I suspect it was only a few minutes in chronological time), and I stared back, playing rabbit to its snake. I could not move to switch on the light, and in any case the creature itself seemed to emit some kind of glow in which I could see the shape of its face and head and the huge eyes, and a dim suggestion of the rest of its body.

While this was happening and I was in a state of some horror due to the unpleasantness the thing generated, some part of my mind was operating independently and was quite aware that I was not seeing the creature with the physical eye, but was experiencing a visual image as one does in dreams, an hallucination of a type.

After what seemed an interminable time the clarity of the thing beside the bed began to fade, its light to dim, and its malevolent emanation to lessen. With this diminution, the room which had been bitterly cold, began to grow warmer. In a few minutes it had disappeared entirely leaving a very shaken and frightened occupier of the bed.

Some two or three years after this incident, I met the person who succeeded me on the staff of this school, and was told that she had had a similar experience in another bedroom in the same wing, though in her case the 'animal' had appeared on the window curtains. From her description, the apparition had been of exactly the same kind as I had seen. Neither of us was able to account for the nature of the experience, and concluded, unsatisfactorily, that we must have picked up an elemental which inhabited this particular bit of space.

One would be hard put to it to define an elemental. The term is usually used to describe a force which appears to be of a primitive kind, a nature spirit or an embodiment of it. Indeed it seemed as though entities of this kind were acknowledged in the pagan religions, and I suspect that their occasional rare surfacings may be due either to archaic memory of pagan beliefs in the subject of the hallucination, or to actual concentrations of energy resulting from ancient rituals in the particular area.

There is, of course, a third and much more disturbing possibility: that these concentrations of (usually highly unpleasant) energy may represent entities of which we know nothing. Our ancestors were more aware of and closer to nature than we can hope to be. Perhaps their goblins and trolls were more a matter of practical experience than highly creative imaginations.

There is a curious corollary to this tale. In the twenty years since the experience occurred I have often wondered at its nature—particularly at the shape and manner of the creature which was its centre. I have seen no beast other than a lemur which resembled it in the slightest. Until three weeks ago, when I received a book of Scottish folk tales to review for a newspaper. Halfway through the book I came upon two stories relating to brownies, the half-mischievous, half-malevolent little creatures who, according to folk-lore would either help or hinder man as the mood took them. Each tale was illustrated, but instead of the usual 'wee folk, small folk' type of fairy picture, the artist had delineated a squat, animal-like creature, with the huge eyes and furred ears of a lemur. It came as a shock, I can tell you, to see that malevolent stare again after so long, that wicked little countenance leering back at me from the page.

Elementals are reported in other shapes, of course, and occasionally these seem clearly to represent some remnants of the pagan culture. Perhaps the truth is that prehistoric man reverenced or feared certain aspects of nature and the concentration of his feelings became imagistic, literally printing encapsulated images of dread or horror upon an area. This is a more comfortable interpretation than facing the fact that before the primitives conjured those entities, such energy-forms may actually have existed!

The last story from Kent was given me by Mrs P. Man of Biddenden, who had heard it told of Appledore, the pretty, straggling village referred to earlier in this chapter.

During World War II soldiers were billeted in an old house in the village. As was usual in such cases, all the men came from the same battalion but men from one unit occupied the rear of the building and those from another took the rooms at the front. Eventually all were posted to France and were at once heavily engaged in action. The batch which had occupied the front of the Appledore house was totally wiped out; those from the rear survived to return.

After the war when it was released for civilian use, newcomers to the district bought the house. It was some time after they moved in that Mr and Mrs Man met them and asked how they liked the place.

There was a moment's pause before the reply came. "It's all right *now*," the new owner said. "But we had to have it exorcized before we could continue to live in it." Apparently in the first weeks of their occupation they had been severely disturbed by screams and yells emanating from the front part of the building, that which had been occupied by the dead soldiers.

I find this an intriguing and puzzling example of a haunting, for it partakes of the nature of a time experience. Men snatched from the relative security and content of pleasant surroundings and thrown immediately into a fair replica of hell upon earth, might have been likely in their closing minutes to have thought of the last good times they had known. But if it is so, it is the first case of its kind I have met where the original venue reproduced the later human condition. My own feeling is that at a time prior to the posting, one or more of the troop may have been troubled by nightmares, knowing what lay ahead, and it is these cries of distress which the house's purchasers heard. This is supposition only. There can be no accurate estimate of the cause of this strange and interesting example of the survival of human emotion.

About to take my leave of Kent, I paid a final visit to the Maydes' Teashop in Biddenden, for a farewell home-made tea and was kindly shown around the private part of the dwelling by the proprietress. Old and beautiful the building certainly is, but the present owner has found no evidence of haunting. I was not surprised, for from the first time of entering I had noticed an atmosphere of great peace and tranquillity in the place. Not just a negative absence of disturbance, but a real and positive sensation. "Almost," I remarked to the owner, "a feeling of devotion." The thought crossed my mind that the atmosphere conveyed three qualities—benevolence, reverence and love, but before I could put the idea into words my guide spoke. "The house is a weaver's house, of course, but it is said to have been the home of a preacher and his family." Hence the atmosphere. I have rarely met such a feeling of serenity. A wonderful house in which to live.

And so out of Kent. Magpies, clerical and flirty, bounced in and out of the hedges. The clapboard and shingle houses, the cone-capped, cinder-coloured oasts, shone wetly in the morning light. The road wound its way westward between the hop-trellises, empty yet of vines. Out of the corner of my eye I could see the desperately pruned apple-trees, their turns and angles still unsoftened by blossom; and until mid-morning the deliberate persistent discouragement of the rain. Then as though by the flick of a switch a shaft of sunlight speared the rain clouds, touching the landscape, lighting its duns to vivid brown, its browns to cinnamon.

Kent is a landscape of land and sky; as Norfolk is a landscape of sky.

Sussex

Although Sussex looks to be of only moderate size on the map, when one comes to travel through it, the distance from one end to the other is considerable. The main roads run from the coast north to London and divide the county like hurdles in a steeplechase. They are all underpinned by the heavy coast road, the A27, which trundles interminably along the southern shore of England, bearing its weight of lorries, coaches and cars as a dragon does armour.

Sussex partakes of some of the character of Kent, though without the latter's air of mystery. Its green and welcoming face has seen a number of invaders over the centuries, for Romans, Vikings and their descendants, the Normans, all marched into this gentle landscape looking for land and plunder. It bears some of the scars still in the form of legends or name-mnemonics.

Not surprisingly, it is a much haunted county, for wherever there is a long history of human habitation, the traces and memories of those contacts appear to remain for indefinite periods of time. As in Suffolk, many of the coastal associations are with smuggling, for its easy access and proximity to France were a temptation irresistible to the impoverished fishing communities. The latter, a tough, self-reliant people, were capable of violence no less than courage when cornered by the law-abiding whose incomes were sizeable enough to guarantee them regular meals.

One such group of smugglers evolved in Bognor, in the days before it acquired its royal possessive, and ran a lucrative trade until a local vicar found matters too much for his conscience. He attempted to put a stop to the activities, and his ban must have had a modicum of success for the local fisher folk laid a curse upon his vicarage and all who should occupy it.

Since that time it seems that the Old Vicarage, Sudley Road, has been an unfortunate place, three incumbents in quick succession having died there, one of them by self-destruction.

The case of the Old Vicarage was brought to my notice by Mrs Irene McFadden of Bognor. Several years ago the house had been in use as an establishment for mentally retarded children and Mrs McFadden worked there as a supervisory nurse. By this time it had the reputation of being haunted. Later it became vacant and eventually fell into disrepair and near dereliction.

It was at about this period that Mrs McFadden again became involved in the place's history. She and a group of friends entered the empty house one night, but at once felt an overpowering sense of evil, and in one particular area—what had been the old servants' staircase—certain of the party thought they heard the sound of footsteps. This was mild enough as experiences go and they were not unduly alarmed.

On another occasion a group of three persons including Irene McFadden, again went over the house, and this time heard the noise of a heavy tread in an upstairs room followed by the sound of something sizeable and apparently cloth-covered being dragged across the floor. This would have been less unnerving had the investigators not just completed an inspection of the entire building and found it empty. With their courage in their hands and their hearts in their mouths they climbed to the affected room: only to discover that the footsteps proceeded to and fro across the room in their presence. This repeated noise, according to Mrs McFadden, continued for four hours, with the witnesses once more in the comparative safety of the hall, embattled but indomitable.

The worst affected area seems undoubtedly to have been the servants' staircase. It was closed at top and foot by doors, and on a third occasion a member of the investigating party had an unnerving encounter involving these doors.

The man concerned, to whom I shall refer as John E., went alone to the stairs and through the lower door which was open and wedged with lino to prevent closure. The door at the top of the staircase was firmly closed. No sooner had John E. set foot upon the stairs than the lower door slammed shut. The door at the top of the stairhead, on the other hand, opened. As if this were not enough preparation for Grand Guignol, the sound of footsteps descending the stairs then became audible, passing John E. *en route*. The latter tore back downstairs, but now the lower door was jammed in the shut position and the demoralized investigator struggled frantically until he could force it open.

After this there was trouble with the windows. First at one end of the hall and then the other, they rattled insistently although the night was still and windless.

Intrepid as Hillary on Everest, the researching group returned to the building the following night. This time they firmly closed the upper door behind them as they descended the affected stairs; only to hear "a great almighty kick on the said door".

There were other incidents. Lights would appear in dark passageways. To quote Irene McFadden, "Lights would light up in a bright white glow and hold that glow. Pinpoints of bright nailheads would glow." The enquirers were undeterred, though their activities were not of a sufficiently professional or organized nature to reach satisfactory conclusions. They tried taking a crucifix into the building and saying a prayer. Finally they consulted a priest who recommended exorcism. It does not seem that this was ever put into practice, though on one or two occasions when prayers were said in the house, the listeners thought they heard a man's voice mumbling, though unintelligibly. At other times water was heard running, lavatories flushing, though the mains water supply had long been disconnected.

Yet again the same group of friends came to the house, apparently fascinated by what they encountered though totally unable to deal with the manifestations. Irene McFadden sat in an old chair, and four men of the group sat upon the actual staircase which was the focal point of the occurrences. Mrs McFadden apparently felt an overwhelming sense of evil and death and wished to leave the place, but before they could do so one of the men of the party, a Canadian, saw standing behind her chair with one hand upon it, the figure of a tall man. Its face was blurred.

On many occasions the sounds of digging were heard from the bottom of the vicarage garden. Apparently this is still so, although the building itself has been demolished.

There now began to be apparent certain effects on the lives of the participants in this ill-advised investigation. One of the group was killed in a motor accident, and the Canadian, Al, and Mrs McFadden herself were injured. My informant is of the opinion that all the group suffered singular bad luck and unhappiness at this time.

The amateur enquiries had reached this stage when Progress, in the form of development contractors, moved in. Bovis Site Contractors began the construction of two large stores (Boots, the Chemists, and W. H. Smith the stationers, I understand) in the street and settled on the empty vicarage as a suitable site office.

About this time Mrs McFadden booked one of the site officials into her hotel as a guest. She knew nothing of his area of work, and it was therefore three months before she heard his story.

It had not taken long for the workmen to realize that their headquarters building was badly haunted. Although the old servants' staircase gave the quickest entrance to the site office, the men refused to use it. All had heard the footsteps and the sound of a heavy bag (described as being similar to that of a sailor's kit-bag) being dragged across the floor. The apparition also had been sighted. Its hand had been particularly noted since one of the fingers wore an ecclesiastical ring.

Once the workmen were in, various materials and impedimenta were apparently kicked audibly about, and cotton and chalk marks laid down as guides to the activity were found disturbed the following morning.

Up to the time of writing these words no explanation has been discovered for the extraordinary series of occurrences which appears to have taken place in the Old Vicarage, Sudley Road, Bognor, though I understand from my informant that research into the vicarage's history is still proceeding. I received from another member of the investigating group, Mr A. Jones of Brighton, confirmation of the incidents quoted by Mrs McFadden.

One is left with a story as confused and detailed as that of Borley Rectory in Essex. And as terrifying. The pattern of the hauntings suggests that the ghost is of a former occupant of the place, and that the action recreates some act anathema to its instigator; murder seems a strong possibility in view of the dragging of a heavy object, the digging in the garden, the sense of evil and death. Perhaps the only way to bring the sequence to an end would be thoroughly to turn over the garden area to see what or who, if anything, lies there. Certainly the manifestation suggests a violent original. A curious case with, as Mrs McFadden points out, a powerful fascination for those whose lives encountered it.

Although baleful presences of this calibre are not uncommon, in general ghosts appear to be indifferent to the living, possibly because so many apparitions are not living entities but mere pattern-pictures projected from the past. That there are exceptions to this generalization is well illustrated by a haunting at Ansty, where a certain farm is reputed to have the ghost of a woman. Mrs Daisy Doyle, now of Billingshurst, was a visitor to it during World War II, when her brother-in-law worked there.

On one of her visits, Daisy was put into the room usually occupied by her ten-year-old nephew, John. During the night she awoke to see the figure of a woman standing by her bed, and although not at all upset by it, she did mention the fact to her relatives the next day. They were much surprised as for several months prior to his aunt's visit, the child had been insisting that a lady came into his bedroom. He had heard her walk down the passage to his door, open it, and after a while return the way she had come. This bedroom of the house (which was Tudor in period) had an old wooden latch which locked by the insertion of a piece of wood behind it. Apparently even if the door were locked it seemed to open and shut during the night yet would still be found locked in the morning. (In some circumstances, apparitions will walk straight through a door or wall, with no nonsense about conventional opening. The Ansty ghost was not of these.) Nothing is known of the history of the house which would account for these manifestations.

From Mrs Doyle also came an account of a haunting at Cowfold Monastery, in which soldiers were billeted during the war. It seems that Alsatian dogs on guard at certain times would growl and raise their hackles without apparent cause. This occurred only in one of the cloisters of the building. The soldiers also appear to have been afraid of this area, though I know of no report of any visual manifestations having taken place.

Seeing these green Sussex lanes in March with enterprising lanceheads of sunlight piercing the patchy clouds one could scarcely conjure the mist and frosts of October. Although Sussex winters are mild compared with those of East Anglia or Northern England, they close the land down into a dark and sullen landscape on end-of-year nights. So found Mr Don Cottrell of Horsham, to whose wife, Bea, I am indebted for the following account.

The incident took place in the October of 1947 a short time before the marriage of Bea to Don Cottrell. After discussing the various wedding arrangements with his fiancée, the young man left to motorcycle back to the village of West Grinstead, some six miles south of Horsham. Before reaching the left-hand turning to his destination, he came to Buck Barn crossroads, where the Horsham–Worthing road is bisected by that from Billingshurst to Haywards Heath. To the right of the crossroads stood a milestone, and as Don Cottrell approached it he was astonished to see an old man seated upon it. It was a cold night with more than a hint of frost, and he was astounded that anyone of that age so raggedly clad should be out in the open. As he drew level with the stone, the man rose and walked out into the road directly in front of him, although he noted that he appeared to glide rather than walk, and above the road rather than upon it. The motorcyclist felt his machine hit something of a deathly coldness before he came abruptly to a halt.

Not unnaturally his first reaction was of horror that he had knocked down and possibly injured or killed a fellow human being. He got off his motorcycle and searched the roadway; he searched the nearer hedgeside and over it; he searched the farther side of the road. All were empty. So was the milestone. There was no one on that stretch of road or its environs except himself.

Had he been given wings he could hardly have covered the ground back to his home more speedily. He was in no doubt but that he had encountered something supernatural. To confirm the extraordinary story, his father immediately drove back to the same spot and thoroughly searched the area of the crossroads. The result was the same. The scene appeared perfectly normal and there was no sign either of an accident or its victim.

Some twenty years later on the Cottrells were entertaining friends to lunch when the raising of the subject of ghost stories brought forth Don Cottrell's own. It came as a surprise to the host and hostess to learn that the tale of the ghost at Buck Barn crossroads had been related on the BBC's Woman's Hour programme a short time before. Apparently the ghost was still appearing in the area at the time of the broadcast.

Since then the country road from Horsham to Worthing has been expanded into a dual carriageway, and although I have heard no recent reports of an apparition there, the area has the reputation of being a persistent accident spot.

One can say that the fact of its location—trunk road crossing minor road—is likely to give rise to accidents. It is also a possibility, however, that some lingering remnants of the original manifestation still operate in the neighbourhood. If hauntings and events of a similar nature take place by means of a 'broadcast' system, then the actual projection must be powered by some form of energy. In view of the electromagnetic nature of the force-field produced by the human organism in life it is likely that that energy is electrical. Any vehicle driving into a force-field of this nature might be subject to temporary malfunction. Accidents in such circumstances would be a strong possibility.

Similar electrical malfunction in cars involved in cases of haunting were observed by me when researching *Haunted East Anglia,* and mechanical failures of a like kind have been reported in connection with UFO encounters.

Almost due south of Horsham and within five miles of the coast at Worthing and Shoreham lies Steyning, and beyond it the village of Wiston. Between the years 1954–58 a cottage in the district was occupied by a Mr and Mrs Kilford, who have now given me the curious story of their residence in this house.

Before moving into their new home the Kilfords decided on redecoration, and in consequence spent several weekends in the task. The cottage was a small one, what is known in agricultural circles as a two-up-and-two-downer. The ground floor contained a sitting-room and kitchen, the latter with egress through the back door, the house's front door opening directly into the sitting-room. This door was kept permanently locked, being fastened with two bolts, a yale lock and one very old lock operated by a huge key. The upstairs accommodation consisted of one fair-sized bedroom and a second room partitioned to make a small bedroom and a bathroom.

The first weekend brought indications of what was to come. The Kilfords, having finished their decorating for the day, decided to drive into Steyning. The cottage was locked up and they left through the back door. However, when they discovered that the lights on their motor-cycle combination appeared to be out of order, they returned to the house with the idea of changing their clothes before catching a bus. They were startled to find that the front door was not only unlocked and unbolted but standing wide open. They concluded that they had omitted to shut it in the first place, and so went through the routine with some precision before again leaving the cottage.

They returned some hours later to find the front door again standing open. That night, the first in their new home, the wife retired to bed before her husband and slept in the small bedroom. She had not gone to sleep when she heard the sound of footsteps coming up the stairs and along the landing to her room. Mrs Kilford thought this was her husband but presently realized that it was not he and then concluded she must have heard the neighbours moving about next door.

This was their initiation. Once they had moved into the cottage the pattern of that first weekend was repeated on several occasions. The Kilfords would go into the sitting-room from the kitchen to find the armchair which habitually stood in front of the door moved to one side, the door curtain pulled back and the door itself standing wide open. On a number of occasions the family cat and dog were discovered in the room with hair bristling.

53

There was one occasion when Mrs Kilford's mother slept in the small bedroom and awoke to see a man standing at the foot of her bed dressed in the style of the early 1920s. Still later in their occupation, the Kilfords' younger daughter saw a man come through the partition wall into her room.

The Kilfords seem to have been sensible, practical people, and they tried to find explanations for the numerous extraordinary incidents which occurred in the cottage—not an easy task when you appear to be sharing your house with an occupant of thirty years earlier. As Mrs Kilford said, "We didn't take a lot of notice until one night I awoke to hear footsteps coming round the bed, and thinking it was my young daughter coming to get in bed with me, said 'Come on, Sue, get in bed'." However, there was no reply. The footsteps stopped at the bedside then started to move back round the bed. Although it was too dark to see anyone on the bed's side of the room, where the window lay was sufficiently light to have shown up the child's outline as she passed it. Mrs Kilford looked towards the window expecting to see her daughter pass in front of it. The footsteps indeed passed and proceeded on out of the door, but no physical outline showed before the low dormer window. Two weeks later precisely the same sequence of events occurred. After this unnerving incident, Mrs Kilford arranged that on any repetition she would awaken her husband so that he could at once put on the light. There was no recurrence, and shortly afterwards the family left the house for good.

Perhaps they were afraid to make enquiries into the cottage's history while they still resided in it for fear of what they might discover. However, once out of it, they found that in the early 1920s a then occupant of the place had been found shot. The death, brought in as accidental, had taken place in the autumn of the year. The manifestations during the Kilfords' occupation had always been in the late summer and early autumn.

Mrs Kilford's balanced and reasonable account of these events suggests either a pattern-haunting or an actual survival of the individual whose life had ended so abruptly in the cottage. From the large number of such cases reported, it does seem that in cases of violent death the human energy (the spirit or soul) as opposed to the matter (or body) of the dead individual often has a tendency to remain in the place where the sudden termination of its life occurred. Why this does not invariably happen is a mystery, but it happens often enough for the enquirer to suspect an 'aware survival'—that is, survival of enough of the psyche to retain the power of independent action. It is this independent action, with its variations and decisions, so that sometimes one and sometimes another kind of manifestation occurs, that distinguishes the apparent survival case from the mechanical pattern-haunting; the latter seeming to be a 'broadcast' strictly related to a part of the surroundings and occurring in exactly the same form on each occasion. The Kilfords' ghost appears to have exhibited enough variety of manifestation to place it in the category of surviving entity.

There is one unexplained factor; that the haunting should be restricted to a certain season. This suggestion of a tie-in with the original occupant's date of death is not particularly surprising, but not particularly welcome, either, when one is trying to discover how the process of haunting works. Like pattern-hauntings, of which they are often a part, anniversary hauntings appear to follow an established rhythm. But how they can do so, why some ghosts should appear only at certain times of the year, is not known. Why, for instance, should the ghost (said to be that of Mary, Queen of Scots, though this is open to doubt) which haunts the Talbot Inn at Oundle, Northamptonshire, appear only in February, the date of the Queen's execution? Why should the gentle spirit which walks Sutherland House, Southwold, make herself felt only on the night before the anniversary of the Battle of Sole Bay?

One seeks logical explanations (for what I believe to be occurrences operating according to an as yet unidentified law of physics) in terms of light, conditions, temperature, weather etc. But these do not always coincide from one year to the next; any more than do the actual dates of hauntings, taking into consideration the calendar variations each fourth year. So this remains a dark area for the investigator, and much concentrated and detailed research needs to be done before enough data is available to be useful.

A perennial fascination of hauntings is the attendant fragments of history which they bring to light. Occasionally these relate to the powerful figures who have influenced the direction of the race's development; more often they speak of the pawns in the game, the peasants, artisans, servants, tradesfolk or clerks who once dead were ever afterwards nameless, remaining if they do so at all, as shadows against a shifting background. But where their echoes have lingered, cling also remnants of a lost way of life, and it is from these we can learn if we pay attention, how our ancestors fared from day to day, what were the matters of importance to them, where their fears and hopes lay, and what they most valued.

In this frenetic, mechanical century which has systematically obliterated the slow, rich beauty of country living, and the deep, innate harmony of spiritual awareness which arose from it, we do not understand how important a part religion played in the lives of our ancestors. Only two generations ago that part was remembered in the very bones, for to our grandfathers Christianity was still a vital force informing all they thought and did, acting as a touchstone for all behaviour, attitudes and relationships. They may not have lived up to its tenets, but neither could they ignore them, for they were built into the very scaffolding of society. And what is incorporated into the structure decides the way the building grows.

But in less than half a century the creation of two millennia has been demolished. Now when we encounter echoes of the past which reveal the degree to which our ancestors worshipped, we either disbelieve or disregard; and certainly do not understand the relationship in which those people stood to their faith.

Between Shoreham and Brighton lies the village of Poling, and in it stands an old house which was once a preceptory of the Knights Hospitallers. The latter was the military order of the knights of the hospital of St John the Baptist, and its members accepted the Augustinian rule in their houses. Founded about 1070, it originally existed to give protection and hospitality to pilgrims and other travellers, and to succour the poor. Its insignia, interestingly enough, was a white cross on a black ground, as that of the Templars was a red cross on a white ground. Their indirect descendants can be seen in the modern Ambulance Order of St John and in the Red Cross Society.

The Hospitallers, in spite of their charitable activities, were mainly concerned in farming their considerable estates (after the fall of the Templars they added the latters' lands to their own, and eventually owned some sixty-five houses in England) and in recruiting for service in the Crusades. The general dissolution of the monasteries in the sixteenth century saw the end of their institution as of their wealth. Now the only trace of this once powerful order lies in the remains of their preceptories or commanderies—the two types of establishment set up by them in England.

The preceptory at Poling is precise in its echoes. Voices are heard singing there with, according to report, a type of organ accompaniment. Although the organ suggests a latter-day church service, apparently the choral music is recognizably a Latin psalm.

Music is frequently an historic remainder (and reminder). Canterbury Cathedral, as already noted, has its medieval singing from the crypt; Fotheringhay Church in Northamptonshire carries echoes of the fourteenth century in the sound of drums and trumpets from within the building. So music appears to be capable of being recorded and replayed as easily as does movement. The extraordinary thing about manifestations of music is that they appear to be coherent and clear, producing recognizable tunes and rhythms. The other form of sound, speech, by contrast is invariably distorted in this type of reproduction. To be able to recognize intelligible speech in a manifestation is rare indeed. Tones can be recognized and some kind of speech pattern, but individual words and sentences usually sound garbled, or as though they had been artificially distorted. The explanation for such distortion could well be a simple physical one, but this aspect of psychic phenomena I hope to discuss later.

Mr A. W. Fayle of Heathfield, who kindly drew my attention to the Poling haunting, also told me of that at Cuckfield Park. This is a reasonably well-known instance, having been catalogued by various writers and ghost-seekers. However, the immediate interest lies in the fact that the ghost has been 'sensed' by the new owner of the Park, who also believes she has seen a shadowy figure moving along passages and stairways in the house ahead of her.

However, another Sussex woman, Miss Frances Blencowe, now dead, but living near Lewes at the time of her own Cuckfield Park experience, appears to have encountered the ghost in fairly substantial form.

From 1654 to the present century Cuckfield was owned by a family named Sergison, and since the Blencowes and Sergisons were connected by marriage, it was natural that on the wedding of one of the Sergison family Miss Blencowe should be invited. The date of this particular event was apparently in 1890, when Frances Blencowe was a young girl.

Being inexperienced in society and shy, Frances was not certain how to greet a lady whom she met upon the stairs. In the event, she did not attempt to speak but merely stood aside for the other to pass, receiving a pleasant smile for her courtesy. Later, at dinner, she looked round for the person she had encountered but the woman was not among those at table. Frances diffidently enquired of her hostess as to the lady's whereabouts, only to be met with a cheerful, "Oh, you must have seen our ghost." The girl thereupon had what she described many years afterwards to Mr Fayle as "a most creepy uncomfortable feeling", though whether in retrospect at having acknowledged and been acknowledged by a ghost, or whether because of some further indication of psychic presence at the moment of her question is not known. "Yesterday upon the stair/I met a man who wasn't there."

Another story well known in this area is that of Nan Tuck of Buxted near Uckfield. There is some doubt about both date and details of the original story, but it relates to the death of a village girl, Nan Tuck, accused of witchcraft, who either died by her own hand or at those of her fellow villagers in what is known locally as Tuck's Wood. It seems most likely that she was lynched by her peers who then sought to exculpate themselves by the suicide charge. However it was, there is now a local legend that at certain times Nan Tuck can be heard and seen running down the lane that bears her name, as she may have run in life before her hunters. I know of no one who has experienced this phantom, however.

There are more modern and better authenticated hauntings in Cuckfield. The sixteenth-century house known as Ockenden Manor is reputed to have a ghost. I first heard about her several years ago when I stayed in the hotel (for this the old house now is), though I spent a peaceful night and saw no sign of the 'grey lady'. When I called again recently to ask about their ghost's health, I was told she had not been seen for some time.

The haunted room, known as the Raymond Room, is an oak-panelled chamber with some beauty. It has a slight atmosphere, but when I visited there was insufficient tension present to suggest an active haunting. The proprietor stated that on one occasion a honeymoon couple was offered the room, but the girl disliked it and refused to sleep in it. One elderly lady who did sleep there asked not to be put in the room again, though apparently she gave no reason for the request. But according to tradition, there is or once was a 'grey lady' occupying the Raymond Room and its nearby landing. As with many long-established manifestations, with the passage of time this one may have become weaker and may now be said to be at vanishing point.

Not so with the haunter of The King's Head in the same village. She is known cheerfully to the pub's employees as Geranium Jane, from the fact that her own demise was said to have been caused by a well-aimed flower-pot from above.

This is one of the few active ghost stories about which some kind of foundation history is known. Jane is thought to have been a serving-maid at the inn (the precise period of her life is not known, though the nineteenth century is suggested) who was seduced by her employer. When she became pregnant and in time demanding, it is rumoured that he quieted her with the geraniums.

Present employees vouch for the fact that parts of the upper building are subject to unexplained noises, that objects unaccountably move from place to place and that certain areas manifest an extreme chill. One of the staff, Mrs Sheila Wakeham, told me that about two months before my visit, there had been an apparent 'intensification of atmosphere', and that these fluctuations in intensity of haunting were characteristic of the case. At this time, Sheila Wakeham had felt unable to stay upstairs alone. There had, she explained, been a number of unexplained noises, lights were switched on and off by unseen agency and the general feeling was intense and unpleasant.

Geranium Jane is not only an audible but a visible ghost, though her appearances seem to be chiefly to men. It has been noted that where a man connected with the hotel is sexually misconducting

The King's Head, Cuckfield, Sussex, where Geranium Jane haunts, seen mainly by men.

himself (a state of affairs with which the ghost appears to have little sympathy!) he is liable to encounter the apparition. One such employee of the hotel found his bed being vigorously pushed around at dead of night, the activity accompanied by a deep sensation of cold within the room.

On another occasion a woman bar-worker had her two children with her in the building during her spell of duty. They had been playing contentedly enough upstairs until about midday, when they came running down calling out that they had just seen a woman walking about with make-up streaming down her face. It is not known whether the 'make-up' resembled blood or not.

The figure has twice been seen by one of the managers, and on several occasions by other persons about the hotel. Usually the sighters are male.

The hotel is thought to have a second ghost, though less well-documented than Geranium Jane. In the long bar downstairs a young boy has occasionally been sighted. He appears to be confined to this particular area and I gathered that though his form has been seen his face has not.

One of my favourite parts of Sussex has always been the neighbourhood of Hassocks and Hurstpierpoint, partly because of my incurable addiction to antique shops (in which the area once abounded) and partly because the uphill-and-downdale nature of the landscape gives the impression, give or take a trunk road or two, that it has not changed its ways for a thousand years. This corner of the county has a determinedly rural air and its villages are true villages rather than dormitory suburbia for large nearby towns. It is not hard to believe that this piece of Sussex felt Roman sandals. The Roman road known as the Sussex Greensand Way passes through Hurstpierpoint from east to west and crosses the nearby estate of Danny.

Hurst, as its inhabitants refer to it, was a manor at the time of the Conquest, owned by Earl Godwin, who was rapidly dispossessed of it in favour of the Norman de Pierpoints. Not that the Norman traces are much in evidence now. Hurst is preponderantly Victorian and Edwardian with an overlay of between-the wars development.

What local supernatural echoes there are belong not to Hurstpierpoint but to Danny House—Daneghitte of 1343, when Simon de Pierpoint received a licence to enclose the wood of that name. A small hunting lodge was built there which, little used, began to fall to ruin. It was rescued in the sixteenth century by a certain Gregory

Dacre, who turned it into an attractive small manor house. It was improved again in the eighteenth century and eventually used by Prime Minister Lloyd George as a country retreat towards the end of World War I.

The ghost of Danny would appear to be romantic rather than political, and her period of origin is not known. She is yet another of the interminable 'grey ladies' who haunt English country houses. As far as I can discover, she is a quiet apparition, as she stands at the top of the stairs in Danny House, waiting for a lover who was killed by some means unknown. I understand she has been seen on several occasions by persons working at the house. For Danny still has an actively useful life as a home for retired people, its building converted into flats by the Mutual Households Association. The idea of such continuity in an era which is noticeably lacking in it is comforting.

Move a mile or two to the west across the main road which connects Brighton with Crawley and London, and you will come to Pyscombe. Local people assert that the area is haunted by the ghost of a girl killed in a motor accident. She is most often seen late at night (presumably the time of her death), and has been encountered within the last few months, though I found no first-hand account of a sighting and the story is therefore hearsay only.

Far from hearsay is the story related by Mr Roy Chambers of Angmering, to whose friend, Mr J. W. Clifton, I am indebted for it. This account was given direct to Mr Clifton for onward transmission to the author, since the original percipient felt himself inadequate to the task of writing it. It is a clear, succinct statement of an event which occurred towards the end of August in, so far as Mr Chambers can remember, the year 1964.

The subject was at that time working on a local farm and set out to go to a barn at a place known as The Pound, the latter being situated in a field which is now converted to nurseries. The exact situation of the field is said to be between the ancient Ecclesden Manor and Highdown Hill, near Angmering.

The time was about seven o'clock in the evening and still full daylight. As Mr Chambers approached the farm gate leading to The Pound, he saw on the other side of it a man dressed in a brown monk's habit, seated on a bank below a hedge, reading what seemed to be a prayer book.

Nothing about the brown-habited man appears to have struck strangely upon Roy Chambers's perceptions, for he proceeded without hesitation to climb over the gate in order to attend to his cowman's duties. Hardly had he done so, than the monkish figure stood up. He was now only two or three yards from it and was discomposed to see that the man was incredibly tall. "So much so and being so close that it frightened me. I began to move off at a brisk pace. I estimate he must have been at least eight and probably nearer nine feet tall. After going not more than ten yards at a near run, I took a look back and was astonished to find that he had completely disappeared, for there was absolutely nowhere he could have vanished in such a short time. I later examined the hedge and it was much too thick to pass through. I ran from the spot feeling quite terrified."

Mr Chambers was deeply shaken by this experience. Frivolous acquaintances later tried to jolly him out of his conviction, suggesting he had either paid a prior visit to the local hostelry or suffered an hallucination. However, he stuck to his story then as now. "I am quite sure I saw what I have described and am ready to swear to the truth of it on oath. I am not an idiot. I remember it very vividly and I am not ashamed to admit I was very, very scared."

When one considers that the figure appeared to be a good three feet taller than the average tall man, Mr Chambers's distress is not surprising. How often in a lifetime does one see a giant, still less an apparitional one?

Later the percipient made local enquiries, and was told by natives of the area that Ecclesden Manor was a former monastic building. There were stories, too, of one monk of giant size. As in similar instances elsewhere, when the monastic orders were dissolved, the monks at Ecclesden apparently resisted their eviction with vigour and a number were killed in the skirmishing which followed. Was the gigantic monk one of these?

It is not easy in the chill rationalism of the present era to conceive of the resentment, misery and fear which the Dissolution generated in the minds of cleric and laymen alike in the sixteenth century. As long as men could remember, as long as their fathers, grandfathers and great-grandfathers had lived and well beyond that, there had been monastic orders in England. The monks were teachers, doctors, ministers, farmers and landlords; and sinners as often as they were saints. But they were an integral part of the social structure. As well imagine life without them and their hospices and monasteries, cells and abbeys as life without a king or a powerful aristocracy. No matter how corrupt or worldly certain of them became, they represented knowledge and a long-standing, long-surviving aspect of civilization; they had carried the tenuous thread of culture through several centuries; they provided handy reference point and touchstone alike for the faithful as for the illiterate, the sick and the dependent; and an occasional useful tool for those with the power and wit to use it. Above all, they were there, immutable as the power of the Crown itself.

Then in a matter of months they were gone, swept into the past, leaving behind an immense vacuum and the panic which was bound to attend its creation. One does not overturn a third of the social order without an uprooting of whatever surrounds and is interwoven with it. The monks were dispossessed, turned out of their traditional homes and way of life and livelihood. They, the long-time ecclesiastic haves, became have-nots, beggars and starvelings. The institutions they had fostered—infirmaries, lazar-houses, hospices, schools—seemed likely to founder with them, and in many cases did so. It would be years before the rent in this particular fabric was repaired. How much thought, one wonders, did Henry VIII give to the consequences of his action, beyond the fact that the Orders were rich and his Treasury needed replenishing?

It would scarcely be surprising if the giant monk of Ecclesden had died fighting the King's Officers. Others had followed the same road—in Lincolnshire and Yorkshire their rebellion was later referred to as the Pilgrimage of Grace—and been assisted in their struggle by local peasantry whose need of the monasteries' survival was as great as the monks' own. The Dissolution of the Monasteries was at once the most destructive and the most revolutionary act of domestic politics undertaken by a Tudor monarch.

One interesting aspect of the Ecclesden manifestation, is that the legend of a giant monk has survived, apparently by word-of-mouth tradition alone, through almost five centuries. The oral traditions of an area are usually worth serious consideration if one desires to learn the intimate details of its history.

The drive along the A27 which parallels England's south coast is nowadays less a scenic pleasure than a monotonous, foot-on-the-floor race from one sizeable town to the next. When it is possible to remove the eyes from the road for a few seconds, one can take in the Downs to the north and, very occasionally, a gleaming strip of English Channel to the south. In the spring the driver is tantalized by verdant glimpses down small country byways as he hurtles past, and it is well worth while to rein the steed in occasionally, desert the battered highway and lose oneself temporarily in the network of lanes around Walberton, Blatchington or Kingston.

As the spring deepens and the sharp yellows mature to a darker gold, the lanes seem to sink lower into their trees in a luxuriously sensuous fashion, as though they had waited all winter for this particular disguise, this comfortable oblivion. Any traveller who forsakes the embattled high road for the lanes may find himself ambling through them for weeks, until their greens brown at the edges and curl into autumn, and the twigs let in the first damp wind from the west.

While I was researching in Sussex the wind seemed semi-permanently damp, though blowing chiefly from the east. I fell once for the lure of the lanes south of the A27, but had a sound excuse as the ghosts were clustered thickly along the coastal areas of the county and the lanes led alluringly to the sea.

About halfway between Worthing and Rustington lies the village of East Preston. In 1970 the district was quieter than it is today, and had still the feeling of an unspoilt countryside. In a house next to the church at East Preston lived Mrs Dorothy Stringer, who told me of a singularly terrifying experience she had had there.

At the time of the occurrence (September 1970 approximately), Mrs Stringer was sleeping in a downstairs bedroom, and on the night in question had left her window open. During the night she awoke to the sensation of something creeping stealthily up her bed from the foot. It seemed, she said, as though the eiderdown were lifted from the bed and dropped upon the floor. She then sensed the 'thing' approaching her throat, making as it travelled "a soft buzzing noise like something electrical".

With a tremendous effort, the percipient managed to raise her hand and switch on the light. As she did so, she "saw a flash of something white go right through the door". She then discovered that the eiderdown was lying flat on her bed, as though newly placed there.

The next morning when the local handyman called at the house to work, it was discovered that the entire contents of a large dustbin standing outside the house were scattered over the surrounding area, though no sound had been heard by an understandably wakeful Mrs Stringer.

The experience described occurred once only and according to the percipient was of a terrifying nature. Mrs Stringer, who impressed me as a sensible, well-balanced person, seemed to have thought the manifestation had some connection with electricity or some kind of machinery, in view of the noise she heard. The house was quite silent when she awoke apart from this particular sound.

She was able to put forward no explanation for this highly unpleasant encounter, beyond a tentative remark that her father-in-law, who had disliked her during his lifetime, was buried in the next door churchyard. As far as she was aware there was no machinery or electrically powered apparatus in the neighbourhood of East Preston.

In answer to questions, a possibly significant fact came to light. I had asked if to the best of her knowledge any other person had had a similar experience in the house. Mrs Stringer's reply was that after she left the premises, a housekeeper was found dead in the very bed which she herself had occupied.

A disturbing story, for whatever it was which troubled that bedroom, the effect it had on the living seems to have been powerful and horrifying. Or perhaps I should use the present tense? I have heard no word from any current occupant of a house next to the churchyard at East Preston. It would be interesting to know if this unpleasant manifestation continues. There can be no enlightenment as to its cause, I think, without further evidence, and in particular further knowledge of the history of the house and its previous occupants.

It is remarkable that a large number of Sussex hauntings seem to occur around the county's coasts. Why this should be so is impossible to guess, for the same factor does not appear to apply in neighbouring counties. Sussex, however, possesses a long coastline, and the sea's presence makes itself felt even when you are out of sight and sound of it. In earlier centuries the coastal dwellers lived off and from the sea—fishing, sailing, smuggling, as opportunity arose and starvation drove. Little wonder, then, that Sussex's coast occasionally holds echoes of harshly violent conditions.

Yet smuggling, an occupation of some hazard, has left fewer imprints upon its former surroundings than have the peacefully ubiquitous monks whose homes peppered Sussex until the sixteenth century.

During the winter of 1950–51, Miss J. Fermor (now of Peacehaven) worked as an assistant in John Beal's, a well-known stationer's shop in East Street, Brighton. During the two weeks before Christmas, Miss Fermor and the shop's manageress, Miss Goodbody, were working late into the evening in order to price the large stock of new diaries which had just been received, it being the custom for the staff to stay late for a few nights until the new stock had been marked up. Each supplier had a different list of goods and prices, and frequent queries arose as the stock was being checked. The usual procedure at Beal's at this time was for the stock to be checked first, then individual diaries marked off and priced against the respective invoice.

The two women were at work in one of two stockrooms from which a flight of stairs led down to the shop premises. At one point during the evening, Miss Goodbody remarked that she appeared to have left a list in the shop, and would have to get it. Miss Fermor heard her go down the stairs and then shortly afterwards the sound of footsteps ascending. Although she thought they approached at a good deal less than Miss Goodbody's usual speed, the younger girl assumed the manageress was reading the invoice *en route*. She therefore did not trouble to turn when the footsteps sounded in the outer stockroom and ascended the two steps into the room where she was working. The girl called out "Is that you, Goody?" though she had no expectation that it would be any other as the two of them were alone in the building. Getting no reply, Miss Fermor turned; and found herself facing a tall dark figure dressed in robes and a cowl. "As far as I could see it had no face. Then the horror of the situation struck me and I fled down to the shop. There was Miss Goodbody at her desk, sorting through papers."

The two women did not work late again.

On later enquiry, the percipient learned that the monk had been seen by other persons in the area. She was shown, also, a number of underground passageways which led away from the neighbourhood of the shop, and although I have not personally inspected this area, it seems likely that it was the site of a monastic foundation and that cellars or a crypt with interconnecting tunnels may have survived.

From this account an interesting fact stands out; that although the cowl and habit of the monk (if such it was) were perfectly materialized, its face was not. This recalls similar cases already detailed when the head and face of an apparition have either been incompletely materialized or not at all. It is not uncommon to find that an apparition materializes only in part, and this may be because, where a pattern-haunting is concerned, either the 'recorder' or its surroundings have been tampered with, repaired or altered in such a way that the entire record of an earlier proceeding is damaged. If, for instance, the level of a floor or ceiling has been raised or lowered, any picture projected by a part of the surroundings will continue to be thrown in precisely its old place. An Elizabethan courtier, therefore, who appeared to walk on *terra firma* before the floor level was lowered, may now find himself gliding gracefully two feet above it. It is also possible for an incomplete picture to be shown by reason of removal of part of the actual recorder, resulting in the appearance of only the upper or lower halves of apparitions, which materialize distressingly unaccompanied by the rest of their anatomy.

Yet for an entire figure to materialize minus only its head or face—or, what is even more suggestive, for the missing portion to be present in the form of a misty shape—leads to the conclusion that there is less a mechanical discrepancy operating than a minor power failure. This is to suppose that materialization of any pictorial representation (whether thought of as hallucinatory or physically visual) requires power for it to operate at all.

We cannot tell, so inadequate is current knowledge on the question, whether the energy used in a non-mechanical (i.e., not 'broadcast' or 'projected' by a recording process) manifestation is subjectively or objectively created. In other words, where an apparition materializes of its own accord we do not know whether it generates the necessary energy within itself to appear in visual form, or whether it requires and is able to use an outside source of energy for the process. All that seems certain at this stage of knowledge, is that energy in some form is used, and that in some cases difficulty seems to be experienced in materializing detailed representations of the head and face.

A conclusion of this nature, speculative as it is, must give rise to interesting lines of thought, and perhaps later, of investigation, since it presupposes that the materializer is of such a kind that it can exercise an intelligent and deliberate control over its appearance.

To drive from West to East Sussex is to see little change of landscape. The scenery is still pleasant, vernal, undulating, with the shoulders of the Downs hunched to the north of the road, swelling into the skyline as though like Browning's giants they lay "Chin upon hand, to see the game at bay . . .". But the downs are not malevolent—at least not explicitly so. Their age is great, and occasionally the trespassing, minuscule human appears to affront it and then to feel the weight of the hills' ancientness fall upon him.

But threats of this nature are different in kind from those arising out of human activities. Indeed, the sensations experienced in the presence of prehistoric sites, associated as they often are with dramatic natural features, are less a threat than a sense of the alien imposed by the very strangeness of their distance in time from us. *Autre temps, autres moeurs.* The human threats are closer and easier to understand and accommodate.

Eastbourne, that elegant refuge for the retired, holds a surprising number of ghostly associations several of which were notified to me by Mr Robert Armstrong, a member of a psychic research group in the town. Although these vary in their circumstantial detail, I am assured that all have been investigated by the local researchers and been thought to be genuine.

A house in Hurst Road was formerly occupied by a Mrs J. Moran, and during the time she lived there she regularly heard the front door open at night and the sound of footsteps walking along the passage and up the stairs. On one occasion, the lady's brother paid her a visit, but after spending part of one night in a room at the top of the stairs, he refused to remain, and at three o'clock in the morning packed his bags and left, not to return again. Curiously, he seems not to have revealed to his sister the nature of his experience in the room, possibly for fear of alarming her to the point where she would have been unable to continue living in the place. As it was, she saw an apparition on several occasions, and became so nervous that she would only sleep in the downstairs front room and would not venture upstairs even in daylight. Eventually, she was re-housed by the local council, presumably at her own request, and has slept peacefully since then. It would be interesting to know whether or not subsequent tenants of the Hurst Road house have suffered any disturbance.

A manifestation equally unpleasant and persistent occurred about 1969 in one of a group of cottages in Watts Lane. About this time a Mr and Mrs McClurg purchased one of the dwellings, but no sooner had they moved in to it than various unscheduled events began to take place. Rooms which were warm suddenly lost their heat and became icy; doors opened and closed without benefit of human agency; bathwater was turned on; and finally Mr McClurg awoke to find an apparitional shape "holding his legs firmly to the bed".

The following day a Roman Catholic priest was called in and he sprinkled each room in the house with holy water. Thereafter the manifestations appeared to cease, though it is worth noting that Mrs McClurg at some time during the next five years moved away from the house for a period. Five years from the date of the exorcism she returned, however, and at once further manifestations began.

The form of the house's late owner was seen to come up the stairs and walk into the bedroom, every detail of his clothing and face being clearly visible. The morning following this occurrence, when the husband had left for work and Mrs McClurg and the children were asleep, the latter (sleeping in the room next to their parents) were awakened by the sound of a voice calling from the attic. This occurrence was repeated on a number of other mornings, and was sometimes accompanied by the lifting and dropping of the hatch-door. On yet another occasion, when five or six people were present in a downstairs room, a heavy coffee table levitated from the ground before dropping to the floor. Shortly afterwards the house was sold and the McClurgs moved out.

It is remarkable that when Mrs McClurg was not living in the house the manifestations were in abeyance. As soon as she returned, they recommenced with apparently renewed vigour. Whether she acted as a kind of agent or medium for them, or whether the presence of her particular type of personality was necessary before the manifestations could occur, there is now no way of knowing, but it seems reasonable to conclude that her presence acted as either a stimulant or a catalyst to whatever emotion or energy was present in the house. This particular cottage is still occupied, I understand.

Another haunting, though of a very different nature, occurred for a while in a nursing-home in Gorringe Road, Eastbourne. One of the residents, an old man, in due course died at the home, but for many months afterwards could be heard in the sitting-room in the evenings. Apparently he never spoke, but other occupants could feel his presence and hear the sound of his breathing. This proved so disconcerting that the room ceased to be used after the evening meal. The building has now changed hands, and one assumes that the old resident has perhaps finally been able to overcome his reluctance to leave his last earthly position.

A house in Alfriston, near Eastbourne appears to have at least three ghosts. Mrs Christine Williams gave me a graphic description of her family's encounters with them during the seven years they spent at Tuckvar, the house concerned. Originally Georgian, the building possesses a Victorian façade and had at one time a stable block of the same period a few yards away across the gravelled drive. This stable has now been demolished.

The Williams family had not been in the house more than a few days, when the eldest girl, aged about six at the time, asked who was the old man she had seen by the garage. From the child's description of an elderly man with white or grey hair wearing a long leather or baize apron almost to his ankles, her mother concluded that it must be a local craftsman who was due to repair the garage roof. It was discovered later, however, that the craftsman had not yet called at the house and that the figure seen must be some other. This was the beginning of a series of experiences with the manifestation outside the house. At this point I will quote from Mrs Williams's letter to me. "Many au pairs came and went, one staying only two days because in the first room I put her in she thought she was choking to death and would not sleep in it, and she didn't like the downstairs room I put her in either. This had been the original kitchen, with inglenook etc. and a door leading to the yard at the top of the drive, opposite the stable block. An American au pair slept there and refused to stay there after she had heard footsteps crunching on the gravel, but had been too afraid to look out. My husband's niece came to stay with her fiancé, and we put him in the downstairs room, after telling him—jokingly!—to look out for ghostly footsteps. Although he never said anything to us, later we heard that he hadn't slept at all, having been terribly scared by the sudden sight of an old man peering in through the window at him. By this time I was sure he was just an old tramp, being far too taken up with the ghost *inside* the house to believe we had two!"

The fact was that Tuckvar had at least two ghosts. The major one inside the building appears to have been that of a tall, grey-haired woman, who regularly came to the bedside of the younger daughter of the family, and tucked her in at night. The little girl told her mother of this, adding on one occasion that the woman had kissed her before leaving the room. The child had been disturbed enough by this to ask her mother not to allow friends to come and look at her in bed. The parents knew that this had not been what had occurred, and they stayed in the bedroom on one night and asked the ghost aloud to go away. From that time, the little girl did not complain of further disturbance. This room, incidentally, was that in which one of the au pairs had felt a choking sensation.

Christine Williams herself shall continue the narrative. "One night some new friends were playing poker quite late and the husband asked which way the toilet was. As I had a good poker hand I did not get up and show him but told him 'Upstairs and second on the left'. When he came back he was strangely quiet and eventually I asked him if he was all right. He said that he had been followed upstairs by a woman in a long, rustling dress, that he had sensed her rather than seen her, but had heard her. She appeared to leave him (discreetly!) on the landing just before he got to the toilet. This man was a down to earth farmer who said he was not given to over-imagination!

"A new baby-sitter complained on our return that while she had been nursing the baby she had seen someone 'flitting about' behind the larder door which was ajar, and never volunteered to baby sit again!

"One night some old friends visited us and my husband saw them out, going down the front path with them. He left the front door open and the porch light on. This was a big lantern we had brought from Venice and gave an excellent light. Once they had gone he realized that he had left the car out, and while driving it up the drive he had seen what he took to be me on the porch. He came into the kitchen and asked me why I had been standing outside on a cold night, and why I had not shut the door and put the light out. I said I had not moved from the kitchen. Later our friends reported that they had thought someone was waving goodbye to them too."

Some time later the Williamses decided to hold an Ouija session in the hope of contacting their indoor ghost. The results were interesting and a shortened version is given below.

(After initial "Is anyone there?" etc.)
A. Yes.
Q. Where did you live?
A. Grant Lodge.
Q. Where is that?
A. Why should I tell you. I live in this house.
Q. Who are you?
A. Rachel Stretton. Class me as your benefactor.
(There was an interruption, then we asked)
Q. Have you left us?
A. Not for a second.
(My husband asked at length if this was the lady seen by our daughter who "tucked the children in" and why she did it etc.)
A. Were not you tucked in?
My husband now impressed for the first time and asked
Q. When did you live here?
A. In seventeen ninety.
Q. Were you the owner of the house or a servant?
A. Stayed for a child who was seven and stopped at seven.
Q. Was the child yours?

A. No.
Q. Are you always here?
A. I will always remain as long as I may.

Although Ouija can often give good results, it can be a two-edged weapon and should never be undertaken lightly. In my view it should not be undertaken at all save by those with considerable knowledge of paranormal matters and their mechanisms. Such séance-type operations appear to generate a collective energy over which the participants have no control, and which seems to be open to use by any surviving entity in the area. The results can be both frightening and unpleasant.

Towards the end of the Williamses' time in the house, the husband met a Canadian immigrant who had been born and brought up in the house, Tuckvar, Alfriston. The latter's first words on meeting Christine Williams were "Tell me, is this house still haunted?" He then went on to tell them what he knew of the background.

His father had been a doctor, and had kept a horse and trap in the stables in the old-fashioned manner. His mother also had two horses and a groom was employed who lived over the stabling area. He was an oldish man who habitually wore a long apron down to his ankles.

Mrs Williams assured me that when giving them this information the doctor's son was quite unaware of any haunting by the man, and merely described what he remembered of him during his own time at Tuckvar. He did, however, confirm his own childhood fear of the bathroom and of the various places which had aroused fear in the Williams children. He particularly mentioned having seen figures moving about the house, and mentioned specifically a top attic room which had been used by a housekeeper.

This had been singled out for mention by Christine Williams's mother (a woman of some psychic sensitivity) as being an unpleasant room with a malicious influence in it. This lady 'felt' that whatever was present inside the room had a connection with the presence outside the house. It was, she said, as though the female were trying to get the male into the room. She appeared to think that there had been a sexual affair between the two. This remains absolutely unproven and no evidence has come to light to reflect on the statement in any way.

In conclusion, Mrs Williams assured me that a pony kept for her own children, behaved in a most unusual manner when shut in the stable. Initially it would refuse to enter and would have to be pushed in. Once inside it kicked and rattled an enamel bucket and eventually threw the top half of the door off its hinges. It had struck Mrs Williams, however, that the responsibility for the last activity might not lie with the pony.

A haunting of a different nature occurred in their house, also—one apparently introduced into it from outside. In about 1968/69 Mrs Williams found herself in need of a good-sized desk, and having failed to buy an antique one on which she had set her heart, she purchased a desk of a similar size and shape from a local second-hand shop. It was a white-painted piece, having two drawers and a stretcher bar for the feet. She understood that it had originally been a dressing-table.

Mrs Williams was and is interested in writing, and during the first few weeks she worked with an unusual degree of intensity at the desk, producing a series of short stories. During this period of activity she became aware of the sound of a cat purring somewhere nearby.

Knowing that an adjacent row of derelict cottages housed stray cats, she assumed one of these was seated on the large windowsill outside the room in which she was sitting. However, there was no sign of the animal when she looked. On several subsequent occasions she heard the purring which sounded both loud and close. It was not until she heard the noise on a day of pouring rain, that she knew the unreality of it. As she herself said, ". . . no cat I ever knew purred in the rain!"

Afterwards she looked round the outside of the building thinking a cat may have found a sheltered spot under the overhanging eaves of the bay-window. She even threw stones up to disturb it, but this brought no response.

Eventually she realized that whenever she got up from the desk the purring ceased. Also it became apparent that the sound was coming from under the desk—precisely the kind of warm, sheltered place which would appeal to a living cat.

At no time did Mr Williams hear the cat, though his wife continued to hear it frequently. In fact after a while she began to feel the animal brushing her legs. "It was the end of summer and I was wearing flip-flop sandals and a pair of acrylic trousers. These cling to the leg when touched and are the sort of thing that seem to hold a lot of static electricity. I could actually feel them moving slightly on my leg however still I kept, just as they would if a real cat had been delicately twining round my feet. Once I got quite a shock when it landed in my lap! There was a sudden 'bump' on my knees and extra weight—but not as much weight, I think, as a real cat would have made. I fancy it got off at once as I didn't feel anything after that."

The Williamses were intending to move house, and shortly after this episode, Mrs Williams called in the owner of the second-hand shop with a view to selling some surplus furniture. During the course of conversation she mentioned the old desk she had purchased and told the woman of her experiences with it, asking if the dealer knew anything of its history.

She was informed that the original owner had been an elderly woman living in a residential area of Eastbourne. She had apparently been a breeder of pug dogs and Siamese cats.

Mrs Williams, in her narration of the story to me, then made an interesting remark. "This was the second time I had told someone about the cat ... and I think I 'told' it away, because it never purred again." This is an unusual interpretation of the reason for a haunting's cessation. In my experience the fact of the desk's being shortly afterwards moved to another setting (in the Williamses' new house) may have accounted for the end of the purring puss. On the other hand, genuine survivals by animals appear to last only a short space of time after death. I myself had a beautiful marmalade cat killed by a careless motorist almost outside my home. For several weeks afterwards not only I, but visitors to the house heard the sound of a cat jumping on and off one of the upstairs beds. This particular cat had been addicted to sleeping on the beds and the sound we later heard had been common in his lifetime. He was a markedly affectionate cat and much attached to the house while he lived. Mrs Williams's desk-loving cat may have been of the same kind, remaining with a favoured piece of furniture rather than a favourite house.

Tuckvar was not the only haunted house in which the Williams family had lived. At one time they had occupied Woodhorne Manor, Arlington, a village about eight miles north of Eastbourne.

Woodhorne was built in 1300, and added to in later periods. A long, low, thatched building it still stands by the side of a stream, a tributary of the Cuckmere, and for a large part of its existence seems to have been owned by the clergy. According to Christine Williams, the deeds of Woodhorne state that the owner may claim a free pew in Chichester Cathedral, and local tradition insists that monks once lived there.

Clerics may not have been the only occupants; the house may also have been used by smugglers, for the Williamses' predecessor in the house when repairing the thatch found a wedge of tobacco the size of a shoe-box hidden beneath the eaves. When found it was green with age. The daughter of the local publican told Mr and Mrs Williams that in her childhood she had played in an underground passage connecting the manor with the church. The habit of running contraband underground and hiding it in a nearby church was common practice wherever smuggling took place, so the smuggling rumour probably has some foundation. The tunnel became unsafe many years ago, however, and was filled in.

So much for the known history of Woodhorne Manor. One mystery remains before the haunting is considered. In two or three places in the garden of the house there are great stones, apparently either millstones or grinding stones. These may have some relevance to what follows.

According to Christine Williams, she was awakened one night at about 1.00 a.m. by the sound of voices arguing loudly in an upstairs room. "They sang, quarrelled, and there was a very definite sound of boots on bare floor boards. It sounded as if two men, one with a deep and another with a high voice, were having a drunken argument." Mrs Williams states that she lay in bed, listening to the row, almost paralysed by fear, for the sounds she heard appeared to come from a room which didn't exist—a room built over the stream which ran by the side of the house.

Her husband did not awaken, and the frightened woman tried to rationalize what she was hearing. Remembering the public house a few yards down the road, she concluded that there had been an unscheduled 'late evening' at the pub and that she was hearing the sounds of drunken revelry—or at least, echoes of those sounds. So thinking she fell asleep.

The following morning she made a point of questioning the publican's daughter, but was told categorically that the hostelry had closed early, "about 9.30, as no-one came in". When Christine Williams related her experience, the other said, "Oh, you must have heard the ghosts of Woodhorne Manor. Lady Pat (a previous owner) was always complaining about them."

Mrs Williams's own experience was confirmed by that of her sister who lived with the family for two years. She later confessed to Christine that during her stay at Woodhorne she had several times heard either arguments or the sound of apparently wild parties from the upstairs rooms, often when no one but herself was in the house.

It is not possible to offer a cut-and-dried explanation for these events, but from Mrs Williams's description of the old millstones which still stand in the garden of Woodhorne, and from the traditional association of the place with both monks and smugglers, the following is put forward as a possible theory to account for the manifestations.

Being constructed immediately beside a stream, it is likely that the original builders intended to utilize the water power for flour-milling purposes. Certainly if they were monks, this intention is likely. If this were carried out, then the mill may have been built *over* the stream as an adjunct to the main building, which would account for the direction of the paranormal sounds if not the sounds themselves. The raucous nature of the latter equates more readily with the lives of smugglers than men of God—though in the Middle Ages the monks were often little better than the laymen they professed to guide.

However, the underground passage seems fairly conclusive evidence that Woodhorne at some time in its history was a smugglers' hideout. I incline to think, therefore, that it is 'the gentlemen' who roister and quarrel in a non-existent room over the Cuckmere tributary. Proof may lie on the bank of the stream opposite to the Manor. I understand this is heavily overgrown, but if it were ever searched and traces of a building's foundations discovered, then it might be assumed that a mill house once was perched over the water. Something in the immediate neighbourhood appears to have recorded scenes from times past and to be sporadically re-broadcasting them.

The eeriness of this type of haunting is pointed up by its apparently non-existent location in space. The fact that the recording is likely to be of voices silent these hundred and fifty years is no less uncanny. Audible manifestations seem to have a particular disturbing effect upon those who encounter them.

Frequently when the subject of hauntings is raised, mention is made of poltergeists. For years the noisy and disturbing manifestations attributed to unruly spirits were thought to be caused by malevolent or mischievous ghosts, but it is now accepted in research circles that this type of activity is probably a subjective projection of energy by a living person. Research carried out in the U.S.A. shows that in many cases of this type of disturbance the affected household contains an adolescent (more frequently female than male), and that there is often a history of emotional stress and tension in the family circumstances.

The resultant outbursts of turbulent physical activity (in which objects may be thrown about, furniture overturned or articles hurled through the air) may be caused by an involuntary explosion of uncontrolled energy by the adolescent; such energy randomly directed may account for the violence experienced within the household. This form of manifestation is often referred to as Recurrent Spontaneous Psychokinesis or R.S.P.K.

However, the term poltergeist is still frequently applied by laymen to any psi activity which involves movement of objects, though such movement is rarely due to a true poltergeist effect and much more often to a run-of-the-mill haunting apparently involving non-living persons.

One such instance was reported to me by Miss Margot Hamilton of Bexhill-on-Sea, who lives in the lower of two flats in a house in Marina Court Avenue, formerly the property of the Rajah of Cooch Behar. The magnate, in fact, had not only lived but died in the house.

In the earlier years of Miss Hamilton's residence there were definite signs of a haunting in the lower flat. The occupant was awakened at 3.00 a.m. one morning by a violent hammering on her door. Her Pekinese dog which slept in the bedroom rushed across the room furiously barking. Miss Hamilton herself, thinking that at the least the hammering indicated an emergency—an accident or illness—in the house, leapt out of bed and ran to open the door. However, no one was there and the building was perfectly silent.

On other occasions when she was standing near the back door the bell would ring violently, but on opening it she would find no sign of a caller.

The heating arrangements were also affected. During one autumn when the weather was particularly warm for October, Miss Hamilton remembers congratulating herself that she would not need to use the night storage heater in her hallway. However, when she checked the apparatus, she found it was indeed switched on, although no one had touched it.

Matters continued to progress thus until one Sunday evening. Miss Hamilton was accustomed to wind her grandfather clock at this time each week, but now was unable to find the key, usually kept on the ledge before the clock face. Her maid was on holiday but on returning was asked about the key's whereabouts. "Oh," she said, "on the way down the stairs I noticed some dust on the top of the clock, so I got the ladder and found the key on top." As far as both women were aware, neither they nor anyone else had placed the key where it was found, and there appeared to be no logical explanation for its altered position.

Soon afterwards the owner applied for help from the church, and a local clergyman conducted a service of exorcism in the building. There has apparently been no further disturbance since this time.

Some weeks later Margot Hamilton wrote to a London friend telling her of these events. The latter, when attending a local church meeting on psychic phenomena, related the story to the Speaker, only to find that he not only knew the house in question, but had spent several days researching there with no result.

Whatever caused the disturbances in the house once owned by the Rajah of Cooch Behar seems now to have departed, but there is little doubt that it falls into the category of a genuine ghost—i.e., a former inhabitant of the place who remained in it after death—rather than a poltergeist manifestation from a living human being. The persistent knockings, ringings and tinkerings with small objects, suggest an attempt to attract the attention of the living; a not unfamiliar state of affairs in such cases.

Not all Sussex's ghosts are by the sea. In the village of South Harting, near the Hampshire border, Rosemary Cottage is said to be haunted, a figure having been seen on the stairs. However, details of both figure and haunting are so vague, that this must be taken as an unsubstantiated account. I was also informed that Lady Hamilton had once stayed here, though if she visited the area at all, it is likely she stayed at the nearby mansion of Uppark. There is a local rumour that this was the case, though if one believes all reports, Emma Hamilton must have been as peripatetic as Elizabeth I. The beds she slept in and the taverns she is said to have visited in company with her legitimate as well as her illegitimate lord are legion. But she was nothing if not colourful, and echoes of her particular piece of history are always welcome, whether or not they concern ghosts. Throughout the course of these researches I met no rumour that her restless spirit survives. Perhaps Calais could tell other stories.

There are also vague rumours concerning an old well in the grounds of Graylingwell Mental Hospital, Chichester. The hospital is said to stand on former monastic land, and the well itself to have been part of the monks' water system. If its name is anything to go by, there must have been a fishpond nearby which housed grayling for the monastic Friday lunch. Perhaps the curious sounds said to have been heard around the well are the patient footsteps of a holy fisherman waiting for his dinner. He does not appear yet to have caught anything.

The well-known parapsychologist, Andrew Green, states that Pevensey Castle in the east of the county is haunted by a woman thought to be a certain Lady Pelham who died in the fourteenth century. Her spectre has been seen gliding along the top of the castle walls. Since these have long been ruined, her progress must be both uneasy and impeded.

The charming small town of Rye, long time a smugglers' centre, is certainly haunted, and by more than one ghost. Apart from any individual spectre, the place is stalked by the spirit of its own past. Its steep, cobbled streets, its handsome church, its timbered and bending buildings all speak of a life lived more fully (and more dangerously) two centuries ago than it is now. There are, I am sure, echoes enough of smuggling in the town to provide some record in terms of psychic survival, but yet it is not surprising to find that the best known ghostly records relate to monks.

The town was the site of an Augustinian Friary and part of this structure still stands. When I first knew it, the place was a small hotel known as the Monastery Guest House, and although of necessity its interior was altered since its ecclesiastical days, one of the outer walls remained an original.

One particular monkish ghost is reported to haunt the present-day guest house, and the story from which it is said to arise is a familiar one. Rye not only boasted a monastery but a nunnery, also, and since what is hardest to come by is always the most alluring, one of the holy brothers came to love one of the holy sisterhood and the desperate lovers planned an elopement. Situated as it is at the sea end of the Romney Marshes, it would be hard to escape from Rye without the assistance of motor, rail or air transport. Escape you could, no doubt, by horse or donkey power, but you would not get far unseen, and anyone possessing a faster horse could catch you up in a mile or two. The marshes are flat, wide and empty of everything save sky, and the snaking River Rother.

The two who had vowed themselves to love only God and honour celibacy were caught and returned to their respective disciplines. There is no record of what became of the girl. The young man is said to have been bricked up alive in the very wall which still stands today. He would not have lived long.

Whether or not the romantic tale is true (and in the nature of humanity, there must have been a number of cases of such nun/

monk involvements during the long heyday of the monastic system), there does seem to be some record of haunting in the area of the old Monastery Guest House.

Former owners of the house are my old friends, Irene and Gerald Young, now living in Devon, and it was Gerald Young who gave me first-hand information concerning the hauntings.

About the year 1958, the Youngs began to be disturbed occasionally in the early hours of the morning (invariably about 2.0 a.m.) by the ringing of the front door bell of the Guest House. Whenever Mr Young answered it there was never anyone there. That is, except for two occasions.

These occurred in 1959 and 1960, and Mr Young's account of them is as follows: "I have occasionally seen what I think to be a foggy appearance of a monk with a rather round face. The 'visibility' was never very clear and has only occurred twice. The apparition was only just before hearing him ring the front door bell, but was never a distinct appearance—only head and shoulders, and only then for a fleeting moment.

"These two instances were at Rye and at approximately 2.00 a.m."

In my questionnaire to him I had asked whether or not there had ever been any conversation exchanged between himself and the apparition. His reply was interesting.

"Never a conversation at all. He always rang the front door bell and went on ringing until I acknowledged him with 'All right, Charlie!', when he just grunted and that was all."

The ghost by now had come to be known locally—or at least to the occupants of the house concerned—as 'Charlie', and seems to have responded to the form of address; or perhaps merely to any form of speech addressed to it.

The Youngs left Rye in 1962, and one would have assumed that their connection with 'Charlie' ended at this point. However, on quite a few occasions over the intervening years, Mr and Mrs Young have heard the familiar ring at the front door of their Devon home. Sometimes a tapping has occurred at their bedroom window, either independently of the ringing bell or simultaneously with it. The last occasion was about three weeks before Mr Young wrote to me. Both ringing and tapping took place on two consecutive nights.

Although this account is indecisive in that it is not conveniently clear-cut, there are certain factors in it of considerable interest. These may be summarized as follows:

1. The apparition materialized on only two known occasions, both

occurring in Rye and associated with the Monastery Guest House. On each occasion, the sighting was exceedingly brief.

2. The materialization seems to have been only partial and indistinct on each occasion. (The adjective 'foggy', or more commonly 'misty', is one often applied to such appearances.)

3. The materialization in Rye appears to have taken place fractionally before the sound of the door bell was heard. Since sound travels at a slower speed than light, this is not to say that the noise of the ringing bell followed the visual appearance. The manifestations may have occurred simultaneously, but been registered by the human recorder (Gerald Young) with an interval between in accordance with the differing light and sound speeds.

4. It is unusual for a haunting specifically associated with place, as is this one, to transfer to another location. Is it perhaps likely that Irene and Gerald Young in Devon are hearing by telepathy or clairaudience the sound of a door bell being rung in Rye? They lived for a number of years in the old building in the latter town, and seemed to have a certain empathy with it.

5. The sound of tapping on their bedroom window appears to be an additional manifestation since their removal to Devon, but it could be that natural causes—branch or twig blown by the wind—account for this, though the coincidence of tapping and bell ringing simultaneously seems unlikely.

6. The 'grunt' in acknowledgement of Gerald Young's remark to the apparition is certainly unusual. Conversation in answer would have been even more so, of course, though an interchange of this kind is not unknown. In a recent book on the nature of time, I recorded such a reported occurrence near Oslo, Norway.

7. There is a constant time factor—2.00 a.m.—for the manifestation.

Although the evidence on this haunting is teasing and inconclusive, there have been a number of sightings reported of ghostly monks in Rye, including one which has been frequently seen in Watchbell Street, and perhaps it can be assumed that some small part of the monastic life lived in the town for so many years has been recorded there. The 'Charlie' manifestation, however, appears to relate to an individual rather than a pattern haunting.

Rye is at one end of Sussex and our last hauntings in the county are at the other. To reach Midhurst it is best to forsake the concrete dragon of the A27 and dive into the lesser roads to the north, crossing and winding, meandering and getting lost in the pleasant maze of lanes and villages which swoop up and down the South Downs. It is good countryside, friendly, old and tame, at least in the daytime, with the villages an interesting mixture of ancient buildings and new inhabitants.

Petworth is typical of the small townships situated on intersecting north/south and east/west highways. I was told there of a shadowy figure which had been seen in a local restaurant—"out of the eye-corners" of the staff. None knew the origin of the haunter, and its presence remained tantalizingly vague. The restaurant ghost at the next town is better documented.

Midhurst is an old market town, one of whose claims to fame is that H. G. Wells attended its grammar school and later taught there as a student teacher.

Intimation of the ghost came to me from Mrs Jane Perry who, with her husband, Ian, had worked in a newly opened restaurant in the town. The Perrys were students and impecunious, and in order to save towards a home decided to take on the additional work. This is Jane Perry's own account of the haunting. "My husband being a student chef soon found himself as head chef and I used to help him prepare for the evenings when we could work all day during our holidays. The kitchen was at the time long and narrow with a doorway minus door leading into the eating part with an L-shaped partition around it to save the kitchen being visible to customers. Often while cooking or chopping food I would look up and see someone standing back away from the doorway in the darker restaurant watching me; on being noticed he would move away rapidly through another door leaving the impression of a tall man dressed in orangey brown and black.

"This did not frighten me and happened so often I took no notice of it, keeping quiet about the whole matter. One day Ian and I were preparing some food, I looked up and the blur of colour was brighter than usual (Ian and I had been laughing and it was almost as if the ghost wished to join in the fun and was too shy. This was a standard feeling of us all in the future). I jumped and said 'Did you see that?' Ian said he had. We then discovered we both had been seeing the same thing ever since we had started working but never even hinted to one another, thinking we were seeing things."

The ghost seems to have been much in evidence in daylight, for Mrs Perry states that she saw it almost every day and on many occasions. Often she thought the figure was a customer, as it appeared even on very busy nights when the restaurant was full. The phantom once kicked the skirt of another waitress as it passed her, from which one assumes that it must have been in close proximity to the living humans in the area most of the time.

Local legend declares that the house was once a smugglers' hideout, the restaurant attached to it being the stables of the building. Nothing is known of any story associated with the surroundings which would explain the haunting. I understand from my correspondent that this one is still active.

Let us end as we began with a ghost from Bognor. This case has its roots in the recent rather than distant past, and was encountered by Mr and Mrs R. F. Burstow who still reside near Bognor Regis. Mr Burstow's account is graphic enough to stand verbatim.

Late in 1947 [said Mr Burstow] my wife and I moved to Bognor from the London area, where I had taken up an appointment with the Local Authority. The following year my wife answered an advertisement for a personal secretary to a practice of doctors in the town. The doctors' residence was a large Victorian house in Clarence Road which is a turning off the High Street and leading to the seafront. The house was three-floored comprising a semi-basement which had been used as living accommodation with a separate entrance below street level at the side of the building, the main entrance from Clarence Road was gained by steps to a double porch. The first floor was at that time surgeries, waiting-room and a small office, back stairs leading to the basement, the second floor was reached by quite an imposing flight of stairs from the entrance hall which was a self-contained flat on two levels. The first level at the top of the stairs had the usual offices with a large window which overlooked quite an extensive, but by then rather overgrown walled garden with garage gates from High Street; there was a large brick double garage and greenhouse built on to the north side of the house with a door leading to what at this time was a waiting-room.

My wife accepted the post, the practice of three doctors was well established. The younger partner residing in the flat above, the senior partner living away from the practice. My wife enjoyed her work and as time progressed she became very friendly with the partners. The young partner had in fact only moved into the flat a short time before my wife took up her duties in 1948, before that the senior of the other two partners had resided there.

One must now delve back into the past history of the house, built in 1875 it had at that time been the seaside home of a relative of the royal family, there are many associations with them in this particular part of Bognor. For a short time in the nineties the house became a private hotel, but by the turn of the century was a doctor's residence; the old practitioner retired in 1929 and the senior partner of the practice, which my wife had joined took over the entire house using the drawing-room as a surgery. The basement area was at that time used for its proper offices as kitchens, scullery, large butler's pantry and living accommodation for the below stairs staff of two, a cook and maid.

I was very interested in the old house and as the basement was no longer used at the time my wife took up her duties a nostalgic browse around was quite frequent. There was a large Victorian dresser in the kitchen and among the miscellaneous odds and ends I came across a photograph of the doctor who had retired in 1929. A typical Victorian family doctor with very distinguished aquiline features, and rather long white hair, correct with top hat and frock coat, the photograph was taken as he was standing near the greenhouse on his way out to pay his daily visits. The basement had at that time a bell system with extensions to all the main rooms.

The young wife of the junior partner living in the top flat became friendly with my wife and in discussion said that she was sure the house was haunted, she hated to be left alone at night. My wife being particularly interested in psychic matters, which may have a bearing on the experience related further on, asked her whether it was an atmospheric feeling or whether she had seen anything visual, she said on two occasions she had glimpsed a tall figure in a contemplative stance, it was male and on the first sighting it was twilight in early winter, the figure standing looking out over the garden from the window on the lower landing, the second occasion was daylight and on looking out of a side window from a bedroom above the greenhouse the figure was standing looking at the garden. In 1955 the doctor and his family left to move into their own house and my wife and I, with a young daughter by now, took possession. We were very happy in our new abode and nothing untoward happened; in fact we never really accepted the ghost story and had quite forgotten it. My little daughter loved living there but on occasions would say she'd had a dream when a nice old gentleman would come and smile at her.

On a particularly busy summer's day in the late fifties my wife was busy typing in her small office with her back to the door which was partly open owing to the heat of the day. Engrossed in her work she became aware of a presence at the door and half turning saw standing a tall old gentleman with white hair who asked her if she would mind him going to have a look at the garden as he had happy memories of it long ago. She cannot recall details as it was but a quick glance as she gave permission and resumed work; she did not see him again.

Years passed by, my daughter was growing up and nothing untoward happened, excepting the accountable reaction of our cat at times when it would back up in fright with fur bristling, staring into the far corner of the lounge or dining-room. In one surgery and in the main hall an offensive smell would occur at odd times which was put down to the drains, which were investigated without success. The senior partner had retired and it was obvious that the partnership would leave the old house and move into a health centre. We in turn were seeking a house of our own.

It was now early 1972 and the big change was imminent, I would stress by the way that I had never seen or heard anything unusual. However my daughter had become unhappy about being in the house by herself as whilst in the kitchen when we were out, a set of kitchen utensils hanging on the wall without warning started swaying violently and doors would bang in the basement for no accountable reason.

We all slept by the way in separate rooms; my wife in the main bedroom whilst I had the adjacent small bedroom, my daughter in the room at the back. On one particular night in January, 1972 I was awakened by a piercing scream from my wife, stumbling half asleep into her room I found her in an emotional state of shock; it appears she was sleeping on her side facing the bay window of the bedroom, curtains were always drawn back at night, so that a fitful light entered the room. She felt a presence in the room and turned over half asleep to face the door and stooping over her was a tall figure of a very elderly man, he had a shock of white hair and seemed to be trying to express something by his anguished look, she quickly buried her head under the sheets and then looked again. He was still there. She screamed; within seconds I was at her bedside but there was nobody and for that matter I have never seen the apparition. I will say however that as I stood roughly in the same position as the visitor I experienced a strong smell of what I can only refer to as urine. This is exactly the same smell that had not been traced on the ground floor. From then on things happened, the sound of heavy objects dropped with no evidence of disturbance; on one occasion I felt someone or thing sitting on my bed and there was the sound of bells ringing which we three heard independently at the same time. It was the bell system in the basement long since dismantled. We moved late in 1972 and the doctors' practice followed, but not before one further incident, when the cleaner arrived one morning (it would be about 7 a.m. in February 1973), she was filling a bucket of water from the sink at the end of a corridor in the basement when she heard slow footsteps coming down the paved passage way, the footsteps stopped just behind her. Rooted to the spot she screamed, she turned; nothing!

The old house is still there, substantially unaltered, offices now on the ground floor and basement, the top floor still a flat. I wonder whether the old doctor has settled down. He loved that house. I recall way back when we first went to live there I removed some old floral china finger plates from a door to carry out some painting and on the back in the doctor's hand were his impressions of day-to-day happenings in Bognor 1903. Latterly I met an old Bognorian who had worked for the doctor as a boy cleaning his car, before telling him my story I asked him to give me a picture of the doctor. Tall, he said and distinguished, long white hair with rather sad aquiline features. Very correct in his Victorian attire.

This is a highly circumstantial and convincing account covering a period of several years. The living person whose ghost appears at the house in Clarence Road died recently enough for his history still to be known in the area. It seems (according to my informant, Mr Burstow) that the old man, who was nearing eighty in 1929 when his successor took over the practice, then moved to East Anglia where he lived for some time in retirement before his death.

From this local knowledge arises a possible explanation for the haunting. In the early 1900s, the doctor took a junior partner, a brilliant man, who lived in a large Victorian house on the opposite side of the road from that of his senior colleague. The joint practice, however, was carried on from the senior partner's residence. After some years, the partnership was dissolved, the younger man setting up in practice on his own account in a house in Victoria Drive, Bognor. Shortly afterwards the younger doctor committed suicide, the coroner's verdict at the subsequent inquest being that he died as a result of overwork. Mr Burstow comments that a room at this house, also, is said to be haunted.

It is the ghost of the old man which lingers in the Clarence Road premises, however, returning from the place of his retirement, East Anglia, to the home he had lived in and loved for so many years. It seems unlikely that the tragic death of his former junior partner is relevant to the haunting, though Mr Burstow's account of the increased intensity and frequency of manifestations towards the end of his family's occupancy, suggests the presence of an aware entity rather than a broadcast pattern haunting. The manifestations exhibit variability; they also appear to suggest a growing desire to communicate. "From then on things happened. . . ."

Is it that the spirit of the old man is trapped in a long-gone situation of his own making? Was he, perhaps, over-possessive of his house and practice in his lifetime, and now through long habit is unable to let go—to escape? How long does it take the human energy form (or spirit, or soul) to realize that with death it is free to move from the places used by its material form, the body? How long does it take a man to understand that he has died?

Thinking thoughts such as these, I drove back along the A27 into Hampshire. Patches of sunlight dappled the road verges, and threw nets down between the leaving trees to capture the grasses. Rounding one corner I saw piled unceremoniously into the foot of the hedge a rough black and white form. The badger's striped mask lay upturned to the sun, seeing nothing. Whatever car had ruined him was by now miles away, for he had been dead some hours. I drove on into the darkening day, towards the welcoming lights of Hayling Island and my sister's home.

Hampshire

Of all the southern counties, Hampshire appears to have the most dignity. It is spacious, varied in scenery and old in history. The heartland of the ancient kingdom of Wessex, it includes within its compass long rolling downlands, the ancient hunting grounds of the New Forest and a coastline dogged by sails, swans and deep-sea liners.

Of its cities, Winchester was once Alfred the Great's capital and his statue benevolently watches over the High Street. Sir Walter Raleigh was condemned to death in 1603 in the Great Hall which formerly belonged to the Norman castle; and in the same building hangs a representation of the Round Table of King Arthur, probably constructed for the flattery and entertainment of Henry VIII. Jane Austen died in the town and Keats once walked in its cathedral precincts. Winchester is a mellow handsome city still.

Portsmouth and Southampton dominate the county's coastline, with their air of ships and sailors and great sea-going affairs. Nelson's little *Victory* lies in dock at Portsmouth, trimly polished, cramped as the inside of a crab's shell. It is, inevitably, a magnet for tourists, who stumble up and down its companionways, with forbidden cameras and minds a-boggle that so small a ship should once see such a battle, hold such a hero.

Hampshire is a good place to drive in, for the long shallow hills alternate with neat small valleys, clear-stream-threaded and laden with snug red farms and heavy woodlands. All year round there is a comfortable feeling of fulfilment, as though two thousand years of agriculture had brought this land to a peak of fertility and its people to a rare degree of contentment.

There are ghosts enough to satisfy the most persistent researcher, and as with Sussex, many of these appear to congregate in the coastal area. I began my enquiry on Hayling Island as a matter of convenience, for I was staying at the home of relatives.

Hayling has an air of belonging to some period of time apart from that of the mainland, a suggestion of self-sufficiency which is common to islands. One approaches it across a long bridge spanning an inlet of the Solent, and in ten minutes' drive can cross to the far side of the island to view that larger block of detached landscape, the Isle of Wight, floating mistily offshore.

Hayling had a railway station up until a few years ago, when the Beeching axe beheaded it from the main body of the network. Now it lies derelict at the back of West Town, its goods yard weed-smothered, its train whistles silent. It is no more atmospheric than one would expect from its history, yet there is a story current that it is haunted by a former railway employee. The shadowy figure of a man has occasionally been seen in and around the station building.

Local opinion seemed to be equally divided between the possible truth and falsehood of the rumour. There was a general feeling, that the old station would be an unpleasant place to visit in darkness. One can place little value on such a comment, since it could apply to many empty buildings at night.

A similar tale came from another part of the island, the village of Northney. Here the church is said to have the ghost of a sailor who haunts the nave. However, there seemed to be no first hand experience of the haunting, and Mr James Poore, one of the church officials, knew of no one who had actually seen the ghost.

In on-the-ground researches though much of the work is abortive, it frequently happens that an enquiry which produces nothing worthwhile of its own, may lead to a more authentic account. It was so in this instance. As a result of my conversations in Northney I was directed to Colonel L. E. Sheppard who lives some distance away and near the actual sea-front.

This gentleman had experienced a supernatural manifestation, which took place in the old Fleet Manor House, reputedly the oldest house on the island, having been built towards the end of the fifteenth century. Colonel Sheppard bought it in 1943 and occupied it until approximately 1960.

As far as is known the place had for years been a yeoman farmer's house but had been built near a priory. The house may originally have been part of priory buildings put to farming use on the Dissolution of the Monasteries. Whatever its history, it appears to have been haunted by the apparition of a man in black. The latter has been seen several times through the years and by a number of people.

During Colonel Sheppard's occupation various occurrences pointed to an active haunting taking place. The family dogs would frequently move aside as though waiting for someone invisible to pass by them.

On one occasion, in the Colonel's presence, one of the animals jumped out of the open window rather than remain in the room. Its owner suspected at the time that the dog could see something which he himself could not.

Many of the manifestations took place in a spare room, and from time to time the figure of a man in black was seen there. The family's daily domestic help apparently saw the figure on several occasions. In spite of these activities, the general atmosphere of the house seems to have been good, with no feeling of distress or fear.

There was one outstanding example of the haunting. On one occasion the Colonel himself felt someone gently stroking his head. This activity had been experienced by other persons when in the house. It does not seem to have been regarded as unpleasant or terrifying by any of the percipients.

Colonel Sheppard's successor in the house was a Captain Illingworth and apparently one of the domestics employed by him also encountered the ghost. She seems to have found the manifestations not to her taste, for after seeing the apparition she immediately handed in her notice and left.

Colonel Sheppard's conclusion was that the ghost might be that of a priest—the black garb and the action of head-stroking (an act of blessing?)—possibly connected with the long-defunct priory. Failing any other explanation, this sounds reasonable. It should be said that during my interview with Colonel Sheppard his sister was present, and able to confirm most of the detail of his account.

As noted earlier the presence in strength of the monastic orders in this area of England has resulted in numerous echoes of their lives remaining associated with buildings and countryside. As far as Hampshire is concerned, however, there seem to be as many modern as ancient hauntings.

An account of this kind was given me by former neighbours of my sister, Mr and Mrs Leonard Cook, who no longer live on the island. Of the two, the husband seems to have been the more receptive to the phenomena, which were associated with a house in Waterlooville, a small township on the mainland facing Hayling across the narrow strait.

The occurrences began in the autumn of 1970, and invariably took place between 10.00 and 10.30 p.m. The house was modern, and as far as the owners were aware there was no tragedy associated with its past.

The ghost of a man in black (possibly a priest or monk of pre-Reformation days) has been seen many times by the owners of Old Fleet Manor House, Hayling Island.

The first they knew of anything out of the ordinary was one night when they were preparing for bed. Mrs Cook had already retired and her husband was coming down the corridor from the bathroom of the house towards their bedroom, when he saw the figure of a woman emerge from a small bedroom ahead and walk towards him as though bound for the kitchen. In utter astonishment, he watched this stranger approach then pass him, leaving as she did so a feeling of intense cold in her wake. According to Mr Cook, the apparition appeared to be of a middle-aged woman dressed in black clothes of a modern style.

The next encounter took place about three weeks later. Again it was the husband who saw the apparition, and again the woman walked down the hall and into the kitchen, apparently repeating the first set of actions exactly, except for the fact that on the second occasion she appeared to be weeping. Once again there was a sense of intense cold.

On a subsequent occasion Mr and Mrs Cook and one of their daughters were seated in their sitting-room which was of the type having a smaller dining area attached, the two portions of the room being divided by an archway. On either side of this structure stood a pedestal, each bearing a bowl of ferns.

The time was between eight and nine o'clock in the evening and all windows and doors were closed. As mother and daughter sat quietly talking together, they were astounded to see the ferns in one of the bowls billow outwards, as though someone had carelessly brushed past them. Mr Cook for his part was perhaps less surprised to see at the same time 'his' lady make a brief appearance in the room before going out into the hall. Although neither mother nor daughter experienced the visual manifestation, all three members of the family noticed the degree of chill which set in immediately after the disturbance of the ferns.

The fourth and final indication that the house was haunted came when the Cooks' sister-in-law came to spend an Easter holiday with them. This lady, a widow, was to stay four or five days in the house, and she was put into the spare (i.e., the haunted) bedroom knowing nothing whatever of the family's previous experiences.

On one morning during her visit, she asked at breakfast time whether anyone had heard her scream in the night. She thought she had had a nightmare for although at the time of the occurrence she believed herself to be awake, it seemed to her that a woman entered her room, stood beside her bed and then attempted to strangle her. She concluded that the experience must have taken place in a dream.

Not long after this occurrence, the Cook family sold the bungalow and moved to Hayling Island. They were naturally curious about the incidents in the Waterlooville property and took some pains to learn the latter's history. Apparently the first owners had been a Mr and Mrs Lewis who had had the bungalow built for them. Mrs Lewis particularly had loved the house and was deeply distressed when a change in her husband's place of work had meant that they must leave the area. Persons who knew the couple had said that the woman 'had cried for a week'. Barely three months after leaving the district, she died.

It seems apparent from the facts of this story, that the wife of the original owner had been emotionally bound to her house in a more than normal manner, and that when forced physically to leave it she found herself mentally unable to do so. The fact of physical death appears to have released that part of her psyche which was orientated upon her old home and enabled it to return there—an activity closed to it while in the physical body.

Little is known of the effects of such emotional bondage in the case of humans, though the deep attachment of animals to places is well documented. Cats in particular will return to a loved place though moved many miles away from it and in spite of severe physical obstacles. Occasionally mankind appears to develop similar attachments and even after death to feel a possessive need for the place beloved in life.

The sense of territory, essentially an animal attribute, appears in some human individuals to develop to the point of fanaticism. It then becomes possessiveness of such intensity that no intruder is tolerated within the bounds of that person's self-defined area. Instances of this are common in life, and seem to appear more frequently among the wealthy and famous than in the ranks of the middle-class, middling-paid and averagely anonymous.

One would have thought that death would dissolve such obsessional bonds, since the latter are generally material in nature. However, this does not seem to be so, and the fact is apparently borne out by an account of a haunting in (again) Waterlooville, sent to me by Mrs Sheila White of Ryde, Isle of Wight.

Sometime in the mid-nineteen twenties, when Mrs White was a child of about twelve, she and her father were taken by a family friend to see a large mansion in Waterlooville. The friend was contemplating buying the property for the sake of its size since he had need to house a large and valuable collection of antiques and family heirlooms.

The house appears to have been singularly unprepossessing on first sight. Huge and rambling, with a flight of stone steps up to the front door, it was found by the young girl, Sheila, to be unpleasantly disturbing even from the outside. The interior atmosphere seemed immediately denser and the intense cold within the building enhanced the visitors' feeling of discomfort. Mrs White remembers clearly even from this distance in time the almost tangible feeling of evil as they mounted the stairs.

The girl's father also felt revulsion and attempted to persuade his friend to abandon any thought of taking the house. Mr Dalton*, however, was not sensitive to such imponderables as atmosphere, and refused to be dissuaded from acquiring what seemed to him a highly suitable background for his family treasures.

Before considering the life of Mr Dalton and his family in the Gothic mansion, let us look at the place's history. Called Hopfield because of its initial situation in an area of hop-gardens, the house was built by a Mr Ferriby* in the early nineteenth century to be a family home *in perpetuo*. Ferriby may have been one of the new breed of rising tradesmen who, minus a long pedigree and ancestral home, sought to provide himself with at least one of the marks of a gentleman. He built the house, brought up his children in it, and finally died in it. Before crossing the ultimate bourne he had made it quite clear to his family that Hopfield was to be the family home for ever. This was what he intended and a Victorian *pater familias* expected his intentions to be honoured to the last letter.

In the case of Hopfield they were, the great grey house remaining in the Ferriby family for many years. It was not until the original builder's grandchildren were well grown that his son decided the place was too large and might be let. He knew of his father's prohibition on selling the place, but saw no reason why it should not be tenanted.

It fell to the first tenants to tell him. A childless couple, both were ardent Spiritualists who might have been expected to take a haunting in their stride. This was no ordinary haunting, however. They complained that the spirit of old Mr Ferriby had appeared in the house, extremely angry and threatening to commit violence if the tenants did not vacate at once.

Apparently the threats were carried out, for the tenants asked permission (which was granted) to sub-let, and moved out forthwith. The sub-tenants were a middle-aged widow and her daughter, a girl in her twenties, but they had been only a short while in the place when the mother was discovered dead in her bed one morning. The daughter left almost immediately.

By this time the Ferribys had come to dislike the idea of moving back into the home constructed (and apparently still used) by their irascible parent. Disregarding the expressed wishes of the long dead man, they put the house up for sale.

It was bought by a retired army captain and his wife. They had lived in it for only a short time, however, when the captain was found dead on the floor of the hall with one of his own Indian daggers in his back. The widow moved out as soon as possible and the murder was never solved.

The sinister Victorian house known as Hopfield, Waterlooville, Hants, in which the ghost of the original owner manifested itself in a number of terrifying encounters, resulting in a series of tragedies to the living inhabitants.

By now Hopfield's reputation was well known and no local buyer would have touched it. It was against the pleading of his family and the advice of his friends that Mr Dalton purchased the building in the nineteen twenties. The new owner had no intention of leaving the house in its original condition. He used his wealth to make extensive alterations, and within a short time transformed it into a beautiful and luxurious home, hardly recognizable as the gaunt mausoleum he had first inspected.

The Daltons had children of the same generation as the young Sheila, and for several years it had been the custom of the families to spend Christmas under the same roof. They were all together for the first Christmas in the rejuvenated Hopfield.

But although materially restored, the basic atmosphere of the place seems to have remained unchanged. The girl Sheila felt the familiar chill in the building in spite of its rich furnishings and central heating. Her small dog, Scraggie, appeared to want to escape from the house and eventually had to be carried upstairs when he refused to walk there on his own account.

She was given a bedroom in a wing of the house which was separated from the main building and shut off by a heavily studded baize door. The dog, Scraggie, stayed with her, having his basket in a corner of the room.

Mrs White admits now that she found her accommodation 'spooky'—the room itself beautiful, but with only a spiral iron staircase leading up to it from below and down to it from the attics above. However, she was cheered by the possession of her first long evening dress and the company of the little dog. She wore her dress for dinner that evening and retired to bed about 10.00 p.m., leaving the adults still downstairs. She read for a while, then turned out the light and went to sleep.

She was awakened by the sound of the dog growling. She reached out for the switch of the bedside lamp but could not find it. She sat up and received a "resounding crack on the head from something which felt like iron". She lay down again. Again she sat up, only to have the same thing happen. She began to feel as though she were in some kind of cage, and a sensation of horror spread through her. The dog's growl grew fiercer. His presence reassured her that she was in her room at Hopfield, but why was she not in bed? For she was certain now that she was not.

Careful feeling around convinced her that she was lying *under* the bed, although it was so low that she could not have rolled underneath accidentally, but would have had to edge her way in; a process which she now accomplished in reverse, switching the bedside light on the moment she emerged from her prison.

The dog was crouched in his basket staring fixedly at the door, his hackles raised and his lips drawn back over his teeth. He was growling deep in his throat. Sheila followed his gaze, and as she watched the door handle turned and the door itself began slowly to open. No one came in. Almost in tears, the girl snatched up her dressing-gown and the dog and bolted for her parents' room. The time, according to her bedside clock, was 1.00 a.m.

For the rest of that night and the remainder of their stay, the girl's father spent the night in her room while she slept with her mother. Nothing was said at any time to their hosts, and the occupants had switched rooms again before the maid brought their early morning tea at eight o'clock. Sheila's father discovered that no matter how many times he closed the door of that particular bedroom it would never stay closed. Eventually he did not bother to shut it.

On many subsequent occasions the girl and her parents stayed at Hopfield. The father and daughter always sensed antagonism in the atmosphere, though the mother apparently did not. Very often their rest was disturbed by noises in the night, but these also were not spoken of to the Daltons.

The account would have been less appalling had this been the end of it. However, more than mere noises were operative at Hopfield. One bright summer day Sheila's parents were informed by telephone that the Daltons' son, a likeable young man, still at Oxford and apparently with a brilliant future ahead of him, had gone into the basement at Hopfield and blown out his brains with a shot-gun. His mother did not recover from his death, and herself died a few weeks later. Shortly afterwards Mr Dalton himself fell dead in his dressing-room. Only the daughter remained alive. The place was again boarded up and left empty and desolate.

What was the cause of the series of tragedies which occurred in this house? Coincidences or malevolence? Judging by its reported past history, hostility seems to have been a strong feature in its atmosphere. Which is perhaps not surprising when one considers the almost paranoiac fervour of Ferriby's sense of possession in relation to the house. Given this kind of concentrated emotion generated by a forceful mind, it seems likely that the surroundings (particularly surroundings which were the target and focus of the emotion) would become charged with the energy directed towards it, with the result that anyone living within its compass and sufficiently sensitive to such things, would inevitably be affected.

There is no doubt that energy-emanations of this type can have a pronounced effect upon sensitive persons. One has only to recall the effect of relatively trivial emotional disturbances upon the individual behaviour pattern to understand the possibilities. A family quarrel, an argument with neighbours or colleagues, can often appear to lead to a series of minor accidents or material consequences. We speak of it being 'one of those days', or of it not being our day or of being accident-prone. I suspect that an encounter with certain kinds of emotional output—anger, hatred, sadistic cruelty, for example—will give rise to a mental response in those who encounter it, of such a nature that their own behaviour and thought processes may be temporarily altered by the type of energy output encountered. So may it have been with Hopfield. In a house so charged with negative if not destructive emotions, it would have been surprising had there not been a consequential response from the inhabitants.

What of Hopfield now? It still stands somewhere in the maze of little dwellings which Waterlooville has become. When Mrs White last saw the house some years ago it had been turned into a series of flats, depressing and dark, with endless flights of stairs closed off at top and foot each marked by a number and an empty milk bottle sentinel outside. What thoughts and feelings are generated now within those walls only the occupants know. Has Ferriby been removed at last from the home he built for his descendants to occupy for ever? Or do mysterious accidents still occur within the cold walls of his *folie de grandeur*?

Waterlooville may be buried beneath its burden of bungalows and semis, but under the housing estates echoes of its former life appear to continue. Another correspondent, Mrs Rosemary Stevens, told me of two further hauntings in the area, both recent.

The house occupied by Mr and Mrs Stevens was built about eighteen years ago in an area once covered by woodland. Their garden still retains a fringe of trees which merges with the main wood at one end. The old woodland path runs through the garden and a stile leads into the wood. Mrs Stevens's own account is worth quoting in full. "Last May the development company who owned the wood, had been working for some weeks—cutting a wide lane through, to mark the line of a proposed new road. Several big trees of course had had to be felled during the process.

"The first time I saw the ghost I returned from work at lunch time on a lovely sunny day. While I was hoovering our dining-room (which looks down the garden through double glass doors) I opened the sliding panels and was quite busy with my task when I suddenly had an overwhelming feeling of being watched. I turned off the hoover and glanced out the doors only to be astonished to see a grey figure—not ten yards away—standing on the lawn—on the line of the old pathway. He was dressed in what looked like a ploughman's smock and some kind of squashed-looking hat. I couldn't see his face clearly but the overall impression was of greyness. There was no feeling of evil but a strange sad emanation from him. He vanished very quickly but not before I was convinced I had seen him."

At this juncture Mrs Stevens was not aware of any possible explanation for what she thought she had seen. However, on the following Saturday she asked her local butcher's roundsman (an elderly countryman who had lived all his life in the area) whether there had been a tragedy in the neighbourhood in earlier days. Without hesitation he related a story told by his own father of a time about a century ago when the Hulbert Road (now a busy link road) was a mere grass track.

   A well-known local cattle drover regularly used the track to drive his herds to market, but on one occasion the cattle were found straying while the drover was missing. A search took place through the woods bordering the Hulbert Road along the track which once crossed the land now occupied by the Stevenses' garden. The man's body was found hanging from a large oak tree, situated (according to the knowledgeable butcher) 'somewhere about here'—i.e., the neighbourhood of the Stevenses' house.

   When Rosemary Stevens told the man of the apparition she had seen, he suggested that the developer's bull-dozer might have destroyed the tree in question and thus precipitated the haunting.

The garden of 64 Ferndale, Waterlooville, Hants, in which the ghost of an old drover appears. The man committed suicide by hanging from a nearby tree when a recognized drovers' road crossed the area now occupied by this garden.

This is not an unreasonable assumption, for as we have seen, interference with material surroundings can not only terminate an established haunting, it may equally easily bring one into being, the theory being in the latter case that the visible or audible impression of an original act or personage may be recorded by the surroundings, but be prevented from projecting by some material barrier—as the picture from a slide-projector may be inhibited by placing an obstacle in front of it.

The likelihood in this case is that a tree standing near the hanging tree may have impeded the latter from 'broadcasting' its information. When the obstructing tree was felled, the tree of the suicide could freely transmit its picture of the sad old drover. However, since the apparition appeared standing on the ground where in life he had so often walked, the picture could have been transmitted by any one of a dozen trees in the neighbourhood. It was not the imprint of the *suicide* which was left, but that of a man thinking and brooding as he stood on the old woodland road—perhaps as he stood on his last cattle-drive.

This is not quite the end of the account, for since hearing the original story from the elderly butcher, Mrs Stevens has several times seen a grey shape in various places in the garden—never again so near and definite as on the first occasion, but identifiable nonetheless by the emanation of sadness which proceeds from it. "The sadness ... is very striking and lasts even when the 'grey patch' has vanished", according to Rosemary Stevens. Although she has drawn her family's attention to the manifestation when it has occurred, at no time has any one of them been able to see the apparition.

The account from this percipient is a clear and balanced one and her assurance to me that she is "of a very down-to-earth frame of mind" is borne out by her careful noting of detail and her forbearance in not mentioning the reason for her enquiry to the butcher until after she had received his own story.

This being so, the second haunting of which she notified me, although having some curious aspects, must be taken seriously.

Mrs Stevens describes the motor mechanic at her local garage as "a young hard-headed man with no nonsensical notions of life". Yet the story he told her is far from usual.

It appears that this man, Robert Spensley*, and his wife were driving along the same Hulbert Road which figures in Rosemary Stevens's own ghost story. The highway takes a good volume of traffic and at the time of the incident (November 1976) visibility was poor, daylight fading into dusk. The road has no footpaths along this stretch for very few pedestrians use it. Robert was suddenly aware of "a girl standing on their side right in their path. He yelled to his wife to stop or swerve, but as she saw nothing she did neither."

The man was so appalled that at the crucial moment he closed his eyes, convinced that they were about to run someone down. However there was no impact and nothing to explain the figure he had seen.

In a state of some disturbance he told the story to one of his workmates. It was some reassurance to Robert that the phantom girl had been seen by other drivers at various times. She was said to be a girl from Leigh Park—a large council estate in nearby Havant—who had been killed while trying to hitch a lift from Waterlooville. Local (unconfirmed) rumour has it that she was struck by a car.

I will quote now from Mrs Stevens's account. "The really incredible part of the story was added later by an equally hard-headed working man who told Robert that one wet evening as he passed the cemetery on the Hulbert Road he was flagged down by a very wet girl asking for a lift to Leigh Park. She got in his car and apparently little was said except the address in Leigh Park to which she wanted to go. When he got there he looked across to open the door for the girl and she wasn't there—only a very wet car seat."

Mrs Stevens rightly comments that the last stroke seems too fantastic even for a haunting. Although I have encountered numerous stories of ghostly hitch-hikers, including those who vanished from cars either before or after arriving at their destination, I have not until now heard of one who left a wet imprint behind or the imprint of a wet behind. I did come across one in East Anglia which caused the temperature inside the car to drop alarmingly, but this hitcher was felt rather than seen and was of a singularly unpleasant nature. It would be interesting to know whether or not any other motorist has picked up this particular phantom girl in wet weather, and with what results.

The stretch of land between Havant and Portsmouth seems to have more than its share of apparently paranormal happenings. In February 1977 an unaccountable series of phenomena took place at 13 Partridge Gardens, Wecock. The latter is an overspill area for Portsmouth, largely occupied by council houses, and was in earlier days agricultural land. It would seem that the many manifestations which have occurred in the district may be left over from the days when Wecock Farm and its accompanying tied cottages occupied the ground.

The Partridge Gardens haunting took the form of gentle and not unpleasant demonstrations of presence. The inhabitants felt someone ruffling their hair or tapping them on the shoulder; objects fell from shelves; once a door refused to close, although unobstructed at the time. The disturbed occupants tried ouija (a dangerous practice for the amateur) and finally called two mediums for assistance. The information elicited was that the presence in the house was that of a young man allegedly murdered, who is said to have given his name as Neil Vickerstaff. By a strange coincidence the family then occupying the house possessed the same surname. What connection there might be between him and them cannot be discovered, though the possibility of a family bond some distance back in time is not impossible. Vickerstaff is a relatively uncommon name in the area.

As a result of these activities and the subsequent publicity, a local clergyman warned against the use of ouija remarking that "a number of residents at Wecock feel there is some kind of strong presence on the estate. This could be a result of people using ouija boards." He went on to say that large estates sometimes attracted harmful forces when there was anger or resentment felt by people living there.

In my view, any such forces may be generated by the living individuals themselves. It has been proven in experiments in Canada, that it is possible for a group of people acting together to produce a corporate power (electrical or electromagnetic in origin, one suspects) which can effect apparently paranormal manifestations. The clergyman's guess that something of this nature (though I believe he is wrong in suggesting outside forces as a source) is operating at Wecock may be correct.

It would be interesting to know more of the history of Wecock, for the place seems to have a surprising number of ghosts—from a phantom coach which bowls along a bridle path to the Keydell spectre. The latter is said to be of a young bride who was killed at Keydell, almost opposite Wecock Farm. According to local tradition the phantom appears (dressed in white naturally) in Lovedean Lane. Mrs Dorothy Eames of Catherington Lane, Horndean, has related how her young brother, a child of about ten at the time, was sent to Waterlooville for fish and chips. On his way back he saw in the roadway the figure of a woman wearing a white cloak which covered its entire head and body. The scared boy ran home.

There is also said to have been a murder at a large house named Armore, not far from Woodcroft Farm. A young lord of the manor is reported to have been killed there and the house itself destroyed by fire. A Mr William Parvin, elder brother of Mrs Eames, vouched for the fact that his grandfather when young went with other local men to this site on four consecutive nights. They apparently saw "a light in some bushes, like a ball of fire. It was about the size of a cricket ball." The men, though alarmed, returned in daylight to make a search of the area, but found nothing to account for what they had seen.

Inevitably when such stories are part of local tradition, little is needed to set their vibrations thrilling again through the everyday lives of the modern inhabitants. It takes only one or two inexplicable happenings, and a stray hint or two from interested friends, to set off a chain reaction of speculation and superstition, both of which can grow into certainty and fear with very little encouragement.

It has been suggested that Wecock was once a Viking burial ground. This is possible historically, as the Isle of Wight was regularly used by the Norsemen as invasion Headquarters. The south coast knew the long ships well and had reason to dread them.

A family living at No 24 Partridge Gardens (that same Partridge Gardens in which the Vickerstaffs discovered their ghost) believes it has more than one spectre in its terraced council house. Mrs Daphne Cripps and her husband, Ian, were non-believers in ghosts before moving there in 1975. Since then however, Ian Cripps has seen the white face of a child at one of the bedroom windows; Daphne Cripps has awakened to see "a tall misty white figure" gliding towards the bed; both have heard footsteps in the house on a number of occasions and felt the traditional chill in the atmosphere immediately before a manifestation.

The Cripps family includes a young child, Darren, who also seems to hear things. One evening when in the bath, he lifted his head and announced "Boy crying", which, since no other child was in the house, was unusual to say the least.

There have been other manifestations, from the parting of the strands of a plastic curtain as though someone were walking through it to the various sounds of footsteps—heavy booted, walking up the stairs, Wellington-booted stalking up and down outside the garage, children's feet pattering overhead when their own child was sound asleep. The Crippses' neighbours apparently are sceptical of the ghosts, but it must be borne in mind that Partridge Gardens lies next to the old bridle track which passes Woodcroft Farm. This is the milieu of the phantom coach, the Keydell bride, the ghost of Armore.

Whether or not the local inhabitants are exaggerating their experiences, either through fear or for other reasons, the evidence points to a certain amount of disturbance of a localized nature, possibly because the area itself has had an unquiet history and retained a few of its many impressions. One would need to live in the district for some time before the wheat could be sorted from the chaff. I understand that one or two local investigation societies are researching the Wecock phenomena, though I think it likely that the bushfire of alarm will not last long. The spurious occurrences (if such there are) will die away leaving a small hard core of actual paranormal incidents. These last may well be of long standing.

If you drive up the A3 to Petersfield you will miss a few haunted villages and some of the prettiest lanes in the south country. However, this should be done in order to visit Chalton. The village is small but its pub, The Red Lion, has what may or may not be a paranormal manifestation. From time to time, and always on a Saturday evening, the sound of knocking has been heard near the main chimney breast. It is a rhythmical sound apparently, and suggests a deliberate activity. However, the landlord is a practical man and consulted a well-known archaeologist with whom he is acquainted, presumably on the assumption that the latter's academic training would be an antidote to flights of superstitious fancy. The professor suggested that the Red Lion may be on a chalk vein which at some distant spot comes near enough to the surface again to support another building. If this should be so, and if that building contains a wood-burning stove, the sound of logs being regularly thrown on the fire might be conducted back along the vein and eventually make itself heard in the first available sounding-board—the old chimney of Chalton's inn.

This is an ingenious explanation, certainly, but sounds about as far-fetched as the average ghost story. A more likely one would be the presence of a loose piece of metal in the chimney which might produce a rattling sound in high wind.

But why should the noise always be heard on a Saturday? No one in the pub when I was there had any explanation to offer, although the landlord did suggest, not unreasonably, that the theoretical wood-burning activities might only take place at the weekend. This was a tantalizing account altogether. One could not be certain that the sound did not arise from natural causes, any more than one could be sure that it did. Have they a rhythmically tapping ghost at the Red Lion, Chalton? (Incidentally, the proliferation of Red Lion inns in the south is said to be due to the fact that this was former John o'Gaunt territory; the prince's emblem was a red lion.)

The second of Chalton's ghosts frequents a short stretch of road running from outside the Red Lion down a short decline. It is said to be the apparition of a horse and cart travelling very fast across the road. Although it has been seen by a local man, Mine Hoste at the Lion dismissed the story, saying that on a wet evening there could be a light either from nearby windows or from a dying sunset, which so reflects in the roadside puddles that an image is thrown up against one of the hedges, giving the impression of a moving vehicle crossing the roadway.

Again an ingenious explanation, but as incomprehensible and unlikely as would be a parapsychological one. It is extraordinary how involved so-called natural explanations of phenomena can be. They end by sounding a good deal more incredible than the supernatural events they are intended to dismiss.

A third ghost at Chalton is said to haunt a house opposite the pub. I understand it takes a psychokinetic form—psychokinesis being the movement of objects from one place to another by unexplained means. In this case, apparently a picture in one room is frequently found detached from its place on the wall and lying in the middle of the floor. I was unable to verify the accuracy of this report since the house's owners were away.

I left Chalton after lunch and trundled pleasantly up and down the close-banked lanes until I came to Buriton. Here I was told of a ghostly monk which had been seen in the grounds of the manor. And of the spectre of a nannie (nurse not goat) said to haunt the house itself. There are still local stories of an underground passage connecting manor house with neighbouring church, and it would seem likely that all this land was monastic in pre-Reformation days.

Some years ago the son of the manor found the entrance to the tunnel and had it opened up. It was shortly afterwards that the owner of a horse in the manor stables saw the figure of a monk wandering around the grounds. From the handed-down reports, the apparition does not seem to have been wearing the usual type of habit; which suggests that he may have been a priest rather than a member of a monastic order. A spectral monk is also said to walk up and down the main street of Buriton village.

Buriton is an attractive small place, with friendly inhabitants, but rural Hampshire is full of such nooks and crannies. I moved on in the gathering twilight of an early April evening to Bramdean, some nine miles from Winchester on the Petersfield side. Here another of the innumerable coach-and-horses ghosts drives across the roadway. (Why always across? Why can't they drive down it?) By this time my interest in coaches and horses was becoming less than enthusiastic.

At Hinton Ampner a short distance away the manor is said to be haunted, certain of the manifestations transferring to the new house when the old (and much troubled) manor was pulled down. They include the classic ingredients of a lady in a rustling silk dress, a man of presumably the same era, and a number of disconcerting noises, including fearful screams and slamming doors. Hippisley-Cox in his *Haunted Britain* concludes that the ghosts were probably those of the fourth Lord Stawell and his sister-in-law and paramour. One wonders what had gone on in the house to give rise to banged doors and unearthly shrieks. The manifestations appear to have been highly unpleasant and disturbing.

By all the laws of probability one has a right to expect many historic survivals in Winchester. It was once thought to have been the site of Arthur's Camelot, though perhaps only on account of the presence in its Great Hall of the pseudo Round Table. During the anarchic struggles between Queen Matilda (otherwise known as Maud) and King Stephen in the twelfth century, the city's Wolvesey Castle was besieged by the royal lady, until relieved by the King's forces which then in turn besieged the besiegers. Some 500 years later on a winter's day, Parliamentary dragoons drove out a force of Royalist cavalry which had been occupying the city and swept into the town. The townsfolk, infuriated by the unruly behaviour of the Cavaliers, are said to have stoned them as they retreated. However, the opposition proved little kindlier, for the Roundheads burned the tapestries, vestments and books in the cathedral, and broke the organ into pieces. Parliamentary activity in the neighbourhood is still commemorated by the district known as Oliver's Battery—traditionally an emplacement for Cromwell's guns, though it is doubtful if the leader were present at this particular skirmish.

I heard no reports of ghostly Royalists or Roundheads appearing in the city, but the ubiquitous monks and nuns are in evidence. The Royal Hotel is said to occupy the site of a former convent, and a procession of (according to reports) monks and nuns has occasionally been seen in the vicinity. However, the combination of the sexes even in high celebrations was uncommon, and I suspect that any procession would be of nuns alone on a convent site.

Drive west from Winchester towards Salisbury, and you will pass through Stockbridge, a long slim market town, with an air of being still absorbed in the nineteenth century. It has at least one echo of pre-Victorian days for a mile or two away lies Redrice School, once a country house owned by George IV. A wooded drive leads up to it and it is here that the ghost of Mrs Fitzherbert has occasionally been seen. This lady, morganatic wife of George when he was still Prince of Wales, has left little mark on history, save as "the lass of Richmond Hill". Hers is a ghost I should like to encounter, for there is in her story something of pathos and grace.

Turning south to Romsey, one may pick up a strange fragment of a haunting at a house built on the site of Romsey Abbey nunnery. It is of Regency construction and one of a terrace of similar dwellings. According to the owner, Lady Kate Kendon*, who has lived in the house with her son for the past seven years, the first indication of anything unusual in connection with the building occurred on 20th May 1977. The house has a small dining-room leading from a drawing-room, with beyond it a passage and cloakroom. Sometime in the evening Lady Kate's son went into the dining-room to draw the curtains, then immediately called to say that there must have been a tom cat in the room. His mother, knowing that no cat had or could have been in the house, since all doors had been kept shut that day, then went into the dining-room, to be met by a very strong ammoniac smell. She then went into the passage beyond, only to be met by another smell, equally strong—that of (in her words) "a dirty, sweaty old tramp".

There seemed nothing to account for either smell, and after a few minutes, mother and son closed the doors and retreated. Impelled by curiosity, however, they returned ten minutes later to investigate further, only to find no trace of either smell in the two rooms concerned.

Though an incident of this kind is trivial in nature, it is interesting as an example of the capacity of smells to linger in an area with as much ease as do visual and audible impressions. There seems to have been no external reason for the smell, and its transience (the smell of tom cat at least is anything but transient) suggests a paranormal cause here.

On my return journey to Hayling I crossed the lovely Meon Valley. The little River Meon was brimming with recent rains, swelling into

107

the water meadows and spreading itself luxuriously over the banks. Two magpies flitted across the road, spluttering when they saw the nearness of the car. This is close, rolling downland country, heavily wooded along sides and crowns, with the lanes living naves of new leaves, greenly architectural. The rooks were nesting high; but when did they not? I have little faith in the particular country adage which promises a fine summer for high rook-nesting. There are always some high nesters among the black population.

I came into Droxford at lunch time and made for the White Hart, a ploughman's lunch and information. A ghostly noose—a hangman's noose?—used to be seen in Droxford Church so they told me, but it has not been heard of for some years. There was no knowledge of its origin among the local people.

Droxford was formerly on a coach route, however, and there is a strong tradition in the village that a coach once overturned in the river drowning its passengers. The incident is said to be repeated on anniversaries of the accident. This haunting, also, seems to have faded, for there is no record of any recent sighting.

The diminishing of these echoes is a common feature of hauntings. If, as is fairly certain, they are electromagnetic in nature and operate from a record or 'charge' in the surroundings, it is not illogical to suppose that in time the strength of that charge will run down. Certainly all paranormal manifestations seem to need the use of— or at least presence of—outside energy to enable them to function. This need not necessarily, I suspect, be human energy, but may be mechanically generated energy such as electricity or heat.

Where the manifestation is of the 'recorded transmission' type, the length of its duration (in terms of years) may depend upon the strength of the original impression—i.e. the power of the energy transmission (frequently emotional in origin) which first caused the impression to be recorded.

I deserted Droxford and the main road to Alton for the byways east of it, and swooped up and down a few wooded hills as the lanes threaded their way through the true pastoral country of the south. What fields there were, were mainly down to pasture. A few cows grazed the water meadows, inching forward after their tongues. There would no doubt be buttercups here in a week or two, brimming the valley bowl with high-polished gold. For the present there was only the flat sheen of water around the feet of the willows. It would be May before the river remnants evaporated, leaving the sharp green growth of spring in their wake, nuzzling the tree roots and furring the bank's edges.

I came into East Meon in mid-afternoon, and was immediately directed to Mrs E. G. Lambert as an inhabitant of long standing, knowledgeable on village matters. I had passed a fine old building on the way into the village and this was originally an ecclesiastical court house, in fact the court house for the See of Winchester. It was said to be haunted which did not surprise me. For many years the place had been used as a farmhouse, and it was not certain whether the ghost belonged to this period or to the ecclesiastical era of its life. However, it was not of this haunting Mrs Lambert told me, but of one closer to her personal life.

After being widowed, she moved to a thatched cottage which had formerly been part of the stables of the New Inn in the village. The front door of this house had a huge bolt to secure it (Mrs Lambert supposed it to be the original fastening), but during the time of her occupation, she always experienced great difficulty in keeping the door closed. The widow slept in a downstairs room, but it was very usual for her to be awakened by the draught from the newly opened front door, although she had religiously bolted it before going to bed the previous night. In answer to my question, she was quite certain that the bolt could not have slipped out of its socket of its own volition, yet she was at a loss (as she had been during her residence in the house) to account for the door's failure to stay shut.

When she left the place it was taken by a family named Burley. Apparently they found an inner door within a hollow wall, and on opening it up discovered stairs leading to an attic. Within this room there was nothing noteworthy save a small pair of boots, sooty and grimed, which they concluded had belonged to some child chimney-sweep of the Victorian era. As it happened, there was a flight of sweep's steps leading into the wide chimney of the house, so the presence of the boots was not as unusual as it might have been.

Apart from her own experience with the recalcitrant door, Mrs Lambert had noticed one other sign of strangeness within the cottage. Her pet cat would suddenly look up startled, its hair standing on end, as though it saw something she could not. What it saw, or sensed, Mrs Lambert never knew. At that time of course she had no knowledge of the little boots lying undiscovered in the attic. No knowledge, either, of what lay immediately above her head as she ate her daily breakfast; that is until the dining-room ceiling fell down one morning. The bricklayer who came to effect repairs found a pile of old lace-bobbins hidden between floor and ceiling.

The little house must at some time have held a cottage industry, and been the home of one of the village lace-makers; though how and why the bobbins had been secreted where they were found is beyond comprehension.

I left Mrs Lambert with reluctance for she was full of wisdom and good nature, country lore and local information; I could profitably have spent the rest of the day listening to her stories of the old days in the Meon Valley. However, I had another call to make—upon Mr and Mrs Sims of the Country Stores.

The last named turned out to be the village shop in the main street and had a history of its own. It was once a public house known as The Trooper, and housed Izaak Walton while he wrote *The Compleat Angler*; no mean claim to fame, that. The infant River Meon flows through the main street, so Walton would have felt much at home and not unhappy while he worked, accompanied as he was by the song of water so near at hand.

Almost next door to the Country Stores is a road known as Temple Lane. It runs down a decline and debouches into the main street, where a small bridge takes pedestrians over the river if they wish to cross. Temple Lane itself holds a scatter of houses, including one in which an old woman had died some time towards the end of 1976.

One afternoon in January 1977, four boys, all fourteen-year-olds, came down the lane towards the main street. They were just out of school and not in any particular hurry to get home or anywhere else. There is a certain attraction about winter afternoons, with their chill dampness and fading light, their lost rich smells of the recent past and their occasional accompaniment of moaning rooks from nearby immemorial elms. Children linger and scuff about in what is left of the dead leaves, or they lean on bridges and stare at water flowing coldly underneath. They only seek to delay the pleasure which lies ahead, of a warm room, the chime of friendly voices and the smell of hot supper cooking on the stove.

So did the four boys this January afternoon, one of them the son of Mr and Mrs Sims. They dawdled down the hill, past the now empty house where the old villager had died, and with a few stops and starts for conversation, points of reference and argument, bent their steps towards the main street and the bridge. However, hardly had they passed the dark house than they became conscious of something unusual occurring. The figure of a woman came out of the house and along the path to the road; it then (so they thought) began to follow them down the slope towards the village street. All four boys saw the shadowy figure, and although they do not seem actively to have identified it at the time with the deceased woman, they all appear to have felt a strong sense of the uncanny.

As a result of this they hid in a gateway until the thing should pass them—which it shortly did. They watched it go down to the bottom of the lane and then cross the village street. They thought it continued to the bridge, but did not wait to make sure. The lads scattered to their houses, in a state of considerable alarm. In fact so badly shaken were they that all four of them (to the surprise of their respective parents) refused to go out in the evening again for several nights. However, boys being as resilient as rubber balls, in a short while they forgot about the shadowy woman and returned to their usual habits.

The evidence in this case, although limited to this one group of boys, is sufficiently detailed to point to some likelihood of a genuine (though I suspect strictly temporary) haunting. Normally with lads of this or any other age one would suspect the irrepressible desire to hoax adults. However, boys are not notably good actors and parents are usually excellent detectives where their young are concerned. The parents in this case seem to have been convinced of the genuineness of their sons' fear.

Although one cannot with certainty say so, it may be relevant that the elderly woman who lived in Temple Lane had been a keen Spiritualist during her lifetime. This ghost, I think, is typical of the kind which lingers for a short while after death in the neighbourhood of its old living place. I suspect that such lingering may be the rule rather than the exception, the actual psyche of the dead person remaining for anything from a few days to several months in its life area, before departing for fresh woods and new pastures. This type of manifestation is as different from the 'recorded' type as a live performance is from that on a gramophone record or tape.

I am saying, without equivocation, that I do believe manifestations of this nature may be taken as one type of evidence (there are others) for survival of physical death by the psyche, spirit, soul, energy or whatever name you care to give the 'aware' part of the self.

When I left the Country Stores lights were beginning to appear in the cottage windows and the soft grey wings of twilight rushed along the village street, blurring the shapes of trees to shadows, muffling the singing Meon to an evening murmur. I did not glance back at Temple Lane, but trod hard on the accelerator and drove north to join the Petersfield road at Langrish, though by the time I reached that attractive place darkness was falling like the sound of a ten-ton bell. I decided to get home to Hayling and continue the ghost hunt in the morning. The lady of Temple Lane had left a deep impression.

When I returned to Langrish the following day, I was glad I had waited. The morning was bright with the promise of sun. A few trees were beginning to show mists of green in the distance, and larks were discovering voices mislaid since the previous summer. I looked out for battling hares but saw none. There was a feeling of stirring life, though, and the few humans about walked with springy steps, calling cheerful greetings to each other. I found myself singing as I drove into Langrish village, which considerably startled an elderly gentleman emerging from the telephone box and failed to improve the temper of an Alsatian dog peering at me suspiciously through a neighbouring fence.

Preliminary enquiries directed me to Bordean House, a large, dignified building on the outskirts of Langrish.

It turned out to be a Sue Ryder Home, though it had been built in 1611 by Roger Langrish, and occupied as a private house for centuries. In 1878 it became the property of a family named Nicholson, but during World War II the building was taken over by the Navy as a rest centre for sailors and W.R.N.S. On de-requisition it became the home of an order of nuns, the Oblates of the Assumption, remaining so until 1976 when it was leased by the Sue Ryder Foundation. Several of the Sisters, now retired, continue to live in the house.

Bordean itself is not of striking beauty, though its proportions are good. An atmosphere surrounds it of serene dignity. And why would it not? The place is superbly set on its hill top, looking out of and into trees, and with a wide circular sweep of drive to accommodate aristocratic carriages before the house.

The ghosts (there are three) do not concern carriages, however. One—I would guess the oldest in terms of survival—is said to be that of a cavalier with a plumed hat and long cloak who frequents the interior; a second is of a white lady who walks from the house and down the drive before disappearing; and the third, about which I could discover very little, arises from a duel between two brothers which resulted in the death of one of them. There is an apparent bloodstain (indelible) on the floor of the chapel to prove the story. No matter how the mark is scrubbed or treated it cannot be got rid of. There are many such throughout Britain.

The tradition of hauntings in the house appears to have survived in well defined form, though none of the present occupants had experienced them at the time of my visit. One night attendant, however, stayed only one night in the place before declaring that she could not continue on account of the unpleasant atmosphere. I thought the feeling of the place taut, a little other-worldly, perhaps, yet not uncomfortable. But this was broad daylight; midnight might be another matter.

The tradition of associating hauntings with the post-midnight hours does have some foundations in fact. The possible reasons for such a time preference are detailed in my book, *The Mask of Time*, and are too complex to go into here. There is no doubt, however, that a larger number of psychic phenomena appears to take place between the hours of midnight and 4.00 a.m. than at other times of the day, and that the reason for this may have a strictly scientific basis.

I left the Meon Valley with regret, for it is a place of singular atmosphere and beauty. Although well populated by small villages, it has retained an air of seclusion, of being set apart from the present century.

By contrast, the Isle of Wight, that little Hampshire south of Hampshire, would seem to be very much of the twentieth century, for it is a popular holiday area, much frequented by yachts, hovercraft and families on vacation. Do not be misled by appearances. The island has an ancient history, and I have told elsewhere how first the Romans, then the Vikings used it as a base. Some echoes of the one or the other still remain, and a correspondent gave me an account of a remarkable experience which befell her and her husband during a night drive over the Downs. However, it is not this which concerns us, but another account, equally interesting, from the same lady.

It was Mrs Sheila White of St Helens who told me the terrifying story of Hopfield at Waterlooville and to her I am indebted for the account of the Blue Lady's dog associated with the house known as Priory on the Isle of Wight.

Priory was, as its name suggests, built on the foundations of a Cluniac monastery, said to have been founded in the eleventh century. Later associations brought it into contact with the contraband trade, and to this day there are stories of buried treasure (associated with the monks) and underground passageways (the work of the smugglers). The ghost story concerns neither of these, but relates to one of Mrs White's ancestors, for the old house was in the possession of her family for many generations.

At the time of her earliest recollections of it, Priory belonged to her cousin Laura, elderly and unmarried, who lived alone in the great house surrounded by a staff of retainers who had served her for many years. If such a lifestyle seems extravagant, it should be said that the date was the early 1920s, and that the châtelaine was merely carrying on the traditions of a family which had occupied Priory for two hundred years.

Sheila's first visit to the house took place when she was a small child, and she appears to have returned at intervals until well into adolescence. In fact not only did an affinity appear to exist between the young Sheila and her elderly cousin, but between the girl and the house, for she loved every stone of it, as did its owner, Cousin Laura. Perhaps the one bond produced the other.

Sheila knew from an early age Priory's reputation for being haunted. A portrait of the ghost's original hung in the dining-room—that of a girl of fourteen or fifteen, dressed in a blue gown with silver lace trimmings, the period being the early eighteenth century. The girl was portrayed on a rustic garden seat with a canary, attached by a satin ribbon to her wrist, perched on her finger. At her feet played a small dog, a King Charles spaniel. Inevitably she was known as the Blue Lady; the young Sheila never learned her ancestor's name.

Of the dog there were more tangible remains, for what had been mortal of him still reposed, stuffed, in a square glass case over the main staircase. His glassy, baleful stare caught the light of her candle when the child retired to bed each night.

It was not the dog which haunted Priory but his young owner. She had been seen on several occasions on the staircase or in the grounds of the house. A happy little ghost, faint and shadowy, and always accompanied by the scent of lavender. Although Sheila herself never saw the Blue Lady, she smelled the perfume and occasionally heard a faint but unmistakable swish of silken skirts.

This was all there was of the ghost until Cousin Laura died—she who had so loved the house and its history. Priory passed into the hands of strangers, being bought by a wealthy American woman, who proceeded to update and 'improve' the building by the addition of various impedimenta of numerous periods. She settled in with a large staff of servants, but all did not go well. The servants began to see and hear a child running along the corridors in the night, an unhappy child, crying aloud for a lost dog. There then began a heavy turnover in servants. It was when the owner's butler—the archetypal old retainer who had been many years in her employ—announced his intention to leave "on account of the noises" that the American took action. She invited Sheila's grandmother, mother and the girl herself to take tea at Priory. The time was now in the late 1930s; high summer—one of the last before World War II broke over and submerged the leisured way of life.

If the old family was curious about the reasons for the new owner's invitation, this was soon satisfied. The American needed to lay the Blue Lady's ghost if she were to live in the house, and in order to do so, required details of the story. Who was the ghost and what was this dog she cried for? Local inhabitants who must have had the information, carefully withheld it. The American was an 'overner'—from over the water; an outsider and not of the island folk. She would get no help from them. Was the dog perhaps the airedale which Cousin Laura had owned? Was there any legend of a dog connected with the place? The weeping child had unnerved her servants, she said. Footsteps had actually passed them in the corridor, accompanied by the sobs of a child, but they had not seen anything.

It was the head gardener, inherited by the American from Sheila's cousin, who remembered the stuffed dog which had hung over the staircase, and it was a considerable time before this could be traced since it had been sold when the house changed hands. Eventually it was run to earth in the shop of an antique dealer in Newport and brought back to Priory, still in its glass case and still balefully glaring out with its glassy eyes. The spaniel was hung again in his traditional position, and from that moment the nocturnal disturbances ceased. The crying child had what she wanted.

The American woman had needed to hear the original story of the ghost from the family to whom it belonged but she laid the spectre by her own wit and sense.

Nowadays Priory belongs to a travel organization and the building is used by hundreds of people during the course of a year. However, Mrs White assures me that every manager who takes over the running of the place is warned never, in any circumstances, to remove the stuffed dog in the glass case from its place at the head of the stairs.

And that, one would imagine, is the end of the haunting of Priory, the beautiful mellow old mansion which looks out over the Solent.

But is it? Some time after receiving Mrs White's fascinating account, I had the following letter from Mr Victor Golding of Kenton, Middlesex.

In the first week of September last year, my wife and I and our two teenage sons were on holiday at the Priory, Seaview, Isle of Wight—a spacious hotel set in well wooded and secluded grounds. Outside the hotel there is a small open sort of courtyard where guests may park their cars.

One morning during the week, my wife and I (in the front) and our elder son, Richard (in the back) were sitting in the car waiting for our younger son, Keith, to come out of the hotel so that we could all go for a drive. No other person was in sight, it was bright daylight and we had good visibility all round.

Suddenly, all of us were aware of someone approaching the side of the car. My wife and I assumed it was Keith and turned sideways for a better look and to open the near door when the person disappeared from sight. Still thinking it was Keith, we thought he had crouched down by the car, out of sight. "What's he playing at now?" I said. Richard replied "It wasn't Keith, it was an old lady." "Where has she gone then?" I asked, as there was still not a soul in sight and hiding underneath cars is not a usual trick of old ladies. Nor was there anywhere else she could have gone without us seeing her.

Although we thought this rather strange, we dismissed it from our minds and a few minutes later Keith appeared in the distance from the hotel and came to the car. To make sure, we asked if he had played a trick on us and come out earlier and hidden somewhere (though we thought this highly improbable). He was clearly as mystified as ourselves, nor had he seen anyone else about.

On the last evening of our holiday, in the course of conversation with a fellow guest, he said "Of course, you know this place is haunted." "No," we answered, "we didn't know," feeling a suitable shiver of apprehension—"who by?"

"An old lady and a dog," he replied. Then the strange event of a few days earlier came to our minds.

Haunted not by a child, you will notice, but by an old lady and a dog. There was a possibility, of course, that the Priory to which Mr Golding referred was not Mrs White's Priory, but further enquiry of both correspondents made it clear that they were one and the same. Mrs White, who until she heard of Victor Golding's experience had no knowledge of an elderly female ghost at the house, is inclined to think the apparition is of her cousin Laura—she who had 'loved every stone of the place'. Of this there can be no certainty, only a strong likelihood. An interesting sequence all round.

To the west of the island lies Freshwater, which has the unusual distinction of housing most of its industrial development in one building—Golden Hill Fort, a hexagonal building originally built as a defence against possible invasion by the Napoleonic forces. Golden Hill Fort during its lifetime has housed both soldiers and sailors, and the place echoed to barked orders and military drill long before the printing machines and knitting machines began their clacking.

In view of such a history it is not surprising the Fort is haunted, though the ghosts appear to belong to different periods of time. As far as I can discover, there are two distinct hauntings. One, reported to me by Mrs Beryl Lake of Freshwater, concerns the experience of a friend's husband who was working in the Fort late one evening (about 11.30 p.m.) on a metal machine. He looked up from his work to see a sailor leaning in the doorway, with his hands folded. It did

Golden Hill Fort, Isle of Wight, originally built as a defence against French invasion, has at least two ghosts. One is that of a sailor said to have been hanged for treason; the other that of a soldier from the First World War.

not occur to the percipient that what he saw was other than mortal, for the man was laughing, seemingly amused. The subject politely asked the sailor if he could help him in any way, and got up from his machine to go towards the door. Before he had reached it the apparition had vanished, leaving, one assumes, a very startled man behind him. My correspondent here informed me that the sailor is one said to have been hanged for treason by his mates (or as a result of court martial, perhaps?) from a flight of steps which can still be seen on the inside of the Fort. (There are also stories of horses' hoofbeats having been heard within the building, and the sound of shouted orders from the barrack square.)

It is not of sailors that Mrs B. M. Bryan writes but of a ticking clock, an opening door and the sound of footsteps. Mrs Bryan, also of Freshwater, has recent information on Golden Fort through her daughter, Maureen, who for some time worked in the building.

Again the main experience occurred during a late work session, though there had been earlier indications that the Fort was occupied by some of its past inhabitants. On one occasion a broken clock began to tick when it should have been incapable of so hectic an activity; on another a door, bolted on the inside, opened of its own accord without any apparent interference with the fastenings. But it was when Miss Bryan was working alone in the fort at about 7.00 p.m. that she heard the sound of footsteps approaching from another room. Knowing that the sound could not have a natural cause, she hurriedly scrambled into her coat and left the building. However, no sooner had she done so, than she remembered that in her hurry to escape she had omitted to switch off a fan heater, a possible fire risk if left. With her courage in her hands and her heart in her mouth she went back up the stairs, grabbed the keys from another section and went into her own room to turn off the heater. No sooner had she done so than she heard the sound of footsteps enter the room in which she stood. At that point Miss Bryan in her anxiety to get away, tripped and fell, badly cutting her head. She then presumably made her escape in disorder and haste.

There have been many reports of both audible and visible manifestations inside the Fort. One such relates to the sighting of a soldier dressed in the uniform of World War I. There would appear, therefore, to be multiple hauntings within the hexagonal building, all pertaining to the military and naval history of the place.

The same correspondent submitted three other accounts of hauntings of which she or members of her family have had personal experience. Mrs Bryan's brother and his wife who lived in a house in Avenue Road, Freshwater, on several occasions saw the figure of a woman beckoning to them, apparently requiring them to follow her into the garden. On no occasion did they do so. Their stay in the building was also accompanied by other disturbing phenomena, mainly relating to doors which appeared to open and close on their own.

When this couple finally left the house, Mr Bryan's sister and her husband moved in. They, too, saw the figure of the beckoning woman, but like their predecessors found themselves without the courage to follow her. Who this woman was in life and what her story does not appear to be known, but the percipients seem to have thought that a well existed in the garden of the house and that her appearance might be connected with it.

Another equally indeterminate haunting was encountered by Maureen Bryan when still a child. She and another girl, both aged twelve or thirteen at the time, went (or were sent; this detail is not clear) to an empty house in an area of Freshwater named Brickfields. It seems that the children forced an entrance, climbing through an open window, before going into one of the bedrooms to search for certain books which were the object of their visit. The first room they visited was empty, but as they were about to go into the next bedroom, they heard a voice calling the name of the second child, Sandra, accompanied by the sound of tearing paper. They then, according to Miss Bryan's own report, saw the figure of a man in this room, and a pair of (apparently) detached hands tearing the wallpaper from one of the walls. Both girls fled, almost falling down the flight of stairs in their terror. They locked themselves in a downstairs room and then climbed out of its window. Again there is no known story attached to this manifestation.

Mrs Bryan herself had an equally eerie encounter when driving back from Binstead one New Year's Night, accompanied by her niece. The time was between midnight and 1.00 a.m. and as they approached a corner opposite the old Calbourne Mill on the Island, they saw what appeared to be two teenagers, dressed as far as I can make out in hooded anoraks. They were, according to Mrs Bryan, "two white luminous figures, no faces or hands apparent, jumping in the road into the headlights of the car. When we were a fraction from them they both jumped up into the hedge." Although the car's occupants discussed going back to investigate the phenomenon, both of them (not surprisingly) decided against.

This particular manifestation, together with a ghostly car which crashes into the hedge and then disappears, has been seen on several occasions. The place appears to be an accident black spot, which is not unusual where hauntings of this type take place. Apart from the result of shock to the drivers of such a sighting, vehicles themselves may be affected by whatever electrical disturbances cause the apparitions in the first place. The fact remains that haunted areas of road appear to develop a bad record for accidents.

The original of the jumping teenagers might well have misjudged their foolish game and have been killed by the original car-driver. The haunting would seem to be a modern one in view of both dress and activity.

Mrs Bryan had one other account to give me of hauntings on the Island. Again the experience had been that of her daughter, Maureen, who appears to have a strong sensitivity in this direction.

It seems that Miss Bryan and her boy friend visited the derelict old Mill at Yarmouth, I.O.W., with the intention of looking round it. The time was early evening and they had been only a short while in the building when Maureen Bryan thought she felt hands touch her throat. The sensation was not a violent one. There was no feeling of strangulation, merely of a pair of hands touching her neck. However, a sensation of this kind when the hands are invisible is not a welcome one, and Miss Bryan was naturally disturbed. Her friend, who felt nothing, was incredulous and somewhat irritated by these feminine imaginings. However, no doubt he regretted his attitude some time later when discussing the Mill with two local youths. They informed him that a party of their friends, students, had been filming the River Yar for some purpose or other and had had permission to spend the night in the Mill. Most of the boys stayed only a short time, however, for they heard what they thought was the sound of rattling chains echoing through the empty building. All but one of the band departed at once for quieter quarters. The remaining lad braved it out, determined to rise above the mere supernatural. That is, until he felt a pair of hands encircle his throat. He left with rather more speed than dignity. According to Maureen Bryan, she had told no one of her own experience in the building, and the second story came to her unsolicited.

The next account takes us to a house not far from Freshwater, though it stands alone between the sea and the foot of Tennyson Downs. In 1974/75, Miss Helen Allan rented West Sea House* which belonged to a friend and her husband. In its early days the place had been a coaching inn, and it stood near enough to that seamark, The Needles, to have gained a reputation as a smuggling headquarters. According to Miss Allan's account, its age (sixteenth- and seventeenth-century) and its rambling nature appealed strongly to her. The entrance at the time of her occupation was through a glass porch, over which was a small bedroom with a similar one next door to it. Originally these had constituted one large room.

On the day in question, Miss Allan had bought a second-hand bicycle, which for want of better storage, she had propped in the porch beneath her bedroom window. That night she went to bed early, retiring at about 9.30 p.m. leaving her bicycle outside and her black labrador dog, Jamie, asleep in his basket in the entrance hall.

At 11.00 p.m. she was awakened by the howling of the labrador as he raced upstairs to her room, and by the sound of some heavy object being apparently dragged by chains across the cobbled space in front of the house. She let in the dog which seemed much alarmed, growling and with his hair standing on end, and then she listened to the noise outside. The thought which occurred to her was not 'Ghosts!' but 'Burglars!', for she remembered her new bicycle and the unlocked front door beside it ("the front door was open; we never locked it"). The sound of the chains moved across the courtyard and then stopped; moved again and then stopped; moved a third time and then stopped directly outside the door. She did not hear them again. Silence fell. Miss Allan went to the window. The cobbles shone wet under a brilliant moon, but the only sound now was the ceaseless complaining of the wind. There was no person in sight.

She thought it possible then that her bicycle had been stolen, but felt no inclination to hurry after the thief in her night attire. Before she fell asleep she pondered briefly on the loudness, the heaviness of the chain sound, knowing that the bicycle chain was a very slight thing indeed.

As it happened her friend, together with the latter's small son and a friend of his, had spent the night in another cottage nearby, and the second little boy had been unable to sleep, crying out that someone was walking about outside the house. The time was about 11.00 p.m.

It is doubtful whether Miss Allan would have thought further about the matter (her bicycle was precisely where she had left it) had not her friend made enquiries of previous owners of the house the next day. From them she learned that both the small bedrooms were haunted, and that that occupied by Miss Allan had been little used in their day. Whenever guests were put into it they were invariably disturbed about 11.00 p.m. There seems little doubt that the inn's smuggling days were responsible for at least part of the manifestations. From which statement it will be apparent that there were others than that heard by Miss Allan and her dog.

During one period of their occupation Miss Allan's friend was engaged in nursing her husband who was seriously ill. The sick man had the second of the two small rooms at the front of the house. Apparently on several occasions the invalid heard someone come along the passage to his room, and thinking it to be his wife, expected her to come in to see him. The footsteps always ceased at the door, however, and later reference to his wife confirmed that she had not been upstairs at the time they were heard.

On another occasion Miss Allan herself heard a sound as though the brass knob on the bathroom door were being rattled. Since the knob was loose, the noise it made was distinctive. Helen Allan assumed the bathroom visitant was a friend of hers, a temporary house-guest, but was confounded when this lady later returned to the house at 6.00 p.m., having been absent for the entire day.

There were other minor occurrences at West Sea House. On one occasion a figure had actually been seen in the road nearby—a figure with no reality in fact, I gather. And Miss Allan had often found lights switched on on the stairs when she came down in the mornings, although she was certain of having put them off the previous night. This is a very common form of manifestation; though it can also be due to defective switches—which I gather was not the case at West Sea House.

The house still stands, still lived in, but whether still haunted or not I do not know. The owner had the house blessed in Miss Allan's presence at one time, which the latter suggests may account for the chain-sound she heard ceasing at the front door.

It would seem from the detail given in this case that a part of the house's history had remained with it, subject to fairly frequent re-broadcasting. An interesting example of this type of haunting.

The Isle of Wight holds another story, intriguing and mysterious—that of Lucy Lightfoot who disappeared at Gatcombe in a time of eclipse and violent storm. It is richly romantic, illogical and decidedly odd, but is a time rather than a ghost story. As far as I know Lucy does not haunt Gatcombe or its neighbourhood so I cannot include her here. We must travel back to the mainland for the last of the Hampshire ghosts, to the village of Boldre, near Lymington, where rumour states that Norman soldiers have sometimes been seen entering the church there. The vicar, however, believes the story concerns Crusaders, and this may well be the truth of the matter. It has not been possible to find any evidence of recent sightings of these apparitions, so their period in time remains indeterminate.

A rich and beautiful county, Hampshire, with room to move and breathe. Its history is as varied as its scenery and it must always have been a pleasant place in which to live—even with the Norsemen hammering at its sea-doors and the Civil Wars turning its handsome landscape into a battlefield.

I drove away from it reluctantly turning my back on the rolling dolphin hills and the tree-furred valleys as the car nosed westward towards Wiltshire and the mystery of the stones of Avebury.

Wiltshire

If you enter Wiltshire as I did, from the north, you may slide past Swindon into the mysterious, green and oblong county with scarcely a ripple of change upon the landscape to mark your passage. Yet change there is. The hills imperceptibly lengthen, grow higher; chalk begins to show under the green acres, and one crosses the long and ancient line of the Ridgeway, that prehistoric causeway which almost bisects England.

Wiltshire has always had the reputation of being a secretive county. Superficially open and accessible, situated as it is on the main route between the delectable south-west peninsula and the rest of England, it yet retains an inwardness, an area of privacy which is neither open nor accessible to the casual visitor.

I had heard the legend of Wiltshire's bastions long before I arrived there, having been warned that it still possessed some dark areas, that witchcraft flourished, superstition abounded. The same tales are told of Norfolk, Essex, Cumbria and elsewhere. Rural places, if they are sufficiently remote, convey hints of their long past as well as of their inhabitants' natural suspicion of strangers.

The very nature of Wiltshire history, however, sets it apart from the rest of the British Isles, for the county seems to have been in prehistoric times a centre of pagan worship, a chosen holy place where the massive henge of Avebury was erected with its attendant monument at Silbury, its settlement on Windmill Hill, and its sanctuary on the very Ridgeway itself. The settlement may have preceded the district's religious development, but there seems no reason to doubt that the region presently became noted as an important cult centre, probably attracting worshippers from considerable distances, even from overseas. As if this were not power enough, almost exactly due south of Avebury lay the second great temple of Wiltshire—Stonehenge.

The presence of such centres of worship must have imposed on the area not only a reputation for sanctity but also a need for secrecy. The sacred and the secret have always been linked. The strength of primitive religions lay in the fact that their holy rites were known only to the elect, the priesthood. So perhaps in this part of Wessex there would gradually be imposed a sense of apartness, of caution, which would be deep enough to survive the vicissitudes of twenty-three centuries.

Thoughts of this nature did not actively occur to me as I drove over the Marlborough Downs into the little grey town beneath them. The day was chequered sun-and-rain, a mid-March day, with the wind still unwarmed and unfriendly. Marlborough was trim, dignified and heavy with cars. I had come to enquire principally about its ghosts—if it had any—and barely noticed the twentieth-century preoccupations. The town is a pleasant place with a wide main street sloping from one side to the other, the ubiquitous motorcar grabbing the middle for itself; a two-hour parking breather there, while traffic flows on either side.

I talked to a number of people in Marlborough, but only one story came to light of a still-active ghost and it related to a building on the high side of the main street. Until recently occupied by a design group run by a local man, Mr Brian Strutt, the property is now in the possession of Motor Aids, a firm selling small parts and equipment for cars. The latter professed to know nothing of any ghost, but on further enquiry it was obvious that such ignorance was more assumed than real.

In medieval times this part of Marlborough High Street was occupied by a chantry chapel belonging to the local monastery, and as usual in such cases, a word-of-mouth story survives of an underground passage connecting chapel and monastery. (Why are these corridors always subterranean and not on the surface?) No passage of any kind has been discovered but the original medieval chapel still stands—a small room, heavily beamed and arched, which during the design group's occupation was used as a drawing office. It was in this period of the room's history that the ghost was seen.

During the firm's residence there, objects frequently moved in the drawing-office, equipment kept in one place being found in another, odd articles disappearing and then reappearing at a later date, with none of the staff being responsible for the activities. On one occasion a young draughtsman was struck sharply by a moving drawing-board, seemingly operating of its own volition. Such occurrences may easily be accidental or explicable by other means. What cannot be so easily explained is the sighting of the figure of a monk, robed in white, which was seen seated at a desk on the farther side of the room. It remained motionless, the cowl up and face concealed, for a few minutes before vanishing as abruptly as it had appeared. As far as I could discover, he was seen once only by one member of the staff, and the sighting therefore has no corroboration.

The chapel gives the impression of having been at some time divided into two portions, and it has a certain dignity and appeal. However, the left-hand side of the room appears to have some atmosphere apart from these—a kind of tension which anyone familiar with paranormal investigations will recognize. The 'monk's corner' lies in deep shadow.

When I visited it the chantry chapel was in process of conversion into a flat for a couple about to be married, and it may be that so much renovation will result in an end to the haunting if haunting it was. The young bride, who appeared on the scene during my visit, refused to countenance the idea of a spectral monk no matter what the colour of his habit. We carried on a conversation in shouts over the noise of hammer, saw and electric drill. I think it unlikely she will see any monkish manifestation once the curtains are up and the carpets down. Structural disturbance of surroundings disposes of ghosts, as I have stated earlier.

If Marlborough town is relatively unhaunted, the country around compensates for the lack. There are numerous tales of ghostly mail coaches pulled either by headless horses or those of the normal kind. The occurrence of headless horses in this type of story is common, though one never hears of ghostly cats and dogs appearing minus their heads. Since beheading was a common form of execution in the past, headless humans frequently crop up in ghost sightings. But whoever heard of horses being beheaded?

The Pewsey road from Marlborough is said to be the site of a coach-and-horses haunting, though I found no witnesses to testify to it. Pewsey itself is a pleasant village, long and straggling, with its considerable history concealed behind a modern façade. One hotel, the Phoenix, is in its present form unhaunted, though it was originally situated on the opposite side of the road and was reputed to have a ghost, though there is some uncertainty as to its identity.

Local tradition states that when Charles II lodged at Fyfield Manor, a few miles distant, his mistress, Nell Gwynne, stayed at the Phoenix hostelry in Pewsey. The haunting is (inevitably) attributed to her, and she is said to have been seen and heard in the old building which now lurks behind a garage's modern frontage.

I looked at what remains of the old structure. It is dilapidated and unused in the main, but shapes of former rooms can still be traced. One of the garage's staff denied all knowledge of the ghost, but the other said he had heard noises in the old part of the place on several occasions; "though," he added as an afterthought, "we usually attribute the sounds to rats." I was not able to find any person who had seen an apparition there.

There are stories in Pewsey itself of various encounters. A local bus driver when taking his vehicle through the nearby village of Oare on one occasion, saw the figure of a woman dressed in white cross the road in front of him and then disappear. He apparently returned home considerably shocked and quite unable to explain the experience. He assumed he had seen a ghost.

Another local man, a Mr Flippance, at the time of the incident described lived in a village house said to have belonged formerly to a Quaker. My informant referred to it simply as 'the Quaker's house'. It seems that on one occasion when about to enter his home, this man thought he saw the figure of the house's original owner standing at the end of a passageway, beside the house. Somewhat agitated, he drew his wife's attention to the shadowy shape standing motionless by the wall. Look as she might, however, the lady could see nothing there, though in order to pacify her husband she agreed that she also could see the apparition. Later she admitted that she had not done so and the passageway had appeared quite empty to her.

I made several attempts to trace the percipient in this case, but was unable to do so and understood he had moved from the district. This particular occurrence therefore relies on hearsay only, and is not satisfactory as evidence.

The term 'Quaker' here may refer to the Huguenot population which poured into England in the seventeenth century, bringing with it a refined and expert knowledge of weaving and a taste for gardening. (It was the Huguenots who instituted the first gardening societies in this country.) Wiltshire has many echoes of the weavers, and indeed their traces lie all over the South and East Anglia, reminders of their origin lingering in names of places and people, and in the distinctive architectural style which they carried from their old to the new land.

Whether the Pewsey percipient saw the image of a true English Quaker or whether the figure represented a Huguenot weaver who had once owned the house, it is not possible to say. However, he was apparently convinced at the time of the occurrence that the image was not of a living being, but was apparitional. Pewsey is certainly in an old weaving area, so the chances are that Mr Flippance's distant predecessor in this house was Huguenot. I was to find echoes of these energetic and interesting people in many other parts of the region.

Another story came from Pewsey village—that of a local man, Mr

Tony Kimber, who, intent on getting a lift back to Pewsey one evening after his day's work, followed a horse and cart for some distance. He tried in vain either to catch up with the vehicle or attract the driver's attention, without success. The carter did not look back or alter his pace in any way. Finally when Mr Kimber had almost despaired of reaching the cart, it turned into an old trackway at the side of the road. Though useless to him now as a means of getting a lift to Pewsey, he was anxious to see where the vehicle was bound for, and as soon as he reached the lane end stared down it after the cart. There was no cart. It and its driver had totally disappeared and the old trackway was empty as far as the eye could see. The Pewsey man was considerably disconcerted.

This type of hallucination, occurring as in this case, at dusk or half light is open to other interpretations than that of haunting. Shadows cast by trees or hedgerows, reflections in roadside puddles, the motion of grass and branches in the wind, can all contribute to a sense of the unreal. Shapes appear to form which in daylight would be seen for what they are; movement takes place which has natural causes, yet suggests activity of another kind. Even taking this into account, however, it is difficult to see how a man could follow an apparent horse and cart for a considerable distance along a metalled road, then see it turn off into a country bridleway and disappear into the evening air. Owl-light, bat-light, maybe these contributed to what the hitch-hiker thought he saw, but a dusk illusion would have been of shorter duration, I think, than was this experience.

On the outer limits of Pewsey, where the houses thin and straggle, stands a neat and venerable inn, The French Horn. The present tenants, a Mr and Mrs Peall, came to the premises in 1976, and were told on arrival that the place had two ghosts. It seems that one of the ghosts is that of a tenant's wife who resided there in the mid nineteen sixties. She is said occasionally to open the front door of the building, come in and look around before once more leaving the way she came.

There is a second haunting, taken more seriously by local people. This is said to be the sound of a baby crying from the upper rooms of the house. The Pealls' predecessors frequently heard it and went upstairs to try to identify the cause. They never found any reason for the sounds. Strangely enough the crying came most usually when the pub was particularly busy, and the sound could always be heard clearly above the noise in the bar. It was remarked on on several occasions by the inn's customers.

Neither haunting has ever been manifest to Mr and Mrs Peall during their occupation of the premises, though Mrs Peall herself had had an interesting experience earlier in her life to which I shall refer later.

I left Pewsey in a flurry of rain to drive to Avebury, and chose a roundabout route through Easton and Burbage which wound through the Savernake Forest. I had heard much about the forest from conversations in the Marlborough area. It was haunted; it was not haunted; it was mysterious and alarming; it was open and friendly. I determined to see for myself. I had heard, too—again in Marlborough—about the ancient manor house of Wolfhall on the outskirts of the forest, which had once been the home of the Seymours, and which was said to hold echoes of its history in the form of hauntings.

The Seymours—Semere or St Maur in its Norman form—married into the Esturmy family, thereby securing for themselves the wardenship of Savernake Forest which had originally been an Esturmy office. They made their home at Wolfhall, a mansion on the forest edge, and grew to great wealth and power through the fortunes of a sixteenth-century daughter of the house, Jane. It is thought that the original manor house of Wolfhall was the scene of the girl's marriage to Henry VIII, and tradition has it that a Wolfhall barn was used as a reception area for guests at the wedding banquet.

The marriage had taken place with indecent haste after the execution of Henry's reigning Queen, Anne Boleyn. Records are undecided as to whether the widower waited one or three days before committing himself at the altar once again. Henry was not a stander-on-ceremony. On the night his first Queen, Catherine of Aragon, died, he had donned a sumptuous yellow suit and given a ball in celebration. Now Anne, the Black Crow, she of the dark eyes and quick movement, had been summarily silenced, he could not wait to elevate her successor to the vacant bed and crown. "Poor, pretty little Jane," (who, in the Holbein portrait, looks singularly uncomely) lived eighteen months after the Wolfhall celebrations, and died giving birth to a delicate Prince of Wales.

Apart from its sometime owners, what of Wolfhall itself? There is a temptation to think that its name relates to wolves from the nearby forest, for when the mansion was built there were still a few such animals left in England. However, in 1086 the manor was listed in Domesday Book as Ulfela, and was written Ulfhall as late as the end of the sixteenth century. Ulph or Ulfela may have related to a personal name—'the place of Ulf'.

However it was, the old house had a long history. In the course of time and neglect, the timbered building partially collapsed in disrepair or was demolished. What stands now as Wolfhall Farm is a composite building with only a part of it medieval. I came across it unawares, not seeking it, which is often the best way to approach a place. I had heard stories of its being strongly haunted, but on making direct enquiries at the house itself, I found such a conflict of opinion on the part of its occupants regarding the truth of the stories that further enquiries seemed impossible. Nothing would have been resolved by pursuing investigations, and I withdrew. However, here for what they are worth are one or two of the reports circulating *outside* Wolfhall regarding its *inside*.

It is said that an eighteen-year-old boy, a member of a family formerly renting part of the house, was on one occasion sleeping in the older part of the building. It seems he awoke in the early hours of the morning to find the clock in the room stopped and his bed purposefully moving—or being moved—across the room. Not exactly a remedy for insomnia, one supposes.

Another youth formerly residing in the house is said to have seen an elderly bearded man somewhere within the building, though neither the location of the room nor an exact description of the apparition is available.

It is also reported that a dog belonging to the present owners has reacted strongly—raised hackles and signs of fear, etc.—in a particular bedroom of the older part of the premises.

Although these fragments are quite useless as evidence of hauntings, I suspect that Wolfhall may hold very precise echoes of its past, and that there may be more than one reminder of the lives lived under its roof. However, an owner's wishes in the matter are entitled to respect. Wolfhall must remain for me an enigma.

I drove on into the forest of Savernake, the origin of whose name is elusive. John Aubrey, the seventeenth-century diarist, ascribes it to the Old English 'sav' (sweet), 'vern' (fern) and 'ake' (oak), which, though an attractive interpretation, is no longer thought to be correct. Its likeness to the Kentish Sevenoaks is marked, and perhaps the latter name has similar origins.

Savernake is part of the primeval forest of Britain and lies to the east of the great dyke known as Wansdyke which runs from Bath to the forest's edge. Wansdyke—Woden's Dyke—is thought to have formed a tribal boundary in ancient times, and it may well have been a defensive structure against invaders, though who were the attackers and who those being attacked is not certain. It may be significant that

Wansdyke links up with the ancient Ridgeway, and that both are in close proximity to that pagan centre of worship, the Avebury complex. The huge dyke may have existed as a protection for the temple as Ridgeway may have been a high road to it. P. C. Walwin in *Savernake Forest* states that Wansdyke was a Roman or Romano-British construction, but does not give her sources for this belief. If the Romans found it necessary to build a defensive earthwork of this nature, it is probable they would utilize any similar structure already existing. The name Woden's Dyke may have become attached later, for Woden was not only the chief of the Norse gods, but also the god of boundaries. The mere fact that it bears the name of a deity suggests that its origins were likely to have been religious.

Roman roads certainly ran through the forest, which in the days when the legions marched through it, would have been a good deal more formidable than it now is. In fact Savernake Forest is beautiful, with open wood and park land, a fine beech and oak growth, and all the chequered shade of a great deciduous woodland. Only the latter can produce in summer the authentic merry light of the old forest, with its moving dapples of sun and shadow like ripples on water. The coniferous woods of modern afforestations are death to light as well as merriment. From these Savernake is relatively free. So, then, the 'open and friendly' forest which I had been promised. But what of its ghosts?

A young lad in Marlborough, Tim Short, told me a strange tale of a headless girl. It seems that while riding through the forest brakes (at a date unspecified), the girl failed to see a low tree in time to avoid it. She rode headlong into the obstacle and the branch broke her neck. Since then, according to local legend, her ghost appears in the forest, headless. Tim had not seen it, nor did I find anyone who had. He had, however, another and more likely tale to tell.

It is not surprising that Savernake is often used as a lovers' rendezvous. On one particular night a local courting couple parked their car in a secluded glade, prepared to stay there for some time. After a short while, the girl of the pair saw a figure approach the car, walk close by it and then past. The figure does not appear to have paid any attention to the car or to its occupants. Startled and apprehensive, the girl drew her companion's notice to the intruder, certain he must have seen the figure which had practically brushed their car as it moved by. The man saw nothing, however, and had seen nothing. Indeed, he refused point blank to believe that any person at all had been anywhere near the car. Nevertheless, the young people did not stay in the glade after the incident. As far as I could discover, no explanation has been given of the identity of the forest walker, though both the car's occupants appeared to think the figure supernatural in origin.

Savernake also holds stories of black dogs and an albino deer. So far as the dogs are concerned, there are few really rural places in Britain which do not retain black dog stories. Variously known as Shuck, the barguest, the trash, the padfoot or galley trot, this huge animal with ember-red staring eyes appears all over these islands, generally as a bringer of bad luck or a harbinger of death. The creature is less a ghost than a folk-memory—possibly of the wolves which once were at home in our native woods, possibly of the wolf-cult of the Celts. The latter peoples included animal worship in their polytheistic religion, and the priests of these cults may have worn an animal headdress appropriate to the god they served. It may have been, also, that sacred animals—possibly the best and largest specimens of their kind—were kept near the holy places of the cult. The Celts were known to make human sacrifices to their gods. It can be conjectured that the idea of ill-luck associated with such animal images is founded on an unconscious memory or a racial memory of the human role in wolf-worship. To see the cult animal at such close quarters would indeed be a sign of early death.

As for the spectral white deer, since Savernake from medieval times has had a sizeable deer population, it would be surprising if an occasional albino had not turned up in the herds. Deer are unobtrusive and silent enough to create an impression of insubstantiality. A white animal slipping through the rides at dusk or after would certainly be noticed, and very likely turned into a ghost by local imaginations.

Savernake has always been a hunting forest, and for much of its existence a royal preserve with strict laws and punishments controlling its use. The reigning monarchs regarded the hunt as their prerogative, and although Savernake was in the charge of a warden, it was actually the property of the Crown until 1547, when absolute ownership was granted by Henry VIII to the then Warden, Edward Seymour, Duke of Somerset, brother of Henry's Queen Jane. This was the Somerset who was to die on the block in 1552 'for plotting to usurp the royal authority'.

As far as is known, no Seymours linger to haunt their ancient territories. Savernake is the home of deer, and a few local legends. The Seymours are commemorated elsewhere.

North-east of the forest lies a house reputedly much haunted. Littlecote Manor's ghosts are too well known to need further elaboration. They are those (1) of the woman whose new-born baby was murdered by being thrown into a fire (mother and child are said to haunt the room where the crime was alleged to have been committed); (2) of 'Wild Will' Darrell, reputedly the father and murderer of the child. Killed while out hunting, he is said to haunt the area of Darrell's Style, accompanied by spectral hounds; (3) of Gerard Lee Bevin, a sometime tenant of the house, who frequents its long Gallery; and (4) of a mysterious lady with a rushlight.

However, an additional and better authenticated phantom than these is that which appears in the garden, judged by the psychic, Tom Corbett, to be the ghost of Mrs Leybourne Popham. Whether or not it is she, I do not know. A correspondent, Mrs Rosemary Stevens of Portsmouth, when telling me of a personal experience in Hampshire, mentioned that a former colleague of hers once worked at Littlecote and flatly discounted the numerous Darrell stories. However, this lady had several times "seen the happy figure of a woman in flowing robes walking between the lavender hedges in the garden".

It would seem from this that at least one of Littlecote's ghosts is still alive and doing well.

I would say at this point that it is little use for the ghost-hunter to rush off to the nearest haunted spot in the expectation of seeing or hearing its ghost. The mere fact of concentrating upon the subject is likely to militate against the chances of an encounter. It is common experience that whatever manifestations are experienced usually occur when the percipient is thinking about something different—when his mind is detached, relaxed, with its gears in neutral. There is thought to be a scientific reason for this aspect of psychic response, to which I hope to return later. It is a common occurrence for psychic researchers to take along endless gear—tape recorders, thermometers, high-speed cameras *et al.*, plus an intense mental alertness for any sight, sound or change in temperature in the haunted area—and yet to have no results to show for their activities at the end of a long night's vigil. This may, of course, be because a haunting is just not operating at the time they choose for their research. It may also be that something in the state of their own mental processes at the time will preclude them from any direct experience, cutting them off from the manifestation as surely as if they had been wearing earplugs or blindfolds.

It can be objected that if the human 'receivers' are unable to operate, there is no valid reason why the mechanical versions should be similarly handicapped. From time to time the latter have certainly registered when the former have not, but there have been many occasions when in a strongly haunted area the machines also have obtained a nil registration. I would suggest that a similar process is operating in such cases as that which inhibits human receptivity. In an attempt to 'play back' results, the wrong frequency is applied. I hope to go into this complicated question in greater detail in Chapter 6.

It is likely then that such echoes as remain from the past (and they are very many) and whatever hints reach us for the future (and they are not uncommon) come when the brain is in idling gear, when the attention is 'open', not focused.

Occasionally as I journeyed through Wiltshire, and through the other southern counties with which this book is concerned, the above issue was raised. Why is it not possible to see ghosts to order? Why do some persons have many such experiences and others none? The answer, I believe, lies in the physical (and I do mean physical) method of the operation of the phenomena, and of the particular type of brain pattern possessed by the investigator.

But to return to our theme. There are some strange tales current in the Warminster area. A cowled figure has been seen on several occasions at No 14 St John's Road in this town. Sometimes it appears in the hall, sometimes on the stairs, but apparently stands quietly with its face concealed before fading away. A monastery once existed in the neighbourhood, and the hooded apparition appears to be left over from pre-Reformation days.

Not all hauntings arise from the distant past. One which appears to be of comparatively recent origin was reported to me by Mrs June Peall, who had told me of the ghosts at The French Horn, Pewsey.

June Peall, born June Rogers, attended Marlborough Grammar School. In approximately 1962, when she was fifteen, she attended an educational course at Urchfont Manor, near Devizes. The old house had been purchased by the Wiltshire County Council to be run as a Further Education Centre and from time to time local schools used it for supplementary work in 'O' and 'A' level courses. The course June Rogers attended was to last five or six days, and during its length she shared a room with one other girl.

On one particular night, June awoke to see a pinkish sphere of light resting against a partition wall inside the room. Since the wall was an internal and artificial division of the room, it was not near a window, and the curious light was therefore not a projection from outside the building nor yet any possible reflection of moonlight. Although the second girl slept through the experience, June Rogers was wide awake. (Even now, fifteen years after the experience, she is adamant about that.)

She lay and watched the sphere in some astonishment. It was visible for about two minutes altogether, and during that time it moved into the room for about two feet then moved back to the wall, into which it gradually began to fade.

The following morning a number of the girls on the course reported having heard tapping sounds during the night, for which neither they nor the house's staff could account. The only enlightenment they had came from the then warden of the manor, who stated that several years before, about the same time of year (May/June), a woman had been found dead in tragic circumstances in the Manor House. Subsequently strange occurrences seemed to take place around the anniversary of this death, though the warden was careful not to mention the fact in advance to students for fear of alarming them.

This was June Peall's account and was all she knew of the story. It was not until I visited Urchfont village and manor that I heard further details which appeared to enlarge on her experience.

It appears that in the summer of 1940, as Italy was about to enter the war, the then owner of the manor and his wife were found dead in the building. The deaths appeared to be the result of a suicide pact, though the sequence had been that the man had shot his wife before killing himself. Local feeling at the time had been that the wife may have been an unwilling partner in the pact. Although it was suggested at the time that the husband's fatal depression may have been caused by financial losses due to failed investments, there is no proof that this was the case.

Later enquiry at the manor produced little further information. The present warden and his deputy have apparently experienced nothing untoward during their residence, and greeted the ghost story with some surprise. The house seems tranquil enough now, so perhaps the lady—if indeed it were she who had become a reluctant ghost—has now left her old home. The manor's cat, a fine and talkative Abyssinian, seemed unperturbed by any extrasensory activities, and animals are often highly responsive to such stimuli.

An interesting feature of Mrs Peall's account is the form taken by the apparition. Balls or spheres of light are not uncommon features of hauntings, as we have seen. This appears to be yet another example of a manifestation which does not proceed beyond the 'glowing energy' stage.

My village informant told me another story of Urchfont. It appeared that some young relatives of hers visited the village in 1950 and knew nothing whatever of the neighbourhood before this date.

The children were walking up a track known as Friar's Lane when they saw a figure ahead of them dressed in what seemed to be a monk's habit. It crossed the lane and went over land belonging to the Manor Farm as it made for the church. The children watched it for a while, until they realized that what they saw did not appear to be walking so much as gliding. At that point, they took fright and ran back home. They were not aware of a local story, long current, that the route taken by the figure was reputedly that of an underground passageway connecting the church with a friary formerly established in the village.

Underground passages are a familiar part of British folk-lore. If even half of those reported actually existed, the island must once have resembled a huge rabbit-warren. However, monasteries and their off-shoots were extensive in both their buildings and the area covered, and it is feasible that a number of cellars, cellar-passages and crypt-like buildings once existed connecting one part of a monastery with another; useful devices all, not only as storage spaces, but as means for conveying men and goods under cover from place to place in bad weather. So the friar's route may have been a familiar passageway in the days when he used it in life.

Other accounts in Wiltshire relate to events which would certainly have sent the good friar in search of bell, book and candle. According to Margaret Royal and Ian Girven in their book, *Local Ghosts*, a group of people had an unusual encounter near Shearwater. While walking in woodland in this area, they came upon two large pools or ponds. The walkers had a strong sensation of being watched from the far side of one of the pools, and as always when in the presence of an unseen, unguessed-at observer, they felt acutely uncomfortable. They walked round to the opposite side of the little lake, but found to their discomfiture that the watcher had changed sides, also. At that point one of the group took a photograph looking across the pool. When it was processed, the picture showed the outline of a figure rising from the water. It appeared to be covered in weeds and wearing a pointed hat.

This is a particularly intriguing manifestation, as it is almost certainly no ghost. But if not a ghost, then what? One has to turn once more to the myths and beliefs of prehistory. In almost all the ancient religions stories of water spirits are found—water-gods, which eventually dwindled into water sprites. In Britain, these nature spirits became nymphs of well or spring, like the Lancashire water-sprite Jenny Greenteeth, who lured unwary travellers into ponds and drowned them. Or became water guardians like Aegir, god of the River Trent, who annually rolled a great wave up the length of his river to drown the unwary. To this day, the Trent bore is referred to as the 'eagre' or 'eager', though few know the origin of the name.

Among the German Celts the water-nymphs were called undines, and were thought to be clothed in weeds. In Scotland the *babd*, a supernatural washerwoman, might be seen by lonely rivers washing bloodstained garments to give warning of death to the observer. Almost any ancient water throughout Europe will have its legend of an attendant deity or 'saint' (Christianity was wise enough to incorporate the old religion into the new, and canonize the pagan spirits when it could not get rid of them), and the old gods are commemorated in many of our British river names—Lud, Don, Dee, Clyde.

The Shearwater apparition, therefore, rising from her mere like the Lady of the Lake, may have been either an archaic memory of the ancient racial belief in water-spirits conjured up by one member of the party and telepathically transmitted to the rest, or may have been an actual manifestation of some entity once connected with the pool.

But the feeling of being watched? And the image on the photograph? The former, the feeling of 'awareness', is akin to the feeling of 'presence' and could well be due to some form of electromagnetism concentrated near the lake. The photographic image is part of a large group of similar occurrences for which there is as yet no known explanation. Perhaps if Sir Bedivere could have photographed the last moments of Excalibur he would have seen not "an arm, clothed in white samite, mystic, wonderful", arising from the bosom of the lake, but a figure in squelching green and dripping weeds, tastefully capped by a conical hat. (Merlin, where are you now?)

Before leaving the Marlborough area I had determined to visit Avebury, the immense stone circle which now incorporates into itself the village of its name. To reach it I passed Preshute, where a local boy, Stephen Raisey, about eighteen months ago saw a large white figure while cycling through the churchyard, and thought the thing to be supernatural. Through Preshute then on to the Chippenham road, and alongside the River Kennet until the right turning which leads to Avebury.

Before you know it, you are into the West Kennet Avenue, that long and impressive double line of stones which marches beside the modern road, swings up the hill and into the great circle itself.

When I came to it the day was chill and windy, and the huge sarsens stood about in the weather, open-faced to each other across the avenue, with the small flurries of rain dodging round them. I left the car and walked for some distance along the avenue. Between four and five thousand years ago men had dragged and hauled the stones here, heavily over the uneasy ground, dug pits for them and tilted them in, levering the huge masses until they stood upright. They stand so now, regular and mysterious, their ancient, enormous significance largely unknown.

There is no doubt in the minds of archaeologists that the Avebury complex (consisting of the Circle and avenues, the West Kennet Long Barrow and the Sanctuary) once constituted a great cult centre, though of what specific kind the cult was and what were its rituals none has knowledge. Many think the shapes of the chosen sarsens

Part of the great henge at Avebury, Wiltshire. In the eighteenth and nineteenth centuries it was used as a site for country fairs and a hallucination of one such has been seen in the ring itself, the booths, lights and music of the fair all being distinctly experienced.

represent a fertility cult; the stones roughly alternate an up-ended diamond shape with a tall pillar, signifying the female and male principles. This would be perfectly consistent with the religion of the time, which is known to have been centred on worship of the Mother- or Earth-goddess. Indeed, nearby Silbury Hill, which appears to have some relationship to the Avebury complex, may have been a deliberate representation of the goddess.

If you walk up either of the two Avenues to its end, you come to one of the four entrances into the Circle. Here half the stones of the outer circle remain, while the two inner circles are only partially complete. It is noticeable also that the stones of the Avenues do not approach their destination in a straight line, but wander somewhat. It has been suggested that these curves indicated a possible serpent cult, and since the snake is itself an ancient symbol of fertility the idea must not be discarded. As for the inner rings, try as one may, one cannot imagine what rites were conducted inside them. Each of the small circles may have had its own function. Sacrifices in one, purification in the other, perhaps?

My own belief is that the Avebury centre was a temple of healing. (It may have had other purposes, too; astronomical, for example.) Both in the stone avenue and in the southernmost small circle, I experimented by leaning with my back in contact with different stones— that is against two stones in the Avenue, and two in the small southern circle. In spite of the coldness of the day, the Avenue stones seemed to exude the sensation of warmth and well-being. After a few minutes I experienced a feeling of mental serenity and considerable physical comfort. Not so with those in the Circle. Here the sensation was far less pleasant, being one of tension and mild unease. I do not attempt to explain these reactions, but merely report them. Stone is noted for its power to retain impressions over very long periods of time. In my experience it is also likely to retain energy, probably absorbed from earlier human activity in the neighbourhood, and to give it out again at intervals.

Though the above are suppositions only and not subject to proof, one looks for factors which may have a bearing on theories. As far as the serpentine approach of the Beckhampton and Kennet Avenues is concerned, it may be significant that a snake was not only an ancient symbol of fertility, but was also the personal symbol of Asclepius, the Greek god of healing*. So perhaps Avebury was a gigantic healing

---

* Similarities between cults among the ancient peoples suggest a distant common origin.

centre as well as a temple and/or calendar.

You would expect a construction so mysterious and long-standing to hold many past imprints in the form of hauntings, but although I heard one or two tales of odd occurrences in cottages which had some of the circle's stones in their building, the only actual ghost story concerning the Avebury Ring related to the experience of a Miss Edith Olivier, a Wiltshire author, who was driving through Avebury sometime during World War I. Dusk was falling, and as she came within sight of the Circle she saw what she took to be a fair erected around and between the stones. She plainly saw the lights of it, and could hear music drifting across from the booths and shows. As she drew level with the Ring, she was astonished to see that it was empty apart from the standing sarsens. There was no sign of a fair, no sound of music, nothing save the great waiting monoliths and the constant wind-plaint between them. She was told later that although it had once been the custom to hold fairs within the Circle, the last had taken place some fifty years before.

There is no doubt that this is a time-dislocation rather than a true haunting, but manifestations of this nature are similar in kind and perhaps in their method of operation. Miss Olivier had momentarily found herself in the nineteenth century instead of the early twentieth.

Another observer, a Miss J. M. Dunn, on a clear moonlit night saw a number of small human figures moving among the stones when no local people were stirring. Small figures. Our Stone Age ancestors perhaps? The little people, whom legend and a succession of larger conquerors turned into the fairies of folk-lore. This is, in any case, how folk-lore begins; a series of half-understood events, incompletely remembered and eventually mistakenly interpreted.

In the wide embrace of the old temple lies the village of Avebury itself, compact, pleasant rather than pretty, but with one or two delightful houses and cottages, plus a dignified church which has Saxon and Norman features. To the left of the church lies the elegant outline of an Elizabethan house, Avebury Manor; slim-gabled, long-windowed, many-chimneyed, it sits squarely athwart its shaved lawns as though it meant to stay there for eternity.

Before the house grew on the site a Benedictine monastery occupied it, a daughter foundation of the community at St George de Bockerville in Normandy. However, the house's echoes relate not to the Benedictines but to the Cavaliers. Avebury Manor was a Royalist stronghold during the Civil Wars, and its then owner, Sir John Stawell, was heavily penalized for his part in supporting Charles I.

The room said to be haunted is known as the Crimson Room, beautiful in the seventeenth-century manner, with a strong feeling of period attached to it. Maybe that feeling is something more, for local legend declares that the ghost is of a girl who loved a young Cavalier. She lost her lover, though whether in battle or by some other means is not known, and subsequently committed suicide by leaping from one of the house windows. The first floor of the manor is not high above ground, but given bad luck and a determined try it would be possible to kill oneself no doubt. Broken heads and broken necks were usually fatal in the seventeenth century.

How much truth is there in the ghost story? A local man, Mr Hugh Rendle, was for a time caretaker, with his wife, of the manor and has had some odd experiences there. It was Mrs Rendle's custom to arrange flowers in the various rooms, and this task was usually performed on a Friday. Time after time she would leave a bowl of roses in the Crimson Room, but when her husband did his rounds of the house the next morning, he would find the flowers in this room pulled out of their bowl and scattered over the floor. Though roses were arranged elsewhere in the house, this was the only place where they were found disturbed.

In reply to my enquiry about the possibility of dogs, cats, burglars, vandals, etc., Mr Rendle said that the room was kept closed and empty and the house securely locked. Nothing else in the building appeared to have been moved at any time. Dogs apparently have shown reluctance to pass the door of this particular room, and a guide employed at the house a few years ago was convinced that the area was haunted.

Mr Rendle had had other strange experiences in Avebury Manor. One of his duties was to feed the house cats each day, and to stoke and clean the Aga cooker in the kitchen. His usual routine was to enter the house through the front door, cross the hall and go into the kitchen, and to do so he had to pass through double doors over a tight-fitting pile carpet. On many occasions when he did so the door would bang behind him, though normally, so tight a fit was it over the carpet that it needed to be moved by hand. On other occasions at night he would go round with a torch on a final security patrol to make certain that all was as it should be; and then have the eerie sensation that he was being followed from room to room. "Someone," he said, "seemed to be walking behind me." A disconcerting feeling when you have only a torch to lighten your darkness.

It is easy to become over-imaginative in old houses, particularly where the latter have a spooky reputation. However, doors which fit tightly over deep-pile carpets do not bang of their own accord; nor do flowers levitate from a vase and scatter themselves about a room.

Hugh Rendle appears to belong to that large group of people whose particular mental processes predispose them to experience the so-called psychic. They will see and hear what is there to be seen and heard when others are blind and deaf to it. The occurrence which made the strongest impression on the mind of this normally down-to-earth man took place some little distance from Avebury itself.

Hugh Rendle was on friendly terms with one of the gardeners at Avebury Manor in the days before he himself worked there, and it was their custom to have an occasional game of darts in a nearby public house. Afterwards the two men would walk part of the way home together. On a certain occasion—Mr Rendle thought it to be in November, 1954—they had reached their usual parting point where Mr Rendle would leave his friend and take a short cut across a field hard by Trusloe Manor. He duly did so, turning left and keeping the manor house on his right. Then he saw about forty yards away on the right-hand side, the figure of a woman; or rather the head and shoulders only. As he drew level with the gate to the manor the woman seemed to come up behind him, put her hands on his shoulders and turn him to face the house as though to make him go towards it. He stood still, then rapidly hurried away, but not before he had looked well at the apparition. "She was wearing long gauntlet gloves and a kind of white lacy shawl. She had a beautiful face."

This was Mr Rendle's description to me of his experience. Kathleen Wiltshire's *Ghosts and Legends of the Wiltshire Countryside* gives a different version in that she states this same percipient to have thought the woman was a nun with a white hood, who attempted to turn him *away* from the gate. Both versions of the story emphasize the beauty of the woman's face. The description given to Mrs Wiltshire suggests that the figure was that of a nun, while the one told to me recalls a seventeenth-century lady of the Royalist party; lace fichu (the percipient called it a shawl) and gauntlet gloves may possibly point to riding costume. Whether the lovely ghost wished the visitor to call at her house or be gone from it we shall never know. Unless she appears again, that is. This particular apparition was seen by at least one other local person, a Mrs Matthews, now dead.

At the top of Avebury village, lying comfortably between the two circles, is the village inn, the Red Lion. There is a tradition that a coach and horses pulls into the pub yard here and can be heard clattering over the cobblestones. It has never been seen, though heard on several occasions.

However, a more interesting story says that about two years ago a customer came into the front dining-room of the inn, had his lunch, and when in the final stages of it was approached by a girl whom he took to be an employee who asked if there were anything further he required. He replied in the negative and the girl departed. A few minutes afterwards he was approached by a second girl and asked precisely the same question. Somewhat surprised he replied that although he required nothing further, he had already been asked by and replied to the first waitress. Which surprised the second questioner, since she was the only waitress on duty, and had seen nothing of any other that lunch time. The first girl had apparently been perceived by the customer alone, was unknown to the rest of the staff, and seems not to have been of the flesh-and-blood world. It is said locally that footsteps are heard in this old building from time to time, and that a girl's face has been observed looking from an upstairs window. Nothing is known of the identity of this apparition, the period to which it belongs or the reason for its presence.

The day of my visit was Sunday 21st March, and the previous night the nation's clocks had been put forward an hour so that the British could get themselves ahead of the sun's time. I have never quite understood the logic of this, but it seems to have something to do with being early to rise and late to bed; or ensuring that the cows shall be milked by sun-up and motorists given an extra hour of jaunting time in the evening. Or something. Whatever it is, there is always a feeling of warm and guilty pleasure about stealing that extra hour from the cosmos. As though we personally were running things to suit ourselves, for a change.

So on Saturday night, 20th March, around midnight, all the clocks at the Red Lion, Avebury, were conscientiously put forward an hour to register the advent of British Summer Time. And at 8.00 a.m. on Sunday 21st March, when the landlord inspected his premises, every clock in the house was found to have been put back again exactly an hour—to the sun's time registered the day before. The two possible explanations for this phenomenon are that either the landlord had forgotten to alter his clocks (which he stoutly denied), or the resident ghost disapproved of new-fangled self-indulgences.

During my visit there was no sign of either the ghostly girl or the phantom four-in-hand; and the clock episode had taken place before I arrived. I did have a good lunch, however, and was reluctant to go out again into the blustery wind which pushed and whistled through the spaces between the standing stones. Perhaps I was loath to leave the Circle itself. Something there is remaining in its vicinity which holds one to the spot, as though by staying in the neighbourhood one could gain some kind of benison. Judging by the crowds of people surging through Avebury at this cold threshold of the spring, the attraction of the place is felt widely. The little museum was filled with people who seemed genuinely as interested in the shards and tools of the Neolithic peoples who once walked here as in evading the pointed teeth of the rain which awaited them outside.

If you return from Avebury down the West Kennet Avenue of sarsens, turning right on to the main road, you will shortly come within sight of one of the most extraordinary hills in England. Silbury Hill is not remarkable for its height, but for the fact that it is entirely man-made. It is now generally believed that the hill is prehistoric in origin and that it may have been of religious significance to its builders.

Various legends have attached to it, the most popular being that it is the burial mound of an ancient king, Sil or Zel, whose body lies deep within the structure. His equally ancient and enormous treasure (gold is spoken of) is said to be buried with him. Unfortunately for romantic imaginations, Silbury has been investigated by eminent archaeologists on several occasions with a nil result as far as treasure is concerned. They had no luck with burials, either. Far from being a Bronze Age barrow, mausoleum for a great king, the hill appears to be just an enormous mound of earth, carefully constructed to be exactly round and to be almost entirely surrounded by water.

It is certainly impressive to look at. I stopped the car a few hundred yards away, fascinated by the regular shape and the sheer towering bulk. It blots out the immediate sky, giving the watcher the sensation of being dwarfed, reduced to paltriness. Which may, of course, have been part of its builders' intention.

But if Silbury is not a round barrow and not a covering for buried treasure, what is it? The best interpretation I have seen is that of Michael Dames who in his book, *The Silbury Treasure*, concludes that the hill is a gigantic monument to the Mother Goddess, the Earth Mother, the source of all fertility. She is that same goddess who appears to have been revered worldwide, for her likeness appears in many prehistoric cultures. Before the sun was worshipped in the form of a male god of light, the Earth was adored as a symbol of fertility. The idea of fertility was epitomized not by coition but by the act of giving birth; hence the female nature of the deity.

Again and again in material representations of the old religion, in many different countries throughout the world certain images recur; concentric circles which can be seen either as eyes or as female breasts; forms of a female body heavy in pregnancy; serpents—still thought by some to represent a snake-cult, but which seem more likely to be a simple phallic symbol, the penis.

A worldwide religion of this nature should surprise no one who gives the matter thought. For what, in a basic and embryo society, would be the most obvious and striking fact of existence as its people knew it? Not the fact that the sun shone, the rain fell, or that death occurred, but the very fact of life itself: that life in all its forms, vegetable, animal and human, was continually being renewed. Birth is even now the strangest mystery of all, far exceeding death in impressiveness. To a primitive race without any understanding of the mechanics of it, the advent of a perfectly formed new creature issuing from the interior of a female adult creature of the same species—be it animal or human— must have been the original divine miracle. It is not difficult to see how the adoration of the female principle began. (Not hard, either, to see how, with growth of knowledge and sophistication, it would be replaced by worship of the male, the Sun, the life-giver.)

According to Dames, Silbury is a monumental earth-sculpture of the mother goddess, and is linked in significance to the Avebury henge and its subsidiary monuments. The idea is plausible and persuasive, for although Silbury's name suggests the burial of an individual Sil, Sel or Zel, the only human bones known to have been excavated from the mound were exhumed in March 1723. "The workmen dug up the body of a great king there buried in the centre, very little below the surface, the bones were extremely rotten so that they crumbled to pieces with the fingers." An ancient British Goddess, Sul, was identified by the Romans with their goddess Minerva; and the word 'selaru' in the Basque language (the most archaic European language) means a granary. Sul, Sel, Sil, therefore, may have been a harvest goddess, representing the fertile earth. As for Silbury's excavated corpse, archaeologists appear to think it of little significance due to its shallow inhumation. There is nothing to say at this date whether the skeleton was even male; the burial could as well have been that of a woman, a great queen.

The Wansdyke also has reports of a funeral cortège, seen on numerous occasions, the coffin topped by a crown or circlet of gold and borne by pall-bearers. Kathleen Wiltshire guesses at Guinevere, escorted on her last journey by Lancelot and his men. A romantic thought. The great queen. I wonder. Aiming for Silbury Hill, perhaps? Yet Guinevere by tradition was buried at Glastonbury which is no great distance from the Wansdyke at this point. Yet let us move away from the spreading net of Avebury and its satellites and look elsewhere.

Legend talks of a ghostly King Sil, however, dressed in golden armour, who rides around the hill on horseback on moon-washed nights. I know of none who has seen this phantom, but local folk say that horses are reluctant to pass the spot. When I left it, the 170-foot mound (undeniably breast-shaped) was presided over by a solitary kestrel, hovering well clear of the summit, his sharp gaze sifting the grasses for a possible scurrier to serve as his dinner. Silbury and Avebury and the region which both occupy represent an old, old mystery which our minds have forgotten, though perhaps our cells have not.

From Avebury I drove to Amesbury. The rain was falling in a cold curtain, the town library was shut and so was the Information Centre; no one knew anything of ghosts in the area. "What about the Abbey?" "Oh, yes, wasn't there a figure seen there once?" But no one knew what kind of figure or if it had ever been seen at all.

Luckily matters are more firmly fixed in the country areas. Roman soldiers are said to march along the old road behind Oldbury Camp, and a shepherd described having seen men with beards, wearing skirts and large helmets with hair on the top—"and a girt bird on a pole, a'front on 'em". Not the usual description of the Roman eagle, but graphic nevertheless.

Wiltshire is a county whose history is very near the surface, and the traveller is continually stumbling on echoes of an older England. There are reminders in names, buildings, and the very landscape itself. The Wansdyke in its journey takes in the ridge of hills overlooking the Vale of Pewsey, and if you travel the road from Devizes to Pewsey village you will pass through Alton Priors. It is charming, sylvan scenery, hill-and-valley country, good sheep land, with little knots of trees gathered conversationally at the feet of the hills.

One of these hills bears the massive carving of a white horse, near to a barrow known locally as Adam's Grave. These great chalk carvings occur in many parts of Britain, and like that of much other property of prehistory, their exact significance has become lost. They may have been the results of acts of worship, they may have been invocations to a god or gods; they almost certainly were religious in origin. The Celts were horse worshippers, but there is no certainty

The White Horse at Alton Priors, Wiltshire, where the sound of ghostly thundering hoof-beats has been heard along the ridge which lies above it.

that they were the carvers into the chalk. So many deities in the old religions appear to have near duplicates in others of the same period or earlier, that a common origin is likely. In the case of the hill-carved horses it may be that the Celts' predecessors were also horse-worshippers. But this is idle speculation, since the exact age of the carvings is unknown.

A woman named Muriel Cobern had a strange experience while walking near the white horse above Alton Priors. She had been visiting the barrow beyond the horse and was returning to her car, when she began to feel ill at ease. There seemed no cause for the discomfort; sheep were grazing placidly around her, and the only sound was the plangent crying of the wind which stalks all high places. Yet still the tension mounted. And then she heard it: the sound of horses' hoof-beats in the distance. The sound grew nearer and louder, until it was unmistakable—the noise of horses' hooves thudding heavily on turf, as though a great many animals were coming full gallop along the ridge towards her. The woman quickened her pace until she was almost running, and still the thundering grew behind her. Then she was clear of Adam's Grave and as abruptly as it had begun, the sound ceased. All was once more calm, still, the upland quiet with the wind singing.

What had she heard? An old ceremony to the horse-god (or goddess—Epona was the Celtic horse-goddess)? It seems likely. Some coincidence of temperature, light, atmospheric conditions, may have reproduced the original circumstances of an ancient custom, resulting in a re-play for the benefit of Muriel Cobern. An inadvertent happening, sparked by no individual, conjured by no particular ghost. The drumming hoof-beats would no doubt have echoed along the hill top even had there been no Miss Cobern to hear them. They may indeed have sounded many hundreds of times over the centuries and been either heard and noticed or not heard at all, depending on the presence of a living human with the right type of mental equipment for receiving the information. There is no reason to think that so-called supernatural events always operate for the benefit of human witnesses. There is evidence pointing to many of them operating involuntarily, automatically, regardless of the presence or absence in the vicinity of the living. Not all, of course, but a considerable number.

Throughout my stay in Wiltshire the weather had been poor even for March, and frequently one saw the hills through a fine net of rain. I drove down to Salisbury alongside the infant River Avon, hardly more than a stream, though approaching Nether Avon it was rain-swollen enough to resemble a tyro river. The usual thin, bitter rain was falling with an icy wind at its back helping it along. Small flights of duck took off over the brimming water meadows, arrowing upwards in a parabola which eventually dropped them into the sedges. Somewhere near the road's edge a song-thrush was valiantly singing out his boundaries in the spiteful weather. It was a taut, green-grey scene as the land waited for the spring.

In Salisbury I parked my car, crossed the market place and made for the cathedral. There is a story that the tomb of a certain Lord Stourton, convicted of murder in 1557 and hanged by a silken rope in Salisbury market-place, is haunted by the image of a noose. Apparently an actual wire noose was for years suspended above the grave, and only removed in the late eighteenth century. Since then its ghostly outline has occasionally been seen above the tomb.

But even stranger than the story of a spectral noose is the fact that the murderer's resting place is also said to be that of the cathedral's founder, St Osmund. It certainly seems likely that its rectangular stone superstructure could once have covered the saint, for there are apertures above the plinth large enough for pilgrims to insert ailing limbs in the hope of a healing miracle. It is known that St Osmund's shrine became a place of pilgrimage.

How could the tomb of a saint—and a healing saint at that—also be that of a murderer? It took some time to unravel the mystery, but I think the confusion may have arisen as follows.

St Osmund's original cathedral was built at Old Sarum, about two miles north of the present cathedral. When the building of the new cathedral began in 1220, the body of its founder was moved from the old to the new site, and reinterred. Later an elaborate stone shrine (presumably that still on view) was erected over the grave and furnished with a reliquary to hold the saint's skull.

In 1790, an architect, James Wyatt, was called in to restore a now dilapidated cathedral, and in his zeal for his task removed the shrine of St Osmund from the south-west side of the Trinity Chapel to the south side of the nave. A black slab of Purbeck stone, the Ledger Stone, now marks the site of the original grave and it may be supposed that the bones of Osmund still lie beneath it. If this is so, then the rectangular shrine with its healing-holes is just an empty superstructure. Or is it? Lord Stourton, murderer though he was, seems to have been buried somewhere in the cathedral itself, and perhaps when Wyatt tidied up the existing graves in the building (i.e., moved them into more convenient places), that of Stourton may have been among them.

By 1790, pilgrims had probably ceased to visit the Osmund shrine, and it would be natural for the reforming architect to house the murderer's remains in a conveniently empty tomb; no matter how eminent its previous owner.

This is guesswork, of course. However, it is fact that several tombs were moved by Wyatt and that Osmund's was among them. The above theory would at least explain why the present shrine of St Osmund is also regarded as the tomb of Lord Stourton, the murderer. Presumably the image of the noose no longer manifests itself, for I heard of no one who had seen it recently.

Parallel with the cathedral lies the King's House, an ancient foundation which is now in use as a training college, though not for much longer. It was, when I visited it, about to be closed for good; a sacrifice to the economic astringencies of the late nineteen seventies. I looked at the medieval hall, hardly recognizable now under its plaster, central heating and twentieth-century improvements. The beamed roof only remained as an echo.

It was in the King's House that Richard III waited to hear the news of Buckingham's execution. The Duke of Buckingham, on whom his king had conferred high honours and friendship, had, after a violent quarrel with Richard, set himself at the head of a rebellion, ostensibly with the intention of placing Henry Tudor on the throne in place of Richard. However, it is not unlikely that Buckingham saw himself as the ultimate ruler of England, since he, like Richard, and more distantly, Tudor, also was descended from Edward III.

Richard, whose fate seems always to have been to be betrayed, crushed the Buckingham rebellion and arrested the figurehead. The latter's silver tongue, which had talked him into Richard's trust and friendship, failed to talk him out of the consequences of his own treason. The King refused to see or speak to him again in spite of his desperate pleadings. Buckingham was duly beheaded in Salisbury market-place. It can have given little pleasure to his sovereign. Harry Buckingham had reminded him of his brother, George of Clarence, of whom he had been fond.

There were no echoes of Richard Plantagenet left in this area, however. In fact the only trace of a ghost is in the building known as the Wardrobe, once also part of the King's House and now in disrepair. The spectral shape of a 'grey lady' has been seen in its upper storey. When I asked him about it, the local car park attendant's eyebrows shot up. "First I've heard of it," he said. "I hope it's not true. I'm often by myself here at night. I don't fancy having a ghost watching me from across the street."

I left him to his worries while I went back again to the cathedral to catch a final echo of Richard of Gloucester. In one of the tombs lies Sir John Cheney, who was standard bearer to Henry Tudor at the battle of Bosworth. Said to be a giant of a man, he was attacked and cut down single-handed by the slight King Richard as he stood between him and the usurping Tudor.

A cathedral official to whom I spoke informed me that Cheney had died many years later in the sixteenth century, the date being so recorded on his tomb. History contradicts: Cheney fell at Bosworth under Richard's devastating onslaught.

"Perhaps it's not the same Cheney," suggested the cathedral man hopefully.

"John Cheney," I said. "He was a huge man, a giant."

My companion looked startled: "Cheney's tomb was opened some years ago," he said. "The size of the skeleton came as a shock. It measured about seven feet."

It was the same John Cheney. He must have died only minutes before Richard himself. The King fell beneath the swords of his erstwhile followers, the Stanleys, who crowned a lifetime of opportunism by changing sides on Bosworth Field in the hope of favours from a grateful Tudor. Richard's fate ran true to the end.

As I left Salisbury, the sun broke through into the grey afternoon and momentarily gilded the cathedral spire. I drove east, towards Winchester and the advancing spring and the tide of blossom.

Surrey and Middlesex

As little as 150 years ago Surrey must have been rural from one end to the other. Now the brimming cauldron of London has spilled over so far into the eastern area that the county proper does not begin until you reach Egham, Oxshott or Warlingham. What remains, however, is beautiful, seductive. The hills are small, close and wooded. The woods are near, crowding and treading on the heels of the roads. The hedges are tapestried with wild clematis and briony, musk rose and bramble. You drive through the green claustrophobia of the lanes searching for the villages, until abruptly the car's nose emerges on to a trunk road; then half the world's automobiles hurtle down on you, hell-bent for nowhere. Like a mole you dive for the green tangle on the farther side and submerge gratefully into the leafage—up and down more lanes, looking for villages.

In this fashion I eventually arrived at Farnham, which is reputed to house several ghosts, though I found little evidence of anything active. A white lady is said to appear occasionally at the top of the church tower and has been seen by some observers to jump off. However, there has been no word of her recently, so the ghost of this particular suicide (which I assume she was) may have ceased to function.

A similarly doubtful haunting concerns Waverley Abbey, where the ghost of a monk, hanged, drawn and quartered, possibly during the Reformation, has been seen walking through the grounds. Since the figure appears to be searching as he goes, local opinion has decided that he seeks for his missing entrails. Though this is a tempting explanation it seems hardly likely. Searching ghosts are more usually concerned with problems which had occupied the mind in life or troubled the conscience. Knowledge that one's innards would be removed before death might generate enough fear to ensure a haunting in the area, but not, I think, one involving a search for the missing physical parts. I suspect so-called searches for missing heads, hands, etc. by apparitions are the interpretations of living observers. The search is more likely to be related to an obsessive activity of the individual when alive—perpetuated after death, possibly by the recording method referred to earlier.

I had heard from a Hampshire correspondent that the Lion and Lamb tearooms in Farnham possessed a ghost; that of a woman who appeared within the building itself or outside in the small courtyard-cum-entrance. In fact there was a highly coloured version of the tale which said that the tearooms' waitresses would go up to her assuming her to be a customer, only to have the lady disappear in front of them.

The proprietor and staff of the tearooms treated this story with some disdain. They knew of rumours of a haunting in the past—the ghostly lady was thought to have been seen standing by the old pump in the courtyard—but no one had seen her recently, and the present incumbents doubt her existence. The Lion and Lamb is a fine old building, one of several which contribute to the grace of Farnham, a town round which the modern maelstrom swirls without

The ghostly form of a woman has sometimes been seen on the top of the church tower at Farnham, Surrey, and on at least one occasion appeared to leap or fall to the ground.

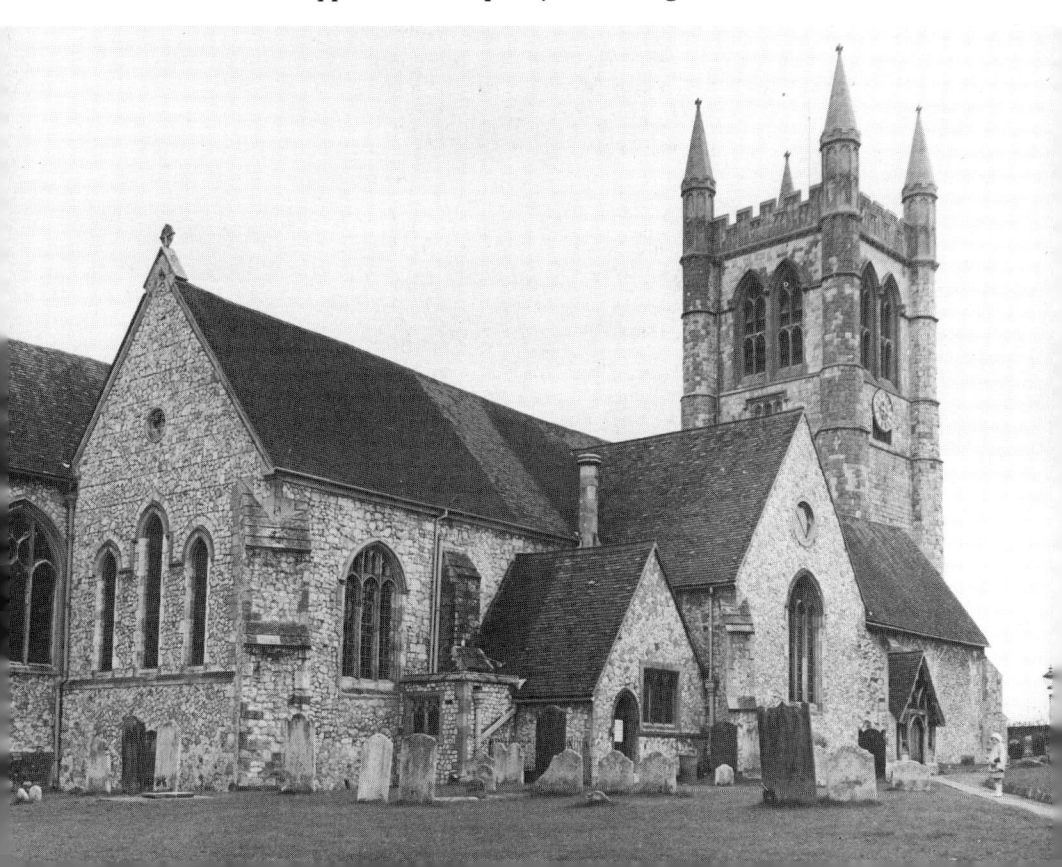

(as yet) spoiling its serene dignity.

The public library has a ghost, I was told by at least three Farnham residents. When I went to Vernon House, however, which houses the library, the identity of their apparition was doubtful. The ill-destined Charles I stayed in the building after his capture and *en route* for London. The shadowy figure seen on the stairs by a cleaner on one occasion was thought possibly to be that of the king. However, since no detailed description of the apparition exists, the assumption is too glib for conviction. This must be a case of 'not proven'.

Another library employee stated that in one room of the building she frequently smelled the perfume of violets and felt a strong sense of presence. However, this also is inconclusive and need not necessarily indicate an operative haunting. It is very tempting where a legend of haunting exists to construe any unusual experience as proof of the rumour. Many apparently supernatural occurrences have natural explanations, however, and investigators do well to consider these before moving in to the more remote field. It is my belief that ultimately *all* so-called supernatural phenomena will prove to have natural causes, but this is too large a subject for inclusion in the present book, and I have in any event discussed it in my book, *The Mask of Time*.

Moving east from Farnham in search of the next sizeable town, one reaches Guildford, but not alas "by green degrees" unless one takes the back roads. Once set wheel on the Hog's Back and you are embarked on a ride as wild as Herne the Hunter's, swept along the high ridge with a superb panorama of scenery on either hand which you are unable to observe in the crazy helter-skelter of the auto-rush. You know the hills are there and the tumbling woods, but there is no time to do more than wish you could take your eyes off the road long enough to look. If you succumb to the temptation it is likely to be your last look at anything. I was resigned to hurtling into Guildford like an eighty-pence rocket when a signpost to the right caught my eye. It said simply "Puttenham". I turned right and sank without trace into greenery and temporary peace and quiet.

Puttenham proved to be minute but charming. I enquired at the local inn for resident ghosts but the landlord denied having any. He suggested I try an ancient cottage a short way up the road, whose owner (known affectionately to the village as Nan) was interested in such matters. Nan, in fact, is interested in many things and takes a lively part in local affairs. She turned out to be Mrs Nan Lethbridge, otherwise Nan Marriott-Watson, the well-known actress and star of many radio, stage and television plays. She was, as the landlord had said, knowledgeable about hauntings, having had several experiences of a psychic nature in her own lifetime.

The Lethbridges formerly lived at Cobham in a house known as Quennells. "It was," Nan said, "a very strange house. You could not stay in the kitchen more than a short time; you had to get out. And people hated using the lavatory there." Not that there was anything wrong *per se* with either room, apparently; merely that a feeling of hostility and discomfort prevailed in both.

The Lethbridges had oil lamps throughout the house, but in one room it was impossible to keep a lamp alight. As fast as it was lit, it would go out. There seemed no logical explanation for this quirk.

"The house did not like us," Nan said simply, and when I pressed her to explain this statement, she qualified it by saying that nothing went right for her family while they were in it. It does not seem that there were either audible or visual manifestations to account for the discomfort, merely an overpowering feeling of presence—the sensation that they were not the sole occupants of Quennells.

That there are such houses is beyond doubt. Most sensitive persons have experienced sensations of mild unease in certain houses; and sometimes the unease is more than mild. People seeking to change houses have occasionally disallowed those uncomfortable sensations on the grounds that a prospective new house was 'pretty', 'suitable', 'convenient' and have moved in in disregard of the inner alarm bell which warned them off the building. Frequently they have later regretted over-riding their intuitive reactions.

In my view, all such reactions should be taken into account. The fact that they appear illogical and inexplicable should not rule them out from serious consideration in questions of judgement. The aesthetic sense which declares a house pretty or charming is just as illogical, but because it stands in good odour with society it will be heeded where the warning sense which announces a wrongness or discomfort in a house will be ignored. This latter sense is discounted because we do not yet understand how it operates, but I believe that it is the result of a physical response to environment just as is the aesthetic sense, the appreciation of beauty. The Lethbridges appear not to have discovered the alien nature of their house until they lived in it. They were sensible enough to leave it after a fairly short occupation.

The Fairweather family of 15 Finches Rise, Merrow, Guildford, were less fortunate. According to an account given by them to the

Surrey Advertiser, they have known their home to be haunted for about twenty years, but seem to have found the fact tolerable until 25th May 1977. On that night, the Fairweathers' daughter and her husband, Mr and Mrs Leslie Hoare, who share the house with the older couple, heard screams coming from the bedroom occupied by their two-year-old son, Jamie. On investigating, they found the child shrieking hysterically, "That's not my daddy. Take him away." The statement might have been less startling had not Mr Fairweather himself seen the apparition of a man "in ancient costume, with a long coat and black hat", though this sighting appears to have taken place on an earlier occasion.

The account seems to have some incoherencies, but perhaps this is not surprising considering the difficulties of describing what is essentially insubstantial. The Fairweathers thought the manifestations had increased with the arrival of their second grandson (five weeks old at the time of the final crisis), although Mrs Fairweather had on one occasion felt to be 'pinned in bed' by some force—which was accompanied by a sensation of intense coldness in the room. There has been an unsuccessful attempt at exorcism, and two priests and a psychic researcher have been consulted without any apparent improvement in the state of affairs at No 15 Finches Rise. The house, on the Bushy Hill estate, is said to occupy the site of a gallows where a highwayman was hanged two hundred years ago.

The story has certain disquieting features; including the fact that James Fairweather attempted to control the manifestation by "swishing towels about" in the bedrooms to get rid of the ghost. The family had also applied to their local council for re-housing several times during the last eight years, on the grounds of the uninhabitability of their current home.

Perhaps the only way to discover the truth of this case is by learning the spot's history prior to the development of the council estate. Was this particular place haunted before No 15 Finches Rise arose upon it? Is it still affected now that the Fairweathers and their family have left it? (They were apparently preparing to leave after the incident with the child.) Further information on these two aspects of the area may clarify the nature of the occurrences at this Guildford address.

There may be a connection between the last haunting and another in Charlock Way, not far from the Fairweathers' home. A woman reported having seen an apparition which appeared "in a golden haze" and Elizabethan trunk hose in the hallway of her house. Local records state that three men were hanged in August 1776, one of whom was the aforementioned highwayman, a certain James Potter. Potter had originally been a coachman at the White Hart Inn nearby, but his venture on to the highway concluded with his robbing a certain William Calvet of eleven guineas and his watch. An expensive excursion for Potter as it turned out. (In no circumstances, however, would an eighteenth-century man be likely to wear Elizabethan costume.)

With him on the gallows were Christopher Ellis, burglar, and Frederick William Gregg, convicted of robbery with violence. Guildford town's archives state: "They were conveyed in a cart to Ganghill Common from the jail at eleven o'clock, where they continued in prayer for half an hour. Gregg particularly begged all young men to avoid bad women that had brought him to his shameful death. They all behaved penitent and were turned off (pushed off the ladder)." More prayer followed, but without the participation of the leading characters.

Which of these three heroes is thought to have reappeared on the site of former activities is not known. Whichever one (or ones) it is, appears to have learned little during the last 200 years.

I was told of another haunting in this town when making enquiries at Chiddingfold. My informant, Mrs Ellen Agar, an employee at that beautiful old hostelry, the Crown Inn, had formerly worked in the offices of the Automobile Association in Guildford. During her time there she and two or three other personnel had encountered a few odd occurrences strongly suggestive of an active haunting.

The main concentration of events seems to have been on the first floor. Lavatories would he heard to flush when the rooms were empty, and Ellen Agar herself was afraid to go into the ladies' lavatory on this particular floor. On one occasion an officer in the building was in the process of turning off the lights for economy reasons, when he thought he heard someone talking behind the lavatory door. Thinking it was Ellen, he called out to her as he passed, but received no reply. He then discovered that she was off duty and thinking there might be an intruder on the premises, he and a colleague opened the door of the toilet. The place was empty, but the lavatory chain was swinging as though it had just been pulled.

Manifestations of this kind are quite common and seemingly purposeless except as a means of attracting attention. There are, of course, possible natural explanations for them. In this case an intruder could have entered the building unseen; but any interloper would hardly advertise his presence by talking aloud in the lavatory or anywhere else. The room may have been used by another member of the staff than Ellen Agar, but in that event one would have assumed a reply would have been given to the officer's challenge.

There have been more decisive manifestations, however, for apparently the wraith of a young woman has been seen in the building, and been heard to say, "Can you help me?" The apparition is said to wear long skirts of a misty grey or mauve colour (typical apparitional appearance) and is small and pale in physique—if a ghost can be said to possess such a thing. Footsteps have also been heard in the building.

One male employee who worked night shift customarily slept upstairs in the Association's rest room. He complained that at certain times of the year the atmosphere in this room became unnaturally cold.

At the time of Ellen Agar's employment, the A.A.'s staff had become disturbed by the situation, though nothing appears to have been done towards remedying it. There had, however, been some attempt to discover the history of the place—a necessary preliminary to understanding the reason for a haunting—and it was believed that the building stood on the site of an old well. That the water table is near the surface is borne out by the fact (according to Mrs Agar) that a pump is installed in the building's basement specifically for keeping down the water level.

The pale ghost is thought to have some association with the well, and there are the usual convenient stories of her having been jilted by a lover. Whether or not the jilting led to a drowning one cannot tell.

In this case, although I tried to get confirmation of the facts from two of the male members of the A.A.'s staff, both were too shy to reply to my letters; which in itself may be of significance.

I had half expected the Crown at Chiddingfold to have a ghost, and indeed some local opinion asserts that it has. However, the present owner denied any possibility of a haunting, and Ellen Agar herself knew of none. It is said to be the oldest pub in Surrey, having been established about 1285. A building of considerable beauty, it looks out over the village Green of Chiddingfold and is well known over a radius of several miles. It must have been a welcome sight for travellers in its early days, when as a hospice attached to Waverley Abbey, it gave shelter to Cistercian monks on their pilgrimage from Winchester to the shrine of St Thomas à Becket at Canterbury. It became an inn in 1385, when the abbey leased the property to one Thomas Gofayre, a brewer. The boy king Edward VI is reputed to have stayed there on a journey from London to Cowdray Castle in 1552.

Before I left the half-timbered grace of this ancient structure, Mrs Ellen Agar told me of one other haunting of her experience. It occurred on a footpath near Sweetwater Lake, Enton, to this lady's two daughters. The girls used this path as a route to school, and at one point it passed through an old kissing-gate, of the kind rapidly disappearing from the English rural scene. On a particular occasion, the girls saw a woman pass through the gate just ahead of them. They seem not to have noticed her presence on the path until they saw her at the gate and then observed her go through it. They followed the lady, being curious about her, but when they themselves reached the kissing-gate the woman had disappeared, although there was nowhere in the immediate vicinity which could have concealed her. There is no proof that what they saw was apparitional, but the likelihood must be admitted. The abrupt appearance and disappearance of figures is a familiar aspect of hallucinations of this type.

A mile or two east of Guildford is the site of a long established haunting. Indeed, it has taken on the texture of legend, partly on account of its age and partly because of a certain romantic quality essential to all self-respecting legends. The place is a sizeable sheet of water, large pond or miniature lake, known as Silent Pool, and lies on the north side of the busy A25 to Dorking. When I visited it on a bright May morning, I had difficulty in believing that the trunk road was at my back, for once climb the path to enter the little glade in which the pool lies, and you might be back in the twelfth century which saw the origins of the haunting.

The story is that Emma, a young village girl, lived in the locality during the times of the Crusades. Richard I, though on the throne, was not at the moment occupying it, being engaged in earning himself his *Coeur de Lion* title on the road to Jerusalem. His younger brother John, unbeloved of history, is reputed to have been behaving wickedly in the county of Surrey at this particular time.

With all the innocence and none of the common sense of village maidens, Emma decided to bathe in Silent Pool minus her clothes. A rash move, as Prince John had spies everywhere. However, she had bathed there often enough before and as far as is known nothing worse than a chill had ever occurred to her.

159

On this occasion she clung as was her wont to the bough of an overhanging tree and dipped in and out of the clear water. When His Grace the Prince appeared with his dastardly band of villains (not villeins) the embarrassed maiden let go of her tree and waded into deeper water to cover her confusion. John, however, was on a horse and rode in after her. Emma got out of her depth, could not swim and gave a loud shriek before she sank.

It so happened that her brother was within earshot, heard the cry and rushed to her rescue. He could not swim, either, so both innocents sank together and were drowned.

Now if you come to Silent Pool on a moonlight night you are likely to see the ghost of the lovely Emma dipping in and out of the water. You may even hear her dying shriek as she goes under.

So much for romance and villainy. Now let us look at the facts. A spring flows into the Silent Pool, and in ancient days the place appears to have been a sacred spot, as such waters often were. In Roman times pilgrims are said to have gone there to buy a mug of 'Roman water'. Later, the rites became transformed by the Christian church into a Palm Sunday Fair. In the nineteenth century this in turn was ended and the fair moved to the nearby village of Albury.

Perhaps the ghost story is merely a development from a pagan legend of a water goddess, the guardian spirit of the pool. Stories of naiads abound in Britain, and some of them are still (like Jenny Greenteeth in Lancashire, who drowns unwary travellers) regarded as evil spirits. Others were rapidly transmuted into saints of the Christian church and their threat neutralized. It may be that the spectral Emma is a faint racial memory of such a pagan spirit. I found no one who had seen this apparition in recent times.

An account of a much more serious nature comes from the neighbourhood of Dorking, a few miles to the east of Silent Pool. It was sent me by Mr C. W. G. Allaston, whose home is now in Littlehampton, Sussex, though at the time of this experience he was living in Bexley, Kent.

On his seventeenth birthday in March 1924, Mr Allaston obtained his first driving licence. In those days the standards of roads, cars and driving were not as high as they are today. What are now 'B' roads were then mere lanes, drivers were not required to pass a test of ability, and cars were primitive in the extreme. Mr Allaston began work as a driver for a car hire firm in Bexley, and was given a Flanders (a forerunner of the Studebaker). "The car," according to Mr Allaston, "had a landau-type body and a sheet of plate glass for windshield, no windscreen wipers, the sides of the driver's cab were fully exposed to the elements, and with the hand brake and gear lever fixed on the offside running board. Lighting was by two brass oil lamps, one either side in the front and another at the rear for tail light. As head lamp a large brass lamp was fitted to the front offside and illuminated by an acetylene gas jet, the gas being supplied from a large brass container fixed on the running board."

One evening the young man was instructed to drive from Bexley to Dorking to pick up a lady and gentleman and bring them back to Bexley—a distance of 35–40 miles. He did as he was bidden, and duly reached the stretch of road between Betchworth and Dorking. The road was narrow, other traffic on it almost non-existent, and the driver's visibility limited by the nature of his car's lighting; he was therefore startled to see in the radius of his single headlamp (about 100 yards) a large shire horse approaching him at full gallop and on a clear collision course. The road was too narrow for the car to manoeuvre, so young Allaston did the only thing left to him—applied the brakes until the car halted.

As his letter makes clear, the lapse of time between Mr Allaston's sighting the horse and stopping the car was only seconds. Then the creature raced by on the offside of the car, its mane and tail flowing behind it. The young man felt considerable fear by this time, for he could not understand how a collision had been avoided. Also his senses informed him that there was something strange about this animal. When he had first seen it 100 yards away, the horse had appeared perfectly solid. As it passed him, however, almost brushing his right shoulder, he had the sensation that there was a transparency about its body—in spite of the fact that it appeared to be in full harness.

The young fellow jumped out of his driving seat into the road, looking back to see if he could discern the animal. Nothing was to be seen. But what was stranger was that nothing could be heard, either; the sound of galloping hooves fading into the distance (which at the least he had expected) was absent. Then he realized that at no time throughout the experience had he heard any sound other than that of the car's engine.

Mr Allaston was brave enough to drive back along the way he had come for a few miles, convinced he would find the horse somewhere by the wayside, but after two miles he gave up the attempt; there was no sign of it.

When he returned with his passengers into Kent, the youth chose a different route. And such was his bewilderment at what he had seen, he did not mention the experience to any except his own family.

Mr Allaston assures me that at this time of his life he did not drink; and that moreover he has and always has had an open mind on the subject of ghosts, neither believing nor disbelieving in their existence. He could hardly, therefore, be said to have been expecting the apparition he encountered that night in 1924.

At the time he was too afraid of ridicule to discuss his experience outside his family. Had he done so or had he reported the matter to the local Press, he might have discovered that a tradition of a spectral horse existed relating to this stretch of road. A manifestation so strong and vivid is likely to have been encountered on more than one occasion in the area.

Mrs Phyllis Hudson of Broadstairs, who had informed me of manifestations in Kent, also told me of incidents at an old house in Westcott, near Dorking. Mrs Hudson was engaged as a nurse by the house's owner, a widow, to care for her during a serious illness. The nurse was surprised to find that the patient's relatives refused to visit her after 7.00 p.m.; that the housekeeper had moved her quarters to another part of the house, and that the family dog would frequently stand at the head of the stairs with its hackles raised. The cause of these extreme reactions was apparently that about 10.00 p.m. each evening, the sound of footsteps could be heard ascending the stairs and walking along to the patient's room. The latter herself stated that her late husband (who had died two years earlier) visited her every night.

Mrs Hudson, an intrepid lady, on two occasions sat at the top of the stairs and listened to the footsteps as they approached, passed and receded. An odd feature of this account is that apparently on the night the widow died the footsteps ceased. Afterwards the garden, which had produced little flower since the husband's death, flowered in great profusion. The man had been a keen gardener. Coincidence? Possibly. A good general flowering season? Perhaps. Neither explanation throws any light on the nightly recurrence of the footsteps.

North Surrey is lost now to London, swept into the uniformity of the suburbs, its original pastoral character totally submerged. Not that all the ghosts stem from the earlier rural background. One, reported to me by Miss Helen Allan, whose experience in the Isle of Wight house has already been related, concerned a house built in 1936 in the district now known as Worcester Park. At the time of this particular manifestation (1937) the area was still one of fields and avenues of venerable oak trees, a semi-rural environment.

The pair of semi-detached houses, one of which was occupied by the Allans, stood in Woodlands Avenue, and the two houses were alike in each possessing a ground floor with french windows opening on to a patio. The difference between them was that the windows in the neighbouring house actually opened, while those in the Allans' were stuck fast.

Mr Allan's aged aunt lived with the family, and this lady apparently had mildly psychotic (Miss Allan's word for it) attacks occasionally, when she believed herself to be the Queen or some other eminent personage, giving her family a somewhat difficult problem for as long as the state lasted.

During the few weeks prior to the incident in question, circumstances in the house had been unusual in that a series of objects appeared and disappeared. These were generally small household articles, dusters, cutlery, etc., yet they caused the family a good deal of irritation, and there was the usual apportionment of blame among its members for the vanishing goods.

According to Miss Allan's account—she was about ten years old at the time—matters came to a climax with some speed. The family was quietly eating its supper one evening when the sound of the bedroom window immediately above was heard "as though it had been flung open, and a very large heavy object (we all thought at once of the aunt) fell out, passed the window, and landed with a crash on the concrete patio". Mr and Mrs Allan dashed out via the back door (the patio doors, of course, were stuck) while their next door neighbours who had also heard the crash, came through their french windows and via a gap in the hedge to the Allans' garden. Both lots of adults were astonished to see the patio quite empty and in its normal state. On investigation, it was found that the elderly aunt was still contentedly in bed and had apparently not moved therefrom. No explanation of this odd occurrence was ever discovered.

Two comments suggest themselves, however. This is an historic area (Nonsuch Palace was not far away and the modern houses could have been built on the site of its Park) and it is possible that some earlier building might have housed an individual who jumped from an upper window. What was heard could have been a 'replay' of an earlier tragedy.

On the other hand certain aspects are suggestive of poltergeist phenomena. These are invariably associated with a young person (generally an adolescent) whose energy appears to be converted spontaneously into violent and noisy movement extraneous to the child. The only child present in the Allans' household as far as I can discover was Helen Allan herself. I am inclined to think however, that the deliberation—and the single occurrence—of the heavy falling object suggests a replay of an earlier incident. Nearer than that one cannot get without further evidence.

Also within the environs of London is the next instance. Mr G. F. Langridge of Croydon moved in 1972 to Thornton Heath occupying a council house there. The manifestations began at two o'clock one August morning when Mr and Mrs Langridge were awakened by the sound of their bedside radio playing classical music at full volume. Mr Langridge, more asleep than awake, got up to turn the instrument off, and then came wide awake as a peculiar realization struck him. The radio was playing music from a foreign station, and the Langridges never listened to other than the English stations. This was the beginning of a series of incidents which lasted the whole time the Langridge family were in occupation and grew progressively more unpleasant as the years passed.

From August until Christmas 1972 the commonest incident was to find that a certain lampshade in the sitting-room had been removed from its stand and placed on the floor, usually several feet away and invariably upside down. This became a nightly occurrence. The Langridges, though worried, were reluctant to speak of the matter outside their home for fear of arousing ridicule.

During the Christmas holiday of that year, on 27th December, Mr Langridge was sweeping the floor of the sitting-room when one of the Christmas decorations hurtled straight at his head, precisely as though it had been deliberately aimed. Since the object was sharp, the percipient might have suffered injury had it made contact. The same evening Mr Langridge was seated on the sofa reading a book, when the Christmas tree standing nearby began to shake violently, apparently of its own volition, showering needles over reader and book alike. After a minute or two this activity ceased and the tree became still once more.

In the New Year of 1973 the footsteps began. They were heard regularly in one of the bedrooms, and although both Mr and Mrs Langridge checked the rooms, nothing was found to account for the noise. It began again immediately they came downstairs, however.

Although uneasy about these strange occurrences, the family seem to have resisted panic. By May of that year, however, the situation was worsening. One of the sons, a handicapped child aged seven, awoke to find a man standing at the foot of his bed wearing, so he said, "old-fashioned clothes". The figure stood motionless for a while staring at the child before disappearing. This occurred again the following month and the little boy was now so frightened that the parents moved him into his brother's room.

On yet another occasion the Langridges were entertaining friends. About 12.30 a.m., all four heard a loud knocking on the outer door. They went together to investigate but found no one there. The visitors left hurriedly and suggested that some form of psychic help should be sought by the occupants. But that same night after the Langridges retired, they heard continual movements about the house. One imagines they lay and listened for a good part of the night in a frame of mind unconducive to sleep.

Throughout this period the lampshade was continually thrown to the ground, the sitting-room door opened and the light switched on. In 1974, in desperation, the occupants had the house blessed, though this seems to have had little effect on the activities inside it.

In August of 1975 Mrs Langridge went on holiday and her husband stayed alone in the house. About 7.30 p.m. one evening when he was in the sitting-room a loud crash reverberated from the kitchen—"as if all the crockery had been scooped off the Welsh dresser and thrown to the floor". It took the startled man some minutes to gather his courage sufficiently to investigate. However all was orderly in the kitchen when he entered, with not a pot out of place.

On a later occasion that year, Mr Langridge renewed the floor covering in the bedroom and left the old lino lying in a roll on the landing. During the night the house occupants were awakened by a scraping sound outside the bedroom door, followed a minute or so later by a heavy crash. Again they were initially too scared to investigate, but when ultimately they did so, they found the lino-roll lying at the foot of the stairs. It had had to travel 3 feet and then turn left along the landing to reach its destination.

Yet again—the sequence was apparently varied and endless—in early 1976 at about 8.30 p.m. when the children were in bed, an exceptionally loud crash was followed by the sitting-room door flying open. One of the family's two sons (not the handicapped child but the other) complained that at that time his bed had been lifted up from the ground. The boy was so upset by the incident that at last the Langridges decided to seek help in their problem.

A medium, Mr Salter of West Norwood, was approached. As a

result of this consultation, the subject in the case, Mr Langridge, was informed that his house was on the site of a farm, and "the spirit of the farmer was very annoyed by us trespassing on his lovely farm. He asked Mr Salter to inform us that we must leave at once. He also gave the medium his name."

At this point G. F. Langridge enquired at the local library to discover if any person named Chatterton had owned a farm in the area at any time. Somewhat inadvisedly he told the librarian his reasons for asking, and a decidedly sceptical official, no doubt with the idea of humouring an eccentric enquirer, duly looked up the records. And then official scepticism vanished, for the archives showed that a man named Chatterton had certainly farmed at Thornton Heath and that the farm had existed where the Langridges' house now stood. The Chattertons had lived there in 1762 and after their deaths had been buried in Croydon parish church.

But worse was yet to be. In June 1976, Mr Langridge was quietly watching television in his sitting-room, when to his utter horror a figure appeared on the screen which had no connection with the subject of the programme. It was that of a man, unusually handsome ("he had fair hair parted on the girl's side") wearing a black jacket with wide, pointed lapels, a high shirt (presumably a stock) with a large black tie. Not, Mr Langridge assured me, a dinner bow-tie, but of an eighteenth-century type.

Mr Langridge sat petrified in front of this apparition. It stared back at him, and handsome it may have been, but according to the mesmerized subject "its eyes were very hard and cold". Three weeks later Mrs Langridge underwent the same experience. Not surprisingly she screamed and was badly shocked. On each occasion the hallucination faded after a moment or two.

Thereafter things grew really bad, as though they had not been bad enough already. On three occasions in one day Mrs Langridge thought she was followed upstairs and also into the kitchen by an elderly grey-haired woman. This apparition had a pleasant enough face but apparently a stern expression. It seems the figure wore "a very old-fashioned pinafore and had her hair in a plaited bun". Mr Langridge's account continues: "She was upstairs when my wife went up and inside a cupboard when my wife opened it. My wife was terrified." I am not surprised.

The Langridges went away for a week, but in their absence lights appeared in the house and a series of loud noises from within the building was heard by the neighbours.

At last the Langridges conceded defeat. The husband applied for a transfer of employment and they moved back into Croydon. He often wonders, so he told me, if the new occupants have been disturbed in any way. With a pestering as strong and defined as this it will be surprising if they have not.

There are certain interesting aspects in this case. It bears a marked similarity to the Hopfield haunting in Waterlooville. Both hauntings suggest that the apparitions were not aware that they were no longer alive. They appear in both cases to have been surviving entities with enough power of will to direct energy—whether their own or mechanical energy such as electricity—to bring about physical effects in the present. Fortunately such cases are rare, but when they occur they seem to be extremely difficult to combat. They are certainly not of the 'if you ignore it, it will go away' variety. Exorcism sometimes but not always brings about the desired result, and the mechanism of this process—assuming it to be successful—is not clearly understood.

A further instance of psychic activity was supplied to me by Mr W. R. Baxter of London Road, West Croydon, and relates to a building near Lambeth Bridge.

In 1976 Mr Baxter worked for a well-known security firm, and in the course of his duties was sent to the new building built on the site of the former Millbank Prison. The time was about two o'clock in the morning, when my correspondent, together with two other men, saw what appeared to be the form of a man, "white and not solid", which, emerging from a wall to one side of them, walked slowly along a gallery before disappearing into a wall at the opposite end.

The apparition materialized again the following night at exactly the same hour, and yet again on the succeeding night. After that it did not appear again. The startled percipients reported the sightings to the building's owners who by enquiry discovered that the plans of the original prison made such a materialization possible. In other words, the two walls through which the figure walked seem originally to have possessed doors, or at least access to the gallery.

The only other knowledge Mr Baxter has of the affair relates to an experience of an office cleaning employee. This particular man was directed to the first floor to clean the staff dining-room in the building. At 11.00 p.m., as he had not returned downstairs, the sergeant of the security firm asked Mr Baxter to go up with him to discover if anything untoward had occurred. When the men reached the dining-room they found the cleaner crouched under a table. He cried out to them to "get me out of here, for God's sake". According to Mr Baxter's account, the man ran out of the room and did not return to his duty. No explanation appears to have been given of this strange behaviour at the time. Since the security guards saw that all the building's doors were locked when they took over evening duty, it is unlikely that any intruder could have entered the place without their knowledge.

There appears to be no known historical explanation for this manifestation. One can only assume that the spectre belongs to the prison period of the building. The present occupiers, I understand, are the Electricity Council, and it is marginally possible that persons in their employ have encountered the ghost. The fact of its being seen by the three men on three separate nights and then not again seems significant, though what the significance is is not clear.

For some reason I find urban hauntings depressing. They invariably seem to relate to sadness, to a feeling of imprisonment and defeat. Not, of course, that the same cannot be said of some country hauntings, though I think less frequently. City spectres, though, are generally attached to buildings while the rural ghosts appear in open spaces as often as closed rooms.

Some such thoughts crossed my mind as I drove towards Godalming on a shower and shine day in May. A pleasant town, this, its narrow streets speaking of less populous days. One listened in vain for the song of a post-horn, the drum-rattle of iron-shod wheels. I stayed in a hotel on the outskirts of the town and was told here of a local house reputedly haunted—the Meath Home, once known as Westbrook Place, now a home for epileptic women and girls.

The house, a fine Palladian building, was originally owned by General James Edward Oglethorpe, the founder and sometime Governor of the State of Georgia. The signs are that the present mansion was built on the site of a much earlier dwelling for at various times during renovation, medieval nails have been found in the old staircase, bones discovered built into a wall (probably animal bones), and an underground passage unearthed which led to the church.

As might be expected, the house's echoes are of the seventeenth century. General Oglethorpe's daughters were ardent Jacobites, and Prince Charles Edward Stuart is said to have visited here. Local word-of-mouth tradition states that the Bonnie Prince frequently walked in the grounds in the evening, wearing a grey cloak. The house's ghost story may have been put about to frighten away the curious, for it also relates to a figure in grey, though of a woman. This phantom is supposed to appear as a harbinger of good news. As far as I could discover she appears very rarely, which may or may not be a comment upon the times in which we find ourselves. The last time she was seen seems to have been by a member of the night staff of the Meath Home, who awoke to find the lady in grey standing at the foot of her bed. Whether the staff member had heard the story before she saw the ghost is not known. Certainly the townspeople know of the legend, but I did not discover anyone who had seen the spectre in recent times—or who knew of any history to which the phantom might with certainty be attached. Westbrook Place is handsome though, and it is not difficult to imagine the young Oglethorpe ladies a-twitter with excitement and hero-worship at the thought of a secret visit from the young prince who was to become the forlorn 'king-over-the-water'.

History is also powerfully remembered at another fine house near Godalming—Loseley Hall, home of the More-Molyneux family since the middle of the sixteenth century when the present building was erected. It is a magnificent Elizabethan manor house, grey and graceful in its rural setting, and with an atmosphere of mellow serenity which is extremely attractive to the casual visitor. Although its age and historic connections make it a show place, Loseley is primarily what it always was, a family home. The present owners, Major and Mrs More-Molyneux, farm their sizeable estate with a high degree of efficiency, concentrating mainly on the production of dairy products springing from the famous herd of Jerseys founded in 1916.

The house itself is a place to fall in love with, for items of beauty and history lie everywhere like rose petals on a day of festival. Queen Elizabeth really did sleep here, as did James I, and the More family as it then was had for many years honourable employment at Court. There was even a connection by marriage with the other More, Henry VIII's Chancellor-of-conscience, Sir Thomas.

It would be surprising if a house of this kind failed to retain some imprint of its previous inhabitants, and there are in fact at Loseley stories relating to three separate ghosts; one is referred to by the family as 'the pleasant lady', the second 'the unpleasant lady'; the third is supposedly the daughter of the last-mentioned, for it is of a child.

The pleasant lady was discovered in portrait form in one of the house's attics, and perhaps it was the removal of the picture which caused its original to appear in the house. She (a woman of the late Victorian era according to her dress) was seen on one occasion by Mrs More-Molyneux outside the door of a bathroom, a gently smiling apparition with a most amiable expression.

The unpleasant lady is a less comfortable phantom. According to tradition the original flesh-and-blood woman in a fit of jealousy drowned her daughter in the moat which at that time surrounded the house. Since then both mother and daughter have occasionally been seen at Loseley, the mother in one particular bedroom.

However, the extraordinary thing is that when one leaves Loseley it is not with the memory of its ghosts uppermost in mind. The deepest impression is made by the warmth and kindness of the

Loseley Park, Guildford, Surrey, is the home of three ghosts: two (the 'Unpleasant Lady' and a child) are said to be mother and daughter; a third, the 'Pleasant Lady', is a later apparition, apparently from Victorian times.

family, the beauty of the house, and the smooth efficiency of its twentieth-century business. Quite a powerful combination to find in rural Surrey.

Anything after Loseley was likely to be an anti-climax, and when I reached the Talbot Inn at Ripley, which I had been assured had the ghost of an old coachman who had fallen downstairs (and presumably killed himself), no one had heard of it or him. What the pub did have was a spinning-wheel tucked under its main staircase, and a bar called Lady Hamilton's Bar. It did not surprise me to be told that the wheel had belonged to Emma, and that she and Nelson had been accustomed to stop at this particular inn on their way to and from the coast. I expressed scepticism at the likelihood of Lady Hamilton's carrying a spinning-wheel about with her, still less using it, but had the feeling I was committing *lèse-majesté* in even thinking such a thought.

If Emma Hamilton's activities as a spinster are doubtful, so are those of Cranleigh's puma as local monster. This is the kind of vague general rumour that has been associated with the area for years without anyone having knowledge of its origin. I did not believe in any puma, whether ghostly or escaped from a zoo. As far as one can tell Cranleigh is bustling and lively and quite unhaunted.

The same cannot be said of Dunsfold, a quiet village a few miles to the west. Here the figure of a monk has been seen walking down the lane near the church. The story is told locally that the original monk had loved a nun at a neighbouring convent, but when his advances were rejected, he took revenge by stealing some object of value (presumably to the Church) and ensuring that it was found in the woman's possession. She was accused of theft, convicted and hanged. Thereafter the vengeful (and by now remorseful) monk killed himself.

Whatever the facts of the original tale, there does seem to be a haunting in the area. The apparition was apparently seen by occupants of the old rectory on one or two occasions, and the local postmistress informed me that her dog reacts violently to attempts to walk him down the lane, refusing point-blank to go. I did not speak directly to any eye-witnesses, however, so the account is mere hearsay.

Dunsfold church, incidentally, is a delightful thirteenth-century building, lying outside the main village, perhaps on an artificial mound sacred in prehistory. A holy well lies just below it, which suggests the place may have been sacred to Brid, the Mother Goddess of our early ancestors. The ancient yew tree outside the church door is impressive and thought to be almost a thousand years old. It is propped by a wooden crutch like a very ancient man.

On my way out of Surrey I passed again through Cranleigh, wishing I could have seen Baynards Park, the Tudor house which once housed the head of Sir Thomas More. After his execution More's head was impaled on Tower Bridge, but his daughter, Margaret Roper, bribed the executioner so that when she passed beneath the bridge in a boat, her father's head was thrown down to her. She then took it to Baynards Park where it remained for some time.

Now the Park is said to house the ghost of More. It is a story worth investigation. However, during my visit to Surrey the building's owner was reluctant to allow strangers to visit the place, so the haunting by Sir Thomas remains just a rumour. A man of such staunch faith, stout courage and high integrity seems an unlikely subject for a haunting, and I suspect, if ghost there is at Baynards, that it is some other than Henry VIII's recalcitrant Chancellor.

The birds were singing as I left Surrey, and somewhere in the woody distance a cuckoo hyphenated with great deliberation. As his distinctive 'cuck-oo' followed me down the Arun Valley, so did the warm heavy scent of centuries old haymakings. The blue distance came nearer, and I moved unregretfully into it.

If Surrey has been decimated by London, the county of Middlesex has been swallowed whole. However, the redrawing of maps and the edicts of Government have not prevented the Post Office and the dwellers in what was once Middlesex from believing in its continued existence. The old postal address is still quoted and honoured, and Middlesex County Cricket Club continues to regard itself as a functioning entity in competition with other county sides.

Correspondents who wrote to me regarding ghosts regarded themselves as Middlesex inhabitants. I shall therefore treat their hauntings accordingly and ignore the fact that the ghosts probably function now in Greater London.

In the year 1935 Mr and Mrs John Wells were living in Isleworth, but due to the fact that Mr Wells's work (he was employed by the Middlesex County Council) kept him primarily in Greenford, they eventually decided to move the necessary five or six miles in order to live there. The couple chose their accommodation from an advertisement in a shop window and went along to view the rooms which were in a house in Lucerne Road*, Greenford, owned by a Mr and Mrs Jack Dawson*.

During their visit John Wells asked if he might use the house lavatory and was accordingly directed to it. However, no sooner had he entered the room than he experienced a feeling of near terror and this remained with him until he left it. To use his words, "I got out just as fast as my legs would carry me".

Shortly afterwards the couple moved into their rented rooms and remained there almost two years. During the whole of this time both husband and wife experienced a feeling of strong fear whenever they used the bathroom, and neither of them spent longer in the place than was absolutely necessary. However, they did not mention to each other the bathroom's uncanny atmosphere for fear of being laughed at. It was not until his wife one night almost ran out of it that John Wells learned that she was as afraid of the place as he was. By this time both of them hated to use the room at all.

A few weeks later a young Irishman came to live in the house. He had come directly from Ireland and knew nothing of the Greenford area. After a few days the owner's wife, Mrs Dawson, asked him why he always ran out of the bathroom as if the devil were after him. "Mrs Dawson," the young man said, "that room is evil." This at least confirmed the opinion of Mr and Mrs Wells.

Shortly afterwards the latter moved back to Isleworth, but now John Wells's work took him often to Twickenham, and it was while working there in the early days of World War II, that he met a workman who had known Jack Dawson. According to this man the house in Lucerne Road, Greenford, had constantly brought ill-luck to its owners. Several builders had been engaged in its erection, and the last comer, who finished the house, got into debt and hanged himself from the lavatory cistern. Jack Dawson himself had had endless bad luck since moving into the place, and had finally been killed by a fall through a manhole.

If such stories are known in advance of occupation, it is likely the inhabitants will create for themselves a feeling of fear and threat. However, in this case nothing was suspected either by Mr and Mrs Wells or by the young Irishman of the house's history. They felt the terror before they knew of the bathroom suicide. It would seem, therefore, that some of the builder's feelings of anguish immediately prior to his death may have remained in the area of the tragedy. A not uncommon occurrence, as we have seen earlier.

One interesting fact about hauntings, is that they do not seem to be the result of intellectual activities of an earlier date, but of emotional ones. That is, whatever record remains in the area appears to do so not as a result of someone's thought processes so much as his feelings—fear, hatred, malevolence, even love and happiness, all seem able to imprint themselves upon surroundings. The reasoning thought processes which do not involve emotion do not seem to register in this way; or if they do, do so much less strongly.

An apparently similarly 'registered' haunting, though of a benevolent kind, took place some years ago at the Middlesex Mother and Baby Home in Ealing, and this report of one sighting was sent me by Mrs Doreen Fleming* of Hampton.

Mrs Fleming, herself pregnant, shared a room with another girl and an older woman, all three expecting babies the following month. One night, Doreen Fleming awoke to see the figure of what she took to be a nun of the nursing order (dressed in a white habit) bending over the patient in the bed farthest from her. She supposed the girl to be in labour and the nurse in attendance, and being tired herself, went back to sleep.

A short while afterwards she awoke again to see the figure in white bending over the woman in the bed next to her. Then it struck the percipient that the coincidence of two of the room's inhabitants being in premature labour on the same night was unlikely. She looked closer at the bending form, and as she did so it began gradually to disappear. Eventually, Doreen Fleming assumed she had been dreaming and went back to sleep.

The following morning, the girl told her room-mates of the incident, and the older woman, who was resident in the area, stated that the house had formerly been a children's home—run by nuns.

Doreen's experience must have been reported to the Home authorities, for this, plus the fact that a similar incident had apparently occurred on the same night in the other wing of the house—to the great alarm of the patients who had had their babies—caused a great furore. Owners of haunted property often find their ghostly guests an inconvenience, causing as they occasionally do, a loss of business patronage or of property value. Mrs Fleming insisted in her letter to me that the figure in white seemed a very comforting one when she saw it, and she had no fear either then or later.

An arresting feature in this case is that the figure disappeared gradually—no immediate vanishing, but a slow fading. Andrew Mackenzie in his *Apparitions and Ghosts* states that the fading of an apparition is characteristic of a manifestation of the dead but not of the living. From my own experience, I would think this true, but there is little evidence available to suggest reasons for this state of affairs.

A very strange experience was reported by Mrs Trudy Kent of Acton regarding a church in the Hanworth Road, Hounslow. During the early part of the war (the year 1940), Mrs Kent was returning home at about 11.30 p.m. At one point her path took her along the Whitton Road, past a small church. As she drew level with the churchyard, she was astonished to see a figure kneeling before a large memorial cross. In spite of the hour of night, the figure shone out clearly, for it appeared to be dressed as a bride with some kind of headdress and a full and glittering veil. No face was visible for the figure had its back towards the percipient.

Mrs Kent turned at right angles, following the churchyard wall, and expected from this fresh viewpoint to see the face of the kneeling woman. However, when she reached the mid-point of the wall the vision had gone. The church environs were totally dark.

Convinced that she had seen a ghost, Mrs Kent yet did not feel at all afraid. She took the first opportunity to make enquiries of the vicar of the particular church in Hanworth Road, telling him of the figure she had observed kneeling before a large cross in his churchyard. She was astonished when he replied that the church had no graves or memorial stones but was in fact a modern church with merely a small garden surrounding it. This the percipient later verified for herself in the light of day.

In reply to my further enquiry, Trudy Kent said she saw only the back view of the apparition and at no time its features. The figure was remarkable for its splendour—"an elaborate bride" according to her account—with its veil "shining like diamanté in floodlight".

That Mrs Kent saw an apparition, probably of a figure which at a previous stage in the history of this area actually existed, seems likely. The splendour of the 'bride' suggests that its original may have been a person of some consequence, and the fact that no ornamental cross stands in the present church garden does not invalidate the possible existence of such a monument at an earlier period. Sacred sites have usually been so for a long time, and it is possible that an earlier version of the church (and an accompanying churchyard, perhaps) once stood beside the Hanworth road. But without a detailed knowledge of its history, it is not possible to guess at the 'bride's' identity or her reason for kneeling where Mrs Kent saw her. Another instance, I think, of an area retaining an imprinted record of its past.

There are many instances of minor hauntings in Middlesex, but few of these have enough evidence behind them to be worth reporting.

One spectre which has repeatedly been seen, however, is the Enfield Flyer, a phantom coach and horses said to drive through eastern Enfield. The vehicle was seen at the end of the last century by three girls and reported again in 1961 by a certain Robert Bird, who encountered it when on his way to a Boys' Brigade meeting. The phantom apparently goes at a spanking pace about two feet above the present road level (the eighteenth-century road level was appropriately higher in order to clear the surrounding marshes) and carries at least three passengers. There are no reported recent sightings.

A better documented ghost is that at the Royal British Legion headquarters, Holtwhites Hill, Enfield. This, known locally as Fred, takes the form of the upper half of a man and has been seen in the spirit cellar (an appropriate place) and felt in a number of other locations. Glasses have been broken on the premises when no one was within reach of them; sounds of heavy booted feet walking in the upstairs bar have been heard; the bar steward asserts that objects (a glass, and on one occasion a bucket of water) have levitated and been thrown down; and the steward's wife on one occasion heard someone enter the kitchen behind her before feeling a touch on her back. The room was in fact empty except for herself.

Apparently there has been the usual movement of small articles from one place to another. I say 'usual' because this type of psychokinetic activity is common in a haunting which appears to be spasmodic and spontaneous rather than worked to a rigid pattern. The very unpredictability of the activities suggests an entity capable of decision-making, which raises the interesting question of whether or not the entity is aware of what it does and can therefore be said to be a surviving energy-form from the time of its body's death.

There is a local tradition that in the days when the building belonged to the Fire Service (before 1972), a fireman was crushed to death by a tender. Is he the haunter of his old quarters? Sudden or violent death often seems to be a factor preceding hauntings. It is as though the abruptness of departure from the physical state cut out a process in preparing for death, the dead one having no time to understand what was about to happen to him. In some cases, the energy or 'soul' part of his composition, would then seem to behave as though it were still living in the physical body. This may be the case in the British Legion building.

Another survival, though of a much less active kind, has been reported from the home of Mr and Mrs Alec Mattingley, Riverdale Court, Enfield. The apparition has been seen by four members of the family over a period of several years, and always appears in the same form of dress—rough outdoor garments resembling those of a gardener or labourer—and always in the same position—at the foot of a bed. In 1972, the percipient was a younger child, Susan, aged twelve, who knew nothing of the ghost and had not heard it spoken of by older members of the family.

At one time the land on which stands the small group of houses forming Riverdale Court was part of the kitchen garden of the old Elizabethan palace at Enfield. Perhaps the apparition is of some outdoor servant of this period, though a description of his upper garment ("a kind of anorak without the hood") suggests a later era. It is not possible to offer any convincing guesses on this one.

In the reign of the first Elizabeth one of the Queen's favourite hunting forests was Enfield Chase. Four hunting lodges were built there for her convenience, and subsequent reigns did not entirely obliterate the buildings. In the nineteenth century, North, South, East and West Lodges stood on the site of the original Elizabethan buildings, and it was North Lodge which apparently retained an echo of its original owner. In February 1975, the *Enfield Gazette* received a letter from one of its readers, Mrs Eileen Spicer (*née* Gundry) of Sevenoaks, whose parents had lived in the house at the turn of the century. At that time the sound of a horse galloping up to the front door of the lodge had been heard on many occasions, though the animal was never seen. The family believed the phantom to be that of the white horse ridden by the Queen herself.

Years afterwards, when digging deeply in the gardens, the Gundrys' gardeners unearthed the skeleton of a horse. Eileen's mother insisted that the animal be given "a decent burial" (a Christian burial?) and thereafter the ghostly galloper was not heard again.

Why Elizabeth I's horse should be buried in the gardens of her hunting lodge is an unanswerable question. But that some particular horse tradition was connected with the building is likely, as Mrs Spicer stated that in her childhood a white marble mantelpiece in the drawing-room bore a relief carving of a horse. Coincidental or significant? The fireplace has vanished now along with its symbol, taken out in the course of later renovation.

A haunting operating until very recently was that at the Crown and Horseshoes, Horseshoe Lane, Enfield, where a small elderly woman was said to materialize occasionally. The figure had been seen by an habitué of the pub, Mr Brian Bullock, while waiting for the return of the landlord prior to opening time. The quite distinct form of a little old lady moved past one of the windows as the man stood outside. He assumed it was of someone in the house, but the building was empty at the time.

The present licensee and his wife, Roy and Sue Williamson, have heard the cellar door bang on many occasions when no one living was near it. Apparently this occurred most frequently at dead of night. The usual feeling of chill hangs about the cellar, and the Williamsons' pet cat and dog cannot be persuaded to go near the place.

As a result of publicity of the incident in the *Enfield Gazette*, that newspaper received a letter from a Mr Claude Cyril Clark of Wellington, New Zealand, to whom the paper had been sent in January 1977, some two years after the first report of the haunting appeared.

As a boy Claude Clark had lived at the Crown and Horseshoes, his parents being its licensees. His mother in particular had spent a considerable amount of time in the cellar to which most of the haunting incidents refer.

There is some tradition at the inn that a female member of the Clark family had threatened to return and haunt the place if ever it were allowed to fall into disrepair. At the time the Williamsons took over, this was precisely its condition. Since then it has been modernized and redecorated and in reply to my enquiry, Mrs Williamson said that little has been heard of the ghost (the mother of Claude Clark?) in recent months.

A small-scale haunting, the type that is common to many public houses which for one reason or another tend to be excessively haunted. This one is of interest by reason of its link-up with a living member of the family previously occupying, Claude Clark, who states that three days before receiving the newspaper report from England, he dreamed of his mother in that very cellar of which the Williamsons complained.

It was Mr and Mrs Sims of East Meon in Hampshire (they who had told me of the haunting by a newly-dead woman in their present village) who had lived in a haunted house in Staines. An old building, it produced a series of strange occurrences from the sound of footsteps to the switching on and off of electric lights (what, I wonder, did ghosts use for demonstration before electricity?). The knocker on an outer door frequently knocked of its own accord, but when investigated no human agency was found to be involved. Mr Sims, a confessed sceptic, attributed this occurrence to the wind. However, there was another occasion when no such easy explanation offered.

The Simses' daughter, Sally, had a child's organ which was kept downstairs. The sound of this instrument was distinctive, and when one morning while the whole family was still in bed, the organ was heard to sound a single note, the child's parents were startled. Since the noise appeared to come from the upstairs quarters, Mr Sims asked his wife if their daughter had the organ in her bedroom. Mrs Sims was quite sure that it was, as it had always been, downstairs. And so it proved when they investigated. However, both parents had distinctly heard a single note played on the instrument, apparently in the upper regions of the house. No explanation was ever found for the incident.

The family felt that the ghost was male, although they could not say why they thought so. It is an arresting feature of hauntings that those being haunted invariably have a fixed idea about the sex of the haunter. Even when the hauntees are several, there is generally agreement about the male- or femaleness of the ghost.

How do they know? If an apparition has been seen, that is one thing, but in cases where there has been no visual manifestation the same certainty seems to be present. A possible parallel in physical terms is that when one has one's back to a door and someone enters, it is possible to make a good guess at the person's sex even without any sight or sound of the intruder. The information must therefore be conveyed to the brain of the room's occupant by other means, and I suggest that the information relaying and receiving is done by the personal electromagnetic fields of occupant and intruder.

These electromagnetic (or e.m.) fields are the product of radiation from the human body, and can be detected by a specialized type of photography known as Kirlian. The individual's field projects from his body for a few inches forming an aura around it. It is this which may be responsible for the giving out and receiving of information by means of a form of radiation.

Since there is some variation between the male and female e.m. fields (the female field projects slightly farther from the body) it is possible that sensitive subjects may be able to detect the difference.

It will be seen from the above paragraph that I believe less in supernatural than in natural explanations for so-called psychic events. Our knowledge of the natural laws governing the universe is still elementary, and the idea of the supernatural has come about as a means of concealing our ignorance from ourselves. 'This is not according to the natural laws, therefore it must be supernatural.' This is not a safe statement to make unless we can be sure we have complete knowledge of the natural laws.

Not all hauntings, as we have seen earlier, relate to happenings in earlier centuries. Our own has produced its quota of ghosts, mainly associated with the industrial/mechanized way of life which has superseded the slow rhythms of agriculture. Mr Victor Worrall of Walmer, near Deal, Kent, wrote to tell me of a London haunting of a fairly typical modern kind.

On an autumn evening in 1938, he and his son were driving home along the road they usually used towards Highgate Village. Dusk was falling but visibility was clear. They turned off the main road (Junction Road) into a secondary highway called Dartmouth Park Hill and began to climb the hill. Let Mr Worrall's own account describe what occurred.

"It is a steep hill and at a certain spot I used to depress the accelerator for extra revs. which enabled my 30 m.p.h. car to climb the hill in top gear. The road ahead was perfectly clear at the time, and there was no mist or fog. I had put my foot on the accelerator, and there was not a vehicle in sight, but in a flash the scene had changed. And it was terrifying. Coming towards us, only a few yards away, was an enormous lorry. It was, I realized in a split second, going to be a head-on crash, as I had no time or room for manoeuvre. I was speechless, but I remember my son saying 'Oh, my God!'. And then the 'crash' came, but it did not crash with us. The whole thing passed through us and as it did so my son and I both turned our heads to look through the back window. There was nothing to be seen. Needless to say, we were both terribly shocked, and immediately afterwards I pulled up on the near side to regain our composure. We were both breathing heavily and hardly able to talk. Here I think I should say that we are both total abstainers, and I am not easily scared. I was the first to speak and said to my son 'You saw what crashed into us, didn't you?' My son replied 'Of course I saw it.' 'And you saw the parking lights on the side of the lorry.' He said 'Yes, it definitely was there, and are we still alive?' That is the question we still ask each other 'Are we still alive?'"

An unnerving experience indeed, and unusual by reason of the fact that the lorry 'passed through' the percipients and their car.

One must conclude in the light of earlier accounts of a similar nature that the projection of the lorry was the result of an accident at this spot, and that by some means the 'imprint' of the vehicle and the action in which it had been engaged was thrown on to the same stretch of road as that concerned in the original incident. This account draws a clear parallel with the slide-projector and screen referred to earlier in this book. The fact that the real-life car of the Worralls drove through the apparition only lends greater point to the theory. It is perfectly possible to drive a vehicle through the picture of a vehicle projected upon a screen. In this case the apparition supplied the picture, as the road the screen. For the 'projector' we should need to look in the immediate vicinity of the Worralls' encounter.

Although the percipients did not appear to know of any former accident at this place, the likelihood is strong that there had been one, and that a coincidence of time, light and possibly weather conditions had reproduced for the drivers in 1938 an occurrence at a point earlier in time. This is a good example of a haunting which is as much a time-dislocation as a true haunting. The percipients experienced the action of a time previous to their own.

From the above it will be apparent how many variations there are in so-called psychic occurrences. Mention has already been made of poltergeist phenomena, and the last account relating to Middlesex appears to be of this nature. As explained earlier, the activities typical of poltergeists are not thought to be connected with the dead but with the living persons. However, since doubt still seems to exist in the public mind on the subject, it may be as well to detail the occurrences at (yet again) Enfield.

The phenomena were first reported by the *Daily Mirror* and then by the *Observer* newspapers and concerned activities in a council house occupied by a divorced woman, Mrs Peggy Hodgson, and her four children (two girls aged thirteen and eleven respectively and two younger boys). The manifestations began in August 1976 with a series of rapping noises, and developed in the usual poltergeist fashion into a series of psychokinetic movements of objects.

It is typical of this type of psychokinesis (spontaneous movements of objects without apparent human aid) that there is violence. Objects both thrown (Lego bricks, marbles, small items of furniture) and moved (beds, chairs, drawers and doors) are impelled with considerable force, enough to cause injury to anyone impeding them. In the Enfield case the demonstrations moved beyond simple psychokinesis; a fireplace was wrenched from its moorings and on one occasion a highly unusual incident occurred. Mrs Hodgson's sister-in-law was making tea in the kitchen when, according to her account, "something appeared in front of my eyes, dropped on to the kitchen unit and bounced once". The lady cried out in alarm and dropped the kettle.

Before any reader denounces materialization as moonshine, let me say that there has recently been a case in India where an Indian religious leader known as Sri Sathya Sai Baba, successfully materialized items of jewellery before the sceptical eyes of two American scientists without, as far as they could tell, any trickery or sleight of hand. They were quite unable to account for the extraordinary happening taking place under their noses.

As far as the Enfield case is concerned, all ideas of ghostly pestering are likely to be unfounded. Poltergeistry is usually a subjective phenomenon, occurring in households where an adolescent child is present, plus a certain amount of emotional strain or maladjustment. There were two adolescents in the Hodgson household, and the family history, according to the newspapers' reports, suggests some emotional stress in the background. In other words the psychokinetic demonstrations may have emanated from one of the young girls.

Such recurrent spontaneous psychokinesis is apparently inadvertent. The subject is unaware of being connected with the happenings and is unable to control them. What seems to occur is a spontaneous throwing-off of energy by the young person (and human energy is perhaps at its strongest at this stage of life), in a random fashion. The consequence is that objects are moved, hurled or overthrown apparently without direction. One cannot, of course, be sure that some subconscious direction or intent is not at work, but if it is, the subject does not appear to be aware of it.

One objection to this particular theory (which is increasingly held in some scientific circles) is that the amount of human energy available in one individual is insufficient for the violent activities typical of poltergeistry. However, as explained in my book, *The Mask of Time*, it may be possible for human energy in some circumstances to use part of the natural energy available in the universe, and in so doing plug in to a power-source of very great potential.

The investigation of this particular phenomenon, like so much other of the apparently supernatural, is still in its early stages. Much will surely be learned before the century's end about the powers which are within and without us. At present we are like children set down in a fantastic shop, whose beautiful, strange and dangerous merchandise seems to us a collection of fascinating toys, to be played with or taken apart as the whim dictates. Our education in such matters has hardly begun.

Berkshire

Until fairly recently, the rolling pastoral landscape of Berkshire ran as far west as the Vale of the White Horse beyond Uffington, but since the reorganization of the county boundaries that venerable animal has retired into Oxfordshire, and Berkshire now ends just north of Lambourn. With as much regard for new boundaries as the General Post Office, I had driven cheerfully up to the White Horse and practically stood in his eye, bent on including in this book one or two of the fascinating stories associated with the considerable prehistoric cult centre. However, local inhabitants quickly pointed out my error, though they hastened to add that they still considered themselves part of Berkshire no matter what the Government decreed.

Reluctantly I left the imposing monument with its forgotten rites and meaning and journeyed south across the falls and swells of the Lambourn Downs to Lambourn town itself. It is a pleasant, tidy small town with a country-market air about it.

There was not much in the way of hauntings, though old Lambourn Place was said to have a ghost in its day. The original house had been fifteenth-century, but this building was demolished in the early nineteenth and a Victorian mansion built on the site. The property was at that time owned by a family named Hippisley, and the last of the direct male line, Henry Hippisley, died about 1890.

This man was unpopular in the district, and was known as a hard man in his dealings with the local people. At one time he had been prosecuted by the Charity Commissioners for defrauding the local almshouses. On another occasion he was said to have taken some of the timber fan-vaulting from the local church for use in building at Lambourn Place. Local inhabitants shook their heads over this sacrilege, prophesying that Henry Hippisley would not prosper.

He appears to have been a man of violent and imperious temper, for when a rumour spread that he had killed one of his servant girls and buried her body in the nearby woods, it was believed. After his death, the last of the Hippisleys was said to have been seen in the neighbourhood of the house he once owned. His appearances seem to have been few, the last just prior to World War II. As far as I could discover there have been no recent sightings. Lambourn Place has been demolished, but when I visited the area the land was about to be built on once more. It will be interesting to see if Henry Hippisley stages a comeback.

A common misconception regarding hauntings is that they always represent the distant past. As the ghostly cars and hitch-hikers prove, this is not the case. Hauntings may not only be of recent date, but may be by recently dead people. A curious account of this nature was sent to me by Mr John Halliday of Wantage, concerning a disused airfield at Grove, near Wantage. (Although this area is now officially in Oxfordshire, I shall include it here, since at the time when the haunting was experienced the place was in the county of Berkshire.)

Mr Halliday worked for the Atomic Energy Authority, which operated an irradiation plant at the Grove airfield, the plant being used for, among other things, the sterilization of animal foodstuffs. The entire plant was housed in an old aircraft hangar, and except for breakdowns was run night and day. During the day a day-shift staff manned it, while from 6.00 to 8.00 a.m. and from 5.00 to 10.15 p.m. only one man was in attendance. During the night the plant ran without supervision, though in the case of a breakdown the night watchman on duty would notify the Duty Officer, so that the latter might deal with the fault.

One summer evening in 1969 at about 9.00 p.m. John Halliday was seated in the office attached to the plant, when he heard what seemed to be the loud murmur of voices outside the office door. (He describes it graphically as the 'rumble' of voices.) It seemed to him to be the sound of a group of people in conversation, and surprised at such an occurrence at that hour of night, he went outside to investigate. Far from finding a small gathering of people beyond the door, he found the hangar absolutely empty. He searched round the various pieces of machinery but with no better result. He then returned to his office and telephoned the gate-house which lay about a mile from the hangar housing the plant. The security officer on duty, in reply to the enquiry, stated that apart from himself and Mr Halliday only a boilerman named Joe Kelly was on the site. And Joe Kelly was seated in the gatehouse with him.

Puzzled, John Halliday during the next few days mentioned the experience to several colleagues, only to be told that it arose either from imagination or from the rumble of the plant as it worked.

He might have been satisfied with this and forgotten the whole matter, had it not been for what took place a month later. Mr Halliday was on the same shift (2.00 p.m. to 10.00 p.m.) and in the same place (the office near the plant) as formerly. The only difference between the two occasions was that on the second the plant had broken down, so that absolute stillness reigned. Then came the sound of voices beyond the office door. John Halliday immediately went outside and searched the hangar as thoroughly as he had before, with the same result. There was no sign of any human being on the premises save himself.

Several weeks passed uneventfully, and then one of the colleagues who had been sceptical of Mr Halliday's first report, approached him saying that he also had now heard the rumble of voices in the hangar and as a result no longer doubted their existence.

Later my correspondent learned that during the last war an American serviceman had hanged himself in this same hangar. At some later stage a Psychic Research organization was called in to investigate certain strange 'happenings', though it is not known what these were or what were the results of the investigation.

It is common for airfields and their buildings to be haunted. They are, after all, places where just in the course of their daily usage human emotions are likely to be heightened, nerves taut—conditions of mind which, when associated with sudden death, appear to be conducive to hauntings.

South-east of Wantage lies Newbury, and the drive takes you over beautiful downland country. Long, shallowly rolling hills, populated by Friesian cattle and a scattering of lambs (no longer small woolly bundles as when I began the journeyings for this book, but bundles grown elderly, portly and sedate).

Newbury itself is a good, neat town, with a pleasant riverside walk and a secretive concealed park. There were swans on the river and a leisurely bowls match in progress the evening I arrived, and having convinced myself that it was too late to begin work that night, I sat and watched both in pleasurable idleness, as the silvery spring sunlight gradually withdrew from the town.

I had been given an excellent account of a haunting by my Hampshire correspondent, Mrs Rosemary Stevens, who was brought up at Winding Wood Farm, Kintbury, near Newbury. As she described it, Winding Wood Farm was then (in 1966/67) a lonely place north of the A4, with a mile or more between houses. The young Rosemary was working then at Denford Park School, and was walking home one evening in late autumn. Her route took her past

Radley Cottages then downhill round a left-hand bend with a coppice on one side and tall, spreading elms on the other. As she came to the bend (known locally as Cox's Corner), she saw what she took for a patch of mist high in the branches of the elm tree nearest to her. It occurred to the girl that mist was out of the question as the rest of the landscape was quite clear. She then told herself that she must be looking at a particularly white owl. However, in the next few seconds this comforting theory was dissipated, also, for as she approached it the white patch began to shape itself into the figure of a man.

Much shaken, the girl hurried past and made her escape, acutely conscious of the white figure thirty feet above her head.

Her family suggested she might have seen Old Cox—he who was associated with the Corner, and who was said to have been a local labourer who had died young after some local scandal had overtaken him. Rosemary, however, was inclined to the view that she had seen the aftermath of a bomber crash in the early years of the war, when a young Canadian rear-gunner had died. The rest of his crew had been brought to Winding Wood, her own farm, for tea and first aid. The method of the gunner's death appears not to be known, but had he baled out and hit the tree, the apparition's height from the ground would be explained.

Nothing further is known of this occurrence, and the sighting appears to have been an isolated one. One singular fact about the date of this particular sighting was that it took place on All Souls' Day, traditionally that of the Feast of the Dead, both in pagan and Christian times.

The Newbury area is no stranger to wars, for during the Civil War of the seventeenth century, heavy fighting took place in the district, with massive (for the time) loss of life. It is therefore not surprising to find that many of the hauntings relate to this period and to one or other of the two battles of Newbury.

I stayed in a small hotel on the Andover road, and its proprietress was most helpful in suggesting possible sources of information for research. It was through her that I met Miss H. M. Purvis, a local historian, of Battery End, and learned at first hand of several nearby hauntings. Battery End, as its name implies, was the site of a Royalist gun battery. Three mounds on the common are said to be the graves of fallen soldiers, though informed opinion believes they are prehistoric round barrows, and any Civil War dead are likely to have been placed in the surrounding ditches. No matter what the truth of this, one fact about Wash Common seems certain; that it saw the death of Lord Falkland, Secretary of State, who during the first Battle of Newbury in 1643, jumped his horse over a hedge where the fighting was hottest and was killed. His body was taken into a nearby farm (known thereafter as Falkland Garth) in which from time to time since then his ghost has been seen.

A Mrs Middlecote, described as "a cheerful extrovert", was employed there as cook during World War II. On one occasion when her employers were out and she was about to leave the house at the end of her day's work, she had the sensation that someone was standing behind her. She turned and saw "a short man dressed in black", but the illusion vanished as abruptly as it had happened. On being shown a picture of Lord Falkland later, she identified it as that of the man she had seen.

One of the areas where the fighting was fiercest in the 1643 battle was around Enborne, and several accounts of hauntings survive in the area. One concerns the lane running beside Cope Hall, which is said to have been heaped with bodies by the battle's end. A shadowy figure has occasionally been seen there. Considering the slaughter it is a wonder the lane is not jammed with shadowy figures. Cope Hall is reputed to have a chilly atmosphere and a legend of ill-luck for its inhabitants, due according to rumour to a murder once committed there.

A more interesting haunting relates to Biggs Cottage, Enborne, which was the headquarters of the Parliamentary commander, the Earl of Essex. In a race for London, the Royalist forces, as dusk was falling, had occupied Newbury just two hours ahead of the Parliamentary army. Essex and his soldiers as tired, soaked and even hungrier than the Royalists, were engaged in battle the next morning, but fought valiantly against an army rapidly running out of ammunition. There were terrible losses on both sides. Lord Falkland, as we have already seen, died of a musket ball, his hope for a rapid end to the war utterly dashed. Prince Rupert, leading the hot-blooded cavalry charges of which he was a master, had an enemy pistol fired at him from point-blank range, but was reprieved when it failed to go off. Essex, discovering the Royalists' lack of ammunition, resumed his march for London, gambling on getting through before the King's forces could prevent him.

Did Essex the night before the battle walk the small length and breadth of Biggs Cottage, calculating his chances? Some stress and emotion must have been felt there, for from time to time the commander has been seen at intervals over the years. There was a record of sightings even before the present day, but two sisters by the name of Hesketh who occupied the place in their retirement both saw the apparition.

The elder sister (now long dead) was the first to see the ghost. She awoke one night to find the figure of a man in her room, standing near the bed; she later described him as "tall and dark". She screamed, and her sister ran upstairs to her, but by the time she reached the bedroom the apparition had gone.

It seems that many years passed without further sighting, until approximately 1973, when the younger Miss Hesketh had a similar experience to that related. She was sleeping in the same bedroom when she awoke to find the figure of a tall man, with long, dark curled hair, standing at one end of the room. He wore a dark cloak "with a badge or insignia in white with a petunia-coloured centre across his chest". Miss Hesketh also thought he wore a "shovel-shaped" hat—by which I can only think she meant the broad-brimmed hat of the times, usually turned up at one, and occasionally at both sides.

As for Essex's personal appearance in life, as a boy he seems to have been dark-haired, though late, ageing portraits show him with lighter or greying hair. The percipient in this case formed the impression that "he was a very pleasant man", as he appeared to be smiling when she saw him. Essex, although kindly, was often gloomy and pessimistic in outlook, so his appearance on this occasion is not characteristic. However, he appears to have been a tall individual, and the costume described by Miss Hesketh fits that of the mid-seventeenth century.

Apparently the figure moved diagonally across the room until it reached the far corner and then disappeared. This abrupt capacity to disappear, incidentally, is one of the disconcerting factors about ghost-seeing. One moment the apparition is there, the next not; the scene is perfectly normal and without an occupant. It is no wonder that such hallucinations are frequently disbelieved. They are too sudden, too discontinuous. Miss Hesketh also referred to the figure's "moving across" the room rather than, as one would expect, "walking across". It is a common phenomenon in such hallucinations that the ghost appears to travel with a gliding movement rather than with the jerkiness of a normal walk. Biggs Cottage, therefore, appears to have the ghost of a seventeenth-century man, possibly but not positively that of Robert Devereux, Earl of Essex, commander of the Parliamentary forces. Why he should haunt in an area where he did not meet death is not clear.

There are still Civil War stories current in the Newbury area, and still with that ring of only-the-day-before-yesterday about them. One such concerns a small troop of Parliamentary infantry, hungry as soldiers usually are, who had somehow secured a pig and managed to roast it in Lushy Gully behind Enborne Lodge. A Royalist cannon ball's trajectory happened to take it in their direction. It hurtled into the pig and carried it away, leaving a startled and dejected group in its wake. Although this story has been current a long time, some verisimilitude was given it for me by Miss Purvis, the local historian. Apparently Edward Gray wrote up the tale in 1830, having been told it by a very old man who had had it as a boy from one of the original soldiers in the Battle of Newbury. Such a spanning of time is just possible, and so extraordinary that it may be a fact. It is interesting to speculate upon. Word of mouth local tradition is never to be dismissed lightly.

This part of Berkshire is full of history, and the following morning I sat under the hooded-gimlet surveillance of a stuffed cobra and the wooden indifference of three hobbit-sized, vaguely oriental figures in the hotel's breakfast room, trying to decide which out of my embarrassment of riches I should tackle next. In the event I drove to Kintbury, a charming small village a short distance from Newbury, and stumbled into some ghostly lore and a community of friendly people.

Kintbury church houses the tomb of a certain Mary Dexter, of whom it is said that when she died her husband's sword, by her own desire, was buried in the grave with her. According to local tradition, if you approach the tomb at midnight, you are likely to hear the rattling of the sword in its burial place. However (again according to local tradition), the sound is likely to be caused by stays on a nearby flagpole as they flap against the wood.

Kintbury derives its name from the river which flows through it, that same Kennet which meanders its mysterious way through Wiltshire. The village itself was settled in Saxon times, coins of the tenth century having been found in the churchyard. The church of St Mary's is heavily Victorianized, though a Norman doorway, a battlemented tower, and a thirteenth-century transept remain.

On arrival in the village I had enquired first at the vicarage and interrupted a parish meeting. However, in spite of this I was given

The Church of St Mary the Virgin, Kintbury, Berkshire, whose graveyard contains the tomb of Mary Dexter

The memorial plaque to Mary Dexter in Kintbury Church. Her tomb is said to hold her husband's sword and it is this weapon which is thought to rattle in its resting place from time to time

a friendly welcome, and both the vicar and his parishioners were able to enlighten me about local hauntings.

On one occasion three or four bellringers had entered the church about 7.30 p.m. for a practice ring. They were somewhat surprised to see a figure wearing a black cloak and a dark, wide-brimmed hat seated in the front pew. In some doubt as to his identity, they questioned each other (strangers stand out in so small a village), but before they could come to a decision the man looked round at them, then arose and walked into the vestry. The villagers followed him a short distance behind, wondering by what right this unknown person should enter a part of their church not open to the public. So close were they that they expected to confront the cloaked man as soon as they set foot inside the vestry. However, the room was empty, and on checking they found all doors into the church locked and no sign of the intruder in any part of the building.

This would appear to be one more echo from the period most potent in the district's history, the Civil War. Who the original cloaked-and-hatted man was no one seems to know. As far as is known, there is no surviving legend of any particular individual of that period associated with the church. He may have been a casual worshipper from one side or the other of the conflict, who for reasons unknown has left a record of his presence in that place.

The bellringers, incidentally, seem to have been quite unaware until the figure disappeared that they were not watching a flesh-and-blood man. Indeed, the manner of seeing ghosts is particularly interesting in that while many people appear to experience a true visual hallucination, actually seeming to *see* the apparition with the naked eye, others experience a kind of mental picture, as though it were a waking dream, which yet contains action, colour, shape and (occasionally) sound. These individuals are more likely to be aware that they are seeing what is not physically present than are those for whom the hallucination appears to be of solid substance and seen with the physical eye.

A week before my visit to the village a young man had died in a local house. There was an element of tragedy about the occurrence, for the youth had been an epileptic and had fallen through the stair banisters, dying as a result of the fall. One of the villagers told me that a woman living in the house declared she heard the sound of the fall being repeated, and during the week following the death had several times thought she heard the young man banging doors as he moved through the house.

This type of activity is not unusual in the vicinity of a sudden death. It is as though the newly dead individual were unprepared for his changed state and continued to behave for a while as though he were still alive. Whatever energy informed the body seems to linger in the area, making its presence felt as it did in life. Generally, such activity ceases in a few days or weeks. Occasionally it will continue for months or even years, as though the individual energy-form were 'stuck' in the situation which he last remembered as a physical being.

This, of course, is surmise only, for we do not yet understand the processes of death and its apparent aftermath. There is evidence, however (and American research has supplied a considerable part of it) that only physical matter—i.e., the body—decays on clinical death. The energy part of the human structure would appear to survive, at least in the short term. Medical staff whose work brings them frequently into touch with the dying and newly dead, have been reported both in this country and in the United States as occasionally seeing apparitions of their patients at the point of or immediately after death. And patients who had 'died' and been resuscitated appear to have recollections of 'leaving' their bodies and observing them from outside—the condition known as an ecsomatic or out-of-the-body state. To remain in the vicinity of the place where one's physical life has been spent—at least until the new situation has been realized and understood—seems not unreasonable.

Some individuals appear to remain for longer periods of time, and these protracted 'survivals at source' seem to be related either to attachment to relatives or to particular places. The latter, as we have seen in the Waterlooville bungalow and Hopfield cases, often relate to obsessions. Indeed, material obsessions appear to account for a number of hauntings, from the house-and-property type to that of the money-and-gold lover. Occasionally there appears to be an obsession with an item of clothing, furniture or letters; or with an animal, as in the case of the child and her dog at Priory, Isle of Wight.

A family survival was related to me by Mrs Jane Hooper of Kintbury, who, living in an old house in the village, occasionally sees a dark slim lady in black standing near her bed. Mrs Hooper also saw the same woman before her marriage, which suggests that the apparition is not attached to the house but to the percipient. In answer to my question, Mrs Hooper said she did possess a jewellery box which had formerly belonged to her great-grandmother, and that this box had been with her both before and after marriage. This lady's sister had also seen a female figure in the house.

It may be that the figure is an ancestral one, and associated with the jewellery box. But whether the box actually 'projects' the figure, or whether the latter is a genuine survival attached to her own family, cannot be said with certainty.

The vicar of Kintbury himself had one or two interesting anecdotes concerning the supernatural. He told me of a man of his acquaintance, a Mr Robert Bright, who at the time of this occurrence lived in Wokingham. Mr Bright, a jolly man, regarded as 'a bit of a lad' by his friends, was not the type of person given to morbid imaginings. However, at one period in his life (exact year unknown), he saw the figure of a man in his room. The apparition apparently shook him by the shoulder, an experience which he naturally found upsetting. This manifestation—both the visible and tangible aspects of it—occurred on several nights, and Mr Bright was shaken in more senses than one. No explanation seems to have been found for the visitations, although the shoulder-shaking sounds much like an attempt to attract attention.

An incident of a more personal kind occurred when the Reverend Albert Millard, Vicar of Kintbury, was newly ordained. He preached the first sermon of his ministry at Cookham in Berkshire, and there was, quite naturally, a number of his and his wife's friends in the congregation. One of these, a lady known to be psychic, told him afterwards that during the sermon she saw the figure of his mother standing below the pulpit as he preached. Had Mr Millard himself seen the figure, it would have been tempting to suppose that the wish was father to the thought, since no doubt regret that his mother could not have lived to see his success must have occurred to him. However, the apparition was seen by someone outside his family. Such continued concern after death for those cared for in life is not uncommon, and often appears to continue for an extended period of time after decease. It does not seem common for the dead actually to be seen by their living relatives, but the sense of presence—usually intense and identifiable to the particular individual personality of the deceased—is certainly not rare.

I left Kintbury with reluctance, for it seemed to represent so much which is old, untouched and serene, epitomizing not only the history of rural Berkshire but of rural England. The drive east, avoiding the trunk roads as far as possible, was something of a compensation, for the countryside was alight with the myriad greens of spring.

Here and there the vivid yellow blaze of charlock sprang into view—whole fields of it, chequering the muted green of young corn and the shouting green of burgeoning beech woods, the tasselled, faintly dusty green of the flowering sycamores. Everything was burningly awake, the land full to bursting with vitality. Good to be alive on a May morning in England, with bird-song blossoming from every scattered woodland and sprawling hedgerow.

Reading came upon me unawares, but even the town gardens looked renewed, and as I was bound for the home of friends I had not seen for many years it was a cheerful entry.

Reading itself has a haunted hotel, The George, and I understand from a former housekeeper there that certain old parts of the building are decidedly uncomfortable. However, a more detailed haunting was given me by Mrs W. Hammond of Reading, concerning the village of Mapledurham, near Caversham. Tradition tells that on New Year's Eve a coach and horses travels from nearby Mapledurham House, and the ghostly sound of wheels and hooves can be heard by anyone in the vicinity.

Mrs Hammond, when she was a child of thirteen or so, regularly used a walk known as the Warren, on her way back from school. On the occasion in question, she and two or three other children were in this lane (a dirt road and narrow) when the subject heard the sound of a horse galloping towards her. Thinking an animal had broken loose from a nearby field, and being afraid of encountering it in full gallop in the narrow track, she flung herself into the bushes at the side. She heard the pounding hooves draw near and pass her; heard, too, the sound of a horse's laboured breathing as it did so. But of the animal itself there was no sign, and eventually the sounds faded into the distance. The child told no one save her mother of this experience.

This account bears a remarkable likeness to that of Mr C. W. G. Allaston who encountered a galloping horse near Dorking, though this gentleman both heard and saw the phantom as it passed him. Hauntings are repetitious, just as events in real life are repetitious. They are no less startling on that account to those who experience them.

A manifestation of a different kind was brought to my notice by the friends with whom I stayed in Reading. It occurred at Finchampstead in the year 1926, at a thatched cottage known as The Forge, and continued almost uninterrupted from February until August of that year. The inhabitants were a wheelwright and his family named Goswell—husband, wife and two daughters, Nellie and Marjorie. A detailed account is given in the Finchampstead Parish Magazine of February 1977, by Mrs Nellie Bird, formerly Goswell, and is worth quoting.

First a bath containing tins was overturned, scattering the tins. Tables were moved, chairs turned somersaults, pictures dropped from walls, a large chest was upturned and emptied, a perambulator insisted on lying on its side, cycles refused to remain upright. When bricks that fell out of a wall were replaced with mortar, no sooner were backs turned than all dropped out again. Bedclothes were dragged across a room. Small objects were flung about.

Writing appeared all over the place, on walls, on doors and on paper such as billheads that were lying about. All these were in the form of instructions, or warnings. One group of these warnings instructed us not to leave the house or go away, while another set of warnings told us to get out and go away. We were also told to take the dog away on a proposed holiday. These writings were made with pencil, or anything that was handy that would scratch or mark. Many of these writings that were on paper or cardboard have been carefully preserved and are kept safely under lock and key.

When things were at their most frightening, we all slept in one bedroom, and one morning the word "Go" was written on the ceiling above us.

A message appeared one day on the coal cellar door saying, "Do not open this door." My mother decided to obey this, but meanwhile things were vanishing all over the house, including an apple pie. This was too much, so she opened the door to find all the stuff stacked there, including the pie. A large metal tray was seen to spin across the hall, to come to rest against a wall. Somebody in the road outside saw a large fire guard flying out of the window.

There were many other incidents, but the one which gives one most food for thought is the matter of the carpenter's bench. This huge carpenter's bench, ten feet long and tremendously heavy, was upended one night. The bench is so heavy that two or three strong men are needed to move it slowly, foot by foot. It is now in use in our garage.

Much of what I have described appeared in various newspapers at the time, but the *Daily Mirror* ran the story more than others. The late Harry Price came down to investigate. The Lady Iris Mountbatten brought along Nell St John Montague, the clairvoyant.

Many spiritualists and investigators also visited the house.

To end on a humorous note. The village constable called to see what it was all about. He found nothing amiss when he looked around, but when he was coming down the stairs, his exit was hastened by a brick which came flying after him.

On the face of it this appears to be just another poltergeist incident (though the dismissive term 'just another' would not be appreciated by anyone living with this type of demonstration). However, there are unusual features. The set of written warnings, contradictory and puzzling; the word "Go" written on the ceiling, are not typical of poltergeistry. However, the mischievous element certainly is. And there were two adolescents present in the family. I am inclined to think it a genuine poltergeist case—recurrent spontaneous (or involuntary) psychokinesis, though there is no certainty that it was such, and the manifestation was so long ago that any hope of further information is forlorn.

Moving north from Finchampstead it is not long before the traveller reaches the Thames Valley. The land begins to flatten out and to lose the distinctive marks of rural Berkshire. There is a faint hint of the metropolitan about it, evidenced in odd stretches of ribbon development and a certain uniformity in the houses. But amid all this there are pockets of rustic survival, where the predominant rhythm is of the earth rather than the machine. One such is Cockpole Green, a pleasant hamlet of mixed development, without anything glaringly up-to-date, and with small copses and ancient farms lying either side the lane connecting it with the main Henley and Reading roads.

A lane (little more than a track) leads off it at one point and emerges in a farmyard, but the farm of which it is part, Putter's Farm, is haunted. I walked down to it on an open, sunny morning and found the farm staff, though busy about their work, willing to talk to me and let me inspect the oldest part of the place—a Tudor building incorporated into the original farmhouse; empty now.

They denied all knowledge of ghosts, but this was not unexpected. Two older inhabitants of the village had a different tale to tell. Mrs E. Butler of Warren Row and Mr Ernest Green of Cockpole Green, both elderly and both familiar with the local history, stated categorically that a horse with chains on the harness walked from the farm to the nearby ridge; Mrs Butler went so far as to warn me: "Better not go up to Putter's at midnight, if you don't want to see the ghost. A horse with clanking chains walks along the ridge."

It was this lady, also, who told me about one room in the old part of Putter's Farmhouse which was always kept locked. It was said to be haunted, though none knew by whom or what. Not, one imagines, by the horse and chains.

The Tudor building looked in urgent need of repair and the whole place had an air of other-worldliness, neglect. Not so the farm itself which was well-worked and trim. Perhaps no local person wants to live in Putter's Farmhouse, and as a result it and its ghost will quietly collapse into the soil. A pity.

The neighbouring hamlet of Littlewick Green is said to have a ghostly hound, the White Dog of Feens which haunts one of the woods. Whenever it howls, it signals the appearance of a phantom hunt which includes a young woman in spectral grey. She is said to be a certain Dorcas Noble who resorted to witchcraft to win back a former lover. I found no one in the area who knew of this haunting, so if it ever operated in the past it does so no longer.

You may drive up to Remenham and meet the Thames itself, but once cross into Henley and you will find yourself in Oxfordshire. On the Berkshire side the Little Angel pub at Remenham is said to house the ghost of a Miss Mary Blandy who, at the prompting of her lover, murdered her father, for reasons unknown. On approaching the pub's landlord personally for information I was brusquely told that he was "too busy seeing to these lads to talk to you". 'These lads' were three cheerful joiners/bricklayers/renovators who would have been quite happy to talk to anybody. But they did not know the ghost story. I suspect the landlord did. I did not find out whether Mary Blandy haunts the pub or why.

The people of Wargrave, some miles upriver from Remenham, were more friendly and co-operative. I called at The Horns inn for coffee, and on admiring the age of the place, was informed that it had once been either part of a hunting-lodge or a verderer's cottage in the great royal forest of Windsor. Alas, it had no ghost, though it seemed an ideal place for one. From here I was directed to the outskirts of the village, to Gibstroude Farm, where I found two strange stories.

The house's inhabitants were charming and friendly, telling the legendary tales as though the latter had not only interest but meaning. They were well aware of the richness which the past may add to the present.

There are two hauntings, one inside (though it is not actually a haunting) and one outside the house. The first concerns a former daughter of the farmhouse who jilted one lover to marry another and much older man. The jilted one, who may have been an artist by profession (he was certainly a more than competent painter) painted a portrait which hung upon the staircase door inside the house—the picture of a man. It seems the artist told his former sweetheart, with some bitter malice, that in time her husband would grow to look like the portrait he had painted. He then presumably left her life not to return to it. The picture remained, however, carrying with it a feeling of ill-omen, not lessened by the fact that whenever the light of a full moon shone upon it, its stern features appeared to come to life. Finally it was removed from the house and stored in a barn where it could not distress the house occupants by its malevolence.

It was in the barn that Mrs Diana Bush found it for me—a dirty scratched canvas, its colours almost black with age, yet with the

Gibstroude Farm, Wargrave, Berkshire, before renovation. The porch was the front entrance and faced the staircase door on which the mysterious male portrait was painted.

features of the face still clear, the eighteenth-century costume still faintly showing beneath the grime and damage.

The countenance it portrayed was not a reassuring one. There was in it a disturbing, sinister quality which would have been inescapable even if the background story had been unknown. I was glad when its face was once more to the barn wall and we could scramble down from the straw blocks and out into the sunlight again.

If the inside ghost is more threat than haunting, the 'outside' ghost is a ghost indeed, for it is that of a woman on horseback, who rides between two large trees across a tract of land known as Hyghams. Little is known of the story's origin, though locals say there is a connection with the farm itself. An old labourer living in the district once refused to take a threshing machine across Hyghams on account of its haunting, and there are village residents who believe they have seen the riding ghost.

Wargrave village seems to have a plethora of phantoms, or at least rumours thereof. I found a haunting at The Bull, where the landlord and several of his customers knew the outline of the story, but none had had personal experience of it. For this I had to go to Mrs Madge Gibbs, who, with her husband, was tenant of the public house for nine years. On several occasions roughly coinciding with the time of Henley Regatta the licensees would hear the sound of a woman sobbing in Room No 2. At first Mr and Mrs Gibbs thought the sound came from their young daughter, who was thirteen at the time, but it was found that the child was not responsible. The weeping continued at intervals seeming to occur on an anniversary, and always from this particular room described by Madge Gibbs as "beamed and eerie". Eventually a knowledgeable local inhabitant told them the supposed story of their weeping ghost.

A former landlady of the inn (date of occupation uncertain) was said to have taken a lover and to have had the fact discovered by her husband. The latter turned her from the house and forbade her to return. She was not, he said, to have or see their child ever again. What happened to the woman is not known, save that in due course she died, without apparently being able to break her husband's ban.

Once dead, she returned to The Bull with a vengeance—seemingly on the anniversary of her expulsion—and can be heard crying heart-brokenly, as she must have cried in life, for the child she had lost.

This is all that is known of the weeping ghost. I was shown the room concerned, and its atmosphere seemed pretty wretched. I did not at this stage know the whole story behind the rumoured hauntings, and my contact with Mrs Gibbs came several weeks later.

This seems to be an authentic case, for many villagers knew of it, and more than one landlord seems to have encountered it. The general opinion (no reason given) was that the haunting originated in the late eighteenth century.

Wargrave is a delightful village to visit. Not only does it have the fat silver Thames swimming through its gardens, it also has a collection of fine old houses, elegant, well kept and dignified. Two which lie near The Bull are Little Gaunt and Gaunt Cottage, once all one house in the possession of that master prince of the south, John of Gaunt. Both are therefore over 500 years old, and there is a tradition that in their time two queens lived here. In fact I heard the original house referred to as Queen Emma's House, though the only Emma I can trace as Queen of England was the widow of Ethelred the Unready, who took as her second husband Canute the Dane. She is an unlikely candidate from the time point of view; unless the Gaunt house replaced an earlier one on the site.

The occupant of Gaunt Cottage told me that a woman in white was said to haunt both her home and its next door counterpart, apparently walking through one building to the other, but the owner of Little Gaunt, who has lived in the house with her family for twenty-four years, is quite certain that her own premises has no ghost. Both houses are beautiful, mellow, serene, and I imagine a joy to inhabit, with or without a spectre.

Wargrave Manor is also rumoured to have some kind of haunting, though no one seemed to know what. "Strange things happen in the night", I was told. So do they anywhere!

A much more reliable haunting is at Barrymores, the fine old house which stands aloof in its walled front garden, with rear lawns running down to and disappearing beneath the Thames. The ghost is said to be that of a 'grey lady', haunting principally the upper rooms and the staircase, but of her exact association with the house nothing is certainly known.

Barrymores was bought by Richard Barry, the seventh Earl of Barrymore, who was (according to Mr John French, the present owner) born on 14th August 1769, succeeding to the title in 1773 before his fourth birthday. He died on 6th March 1793, having spent his twenty-three years in riotous and extravagant living. The cause of death? Suicide by shooting. The reason? The young man was hopelessly in debt and hard pressed by creditors; not an unusual state of affairs among young men of his class and time.

His burial was a curious business, for instead of an interment in the family vault, he was buried in the local parish church at dead of night—under the flagstones. This procedure was designed to thwart the swarming creditors, who it was feared might steal the body and hold it for ransom.

In these circumstances, one would expect the haunter to be Richard Barry rather than an undefined 'grey lady', but as far as is known he does not frequent his old home.

When Mr and Mrs French bought the house in (about) 1975, they undertook some restoration and during the course of it found seven crucifixes on the wall of one room, and the cover of a bible with a picture of the Madonna painted on board under the floor of another.

They had not been in occupation long before noticing that certain of the house keys kept disappearing. They would later be found in a pile in a room on the second floor. Occasionally even now people notice out of their eye-corners that objects are moving, apparently of their own accord. Others have had the sensation that someone is standing directly behind them. A discomfiting feeling. Women seem to be singled out for especial treatment, for it is they who have felt someone brusquely pushing past them on the stairs.

Who the 'grey lady' is no one knows; though she seems to be a real entity to the inhabitants of Barrymores. The latter are interested in the history of their house and do not appear to be at all disturbed by their ghost. There was an undeniable feeling in two areas of the house of 'presence', almost of being watched. The sensation was not one of hostility, however. The Frenches' boxer dog, incidentally, has a dislike for one of the upper rooms and refuses to stay in it.

One could spend days in Wargrave and never exhaust its possibilities, either of history or interest, but I had to move on—back towards Windsor Forest and the old grey castle which dominates that royal landscape. On the way I called at the Bird in Hand at Knowl Hill, where a highwayman is believed to haunt. He fell downstairs when drunk and killed himself, it seems, though no one seemed to know much about his story or his ghost. Sad, that. You would think a highwayman would have been famous for something, if only for nuisance value. I turned east for Windsor and Herne the Hunter and the Great Park and the memories of generations of sovereigns hunting their deer or trotting peaceably down the green rides after a hard day in the field.

According to some authorities Windsor, both castle and park, is full of ghosts. Elizabeth I is reputed to haunt the library and occasionally the castle walls, Charles I is said to frequent the Canon's House, and George III to linger in the room in which he spent so many years of sickness. However, someone who is in the best possible position to know, assured me that the castle is not haunted. The matter must rest there.

The Great Park, however, is undoubtedly stalked by Herne the Hunter. Herne, said to be a forester to Richard II, appears dressed in deerskin and wearing the stag's antlers upon his head. He is frequently on horseback and sometimes accompanied by ghostly hounds.

No matter what he seems to be or legend states he is, Herne is actually of ancient lineage. He represents the Norse god, Odin, who rode the Wild Hunt down the sky on nights of winter storm. But even before that, he was the horned god of primitive man, maybe palaeolithic in origin, an incarnation of the animal to be hunted, a representation of a nature spirit. So this pagan god survived into medieval times, when he was regarded by the Church as a devil. Survives still into modern times when he is called a ghost, a supernatural spirit. Yet in honest fact, those who see Herne in the twentieth century are probably calling up a racial memory or an archetypal image of what was once an object of reverence and religious meaning to the northern races. He has been seen in Windsor Forest within the last few years, but how his image is produced— whether by an inherited memory in the brain of the individual percipient, or by a racial memory handed down through the very genes themselves cannot be said. What he is not I think, is the ghost of a Plantagenet verderer who hanged himself from a forest oak. Cernunnos, the Celtic god of the underworld, he just might be, with a grove once sacred to his worship in the ancient park. But older still I think he is, belonging to the days when all men were hunters and all deer their quarry; the horned god, the god of the hunt.

But we will leave the park, the forest and the castle to enquire into one last haunting—of a private house and garden in Windsor town itself.

Maidlea Cottage* in the early nineteen seventies was owned by Mr and Mrs Wakefield-Smith. A large house rather than a cottage, it stood on the outskirts of the park and at the time (August 1971) of which Mrs Joanna Wakefield-Smith told me it appears to have been very much haunted.

There was a constant feeling of animosity, amounting almost to hostility in the house. This coupled with sensations of extreme cold even with a gas fire and a fire of logs blazing, made the occupants aware of something abnormal about the place.

On one occasion a foreign guest in the house asked the identity of the gentleman standing in one corner of the room as he had not seen the man present at dinner. No one else was aware of any 'gentleman in the corner'. The guest described the mysterious figure as a tall man in a dark cloak.

On one occasion both the owner and a guest ran into the hall in the early hours of the morning, each thinking his name had been called. There seem to have been many minor incidents of this nature, which all point to an active haunting within the house itself, although other than the 'cloaked man' description there does not seem to have been any indication of the identity of the ghost. Whoever he was, he had an unhappy effect on the place and its living inhabitants.

The garden of Maidlea Cottage produced a manifestation of another kind. On one occasion Mr and Mrs Wakefield-Smith had walked to the end of their garden, when abruptly they appeared to walk into an area of great heat and noise. It seemed to both of them that they were in the middle of a battle, for they could hear the clash of metal, as of weapons on armour and feel the surge of frenzied activity around them. Then as suddenly as it began, the manifestation ceased. The garden was peaceful, still, tranquil.

In answer to my question, Mrs Wakefield-Smith said that a local tradition existed of a battle in the area between the Romans and the native Britons. She thought she and her husband might somehow have 'tuned in' to this event.

What is described here is typical of a time-dislocation or -slip. The subjects appear to pass from one aspect of time (the present) to another (in this case the past; although it is also possible to experience the future in a similar fashion). Such experiences last only a few seconds in terms of chronological time, and although they have superficial similarities to ghost encounters, they do not appear to be hauntings of the kind we have examined. They relate to the peculiar properties of time, and possibly also to the functioning of our human brains.

Where the past rather than the future is involved, however, it may be that some kind of recording process operates, as in certain types of personalized haunting.

In the course of this book we have encountered several different types of paranormal phenomena which are generally regarded as

hauntings. The reader will have noted the various differences between them which make it unlikely that all occur in the same manner. The following list, though incomplete, will give some idea of the range covered.
1. Recurrent haunting by a static figure, always appearing in the same position.
2. Recurrent haunting by a moving figure, always engaged in the same actions.
3. Recurrent haunting by a static figure, appearing in different positions and places within a limited area.
4. Recurrent haunting by a moving figure in different actions and places within a limited area.
5. One single appearance, either of static or moving kind.
6. A limited number of appearances, either static or mobile, for a period immediately after death (the duration of the haunting may vary from a few days to several months).
7. Partial materializations: (a) either part of figure or (b) whole figure minus head or face.
8. Manifestations in the form of light—ball of light, flashes of light, small moving (usually bluish) lights or human head and face surrounded by light.
9. Manifestations in the form of sound—footsteps, crashes, opening and closing of doors, music, speech etc.
10. Manifestations in the form of smells—flowers, cooking, decay, biological, incense.
11. Manifestations in the form of touch—being shaken, pushed or held down.
12. Vanishing apparitions: (a) disappearing immediately, (b) slowly becoming transparent and fading.
(Apparitions may appear in similar fashion—either at once or by degrees, though the latter seems to be rare).

It will be seen from the above how wide the range of phenomena is and from the contents of this book as a whole how numerous the occurrences are. Although there would seem to be certain factors common to some types, they are not common to all, but one element does appear to be constant; that energy in some form is necessary in order that the phenomena shall work at all. The drop in temperature showing heat loss in the area of a haunting is almost universal. In addition other forms of energy—electricity and, more rarely, gas— are often affected. If this is accepted then it seems likely that some physical basis—physical in the sense of deriving from physics and biology—for recurrent paranormal phenomena exists.

Earlier mention has been made of the apparent distortion in audible manifestations; footsteps and other noises sound hollow, unreal, and there is a curious quality of reverberation—almost of vibration—involved. Speech invariably sounds distorted, its rhythms being recognizably those of speech but its details blurred and indistinguishable. (There are rare exceptions. Music, curiously enough, does not seem to suffer these limitations.)

If, as suggested above, the phenomena operate electrically, then it is feasible that in audible cases the sound waves produced might be distorted. This would seem particularly likely where the 'recorded' type of transmission is involved. (Instance the mysterious airfield noises which revealed themselves on the tape recorder only when the latter was operated at a certain frequency. The wrong frequency in playback then resulted in silence. Perhaps it can also result in distortion.)

One factor of absorbing interest remains. Why is it that certain of the human population experience the paranormal while others never do? The explanation most likely is biological. The human brain habitually uses four different electrical frequencies. These are known as the alpha, beta, delta and theta wavelengths. Of the four, alpha, the 'a' wavelength, appears to be most closely associated with so-called psychic ability, often seeming to be present in the subject just prior to a paranormal experience. This is a wavelength associated, also, with meditation; it seems to represent the brain's 'idling gear', when intense concentration is not taking place. And how often have we heard a subject say after experiencing some aspect of the paranormal, "I was not thinking about anything particular at the time." In other words he was not concentrating. This frequency, though common in most adults is rarely used by others. It may be the latter who do not experience psychic phenomena.

It was that good writer on the subject, Andrew Mackenzie, who used the Oxford English Dictionary definition of an illusion. "Illusion: apparent perception of external object not actually present." He went on to say that a person may see an apparition in relation to his immediate surroundings in such a clear and detailed fashion that he believes it to be real, though it is actually an hallucination of sight. But by this definition so is watching a film or television, yet few of us would consider ourselves hallucinated. We know from experience that somewhere a natural law is being used and operated by men to produce this 'hallucination of sight'.

So may it be with the various forms of haunting we have considered. Somewhere a natural law may be operating of which we have as yet fragmentary or no knowledge, to produce what we believe we see and hear 'by hallucination' or by 'psychic' means.

There are signs that man's eternal curiosity about the world, the universe and his own insignificant self is slowly leading him towards a full realization of the natural laws; laws which govern not only the known, explored ways, but those which are as yet unknown and deeply mysterious.

Thoughts of this kind, which at best can be little more than speculations, occupied my mind as I turned the car into its homeward tracks. Berkshire's grass verges were fringed with cow-parsley and dandelion, its water-meadows gilded with a surface sprinkling of buttercups. Fat white clouds bowled along before the wind, a sky imitation of the dancing young lambs I had seen in March.

It was May now. The woods and hedges, the very air itself seemed full of birds; magpies, wagtails, thrushes, blackbirds, fluting, fluttering, flying and crying until the spring seemed full of them and they to hold in themselves all that was spring.

However much the world beyond impinges on our own, however much it teases our curiosity or emphasizes our ignorance of what we are, it does not take away from the immense wonder of merely being alive; in England; on a May morning; in the warm South.

Bibliography

The Avebury Monuments (Dept. of Environment, HMSO 1976)
Barham, Tony, *Witchcraft in the Thames Valley* (Spur)
Bord, Janet and Colin, *The Secret Country* (Paul Elek, 1966)
Dames, Michael, *The Silbury Treasure* (Thames & Hudson, 1976)
Finchampstead *Parish Magazine* (February, 1977)
Folklore, Myths and Legends of Britain (Readers Digest, 1973)
Forman, Joan, *Haunted East Anglia* (Jarrold Colour Publications, 1985)
— —, *The Mask of Time* (Macdonald & Jane's, 1978)
Green, Andrew, *Shire Album 7, Haunted Houses* (Shire Publications, 1971)
Hadingham, Evan, *Circles and Standing Stones* (Heinemann, 1975)
Herm, Gerhard, *The Celts* (Weidenfeld & Nicolson, 1976)
Hogg, Garry, *A Guide to English Country Houses* (Country Life, 1969)
Mackenzie, Andrew, *The Unexplained* (Arthur Barker)
Mee, Arthur, *Kent* (Hodder & Stoughton, 1969)
Parker, Michael St John, *City of Pilgrims* (Dean and Chapter of Canterbury, and Pitkin Pictorials, 1973)
Purvis, H. M., *A Score of Spooks* (1976)
Walwin, P. C., *Savernake Forest* (P. C. Walwin, 1976)
The Story of Stephen Langton and Silent Pool (Shere and District Rural Preservation Society)
Wiltshire, Kathleen, *Ghosts and Legends of the Wiltshire Countryside* (Compton Russell, 1973)

Index

Adam's Grave, 146–7
Albury, 160
Alfriston, 69
Alton Priors, 36, 146–8
Amesbury, 146
Angmering, 61
Anne Boleyn, 129
Ansty, 50–51
Appledore, 15, 44
Arlington, 74
Aubrey, John, 130
Avebury, 137–44
Avon, River, 147

Baker, Colin, 16
Baynard's Park, 172
Benenden, 10
Bethersden, 10
Bexley, 160–2
Biddenden, 10, 45
Binstead, I.O.W., 119
Bluebell Hill, 17–18
Bognor, 47–50, 83–7
Bonnie Prince Charlie, 168–9
Bordean House, Langrish, 112
Borley Rectory, Essex, 50
Bosworth Field, 150–1
Bramdean, 106
Brighton, 65
Broadstairs, 19
Buckingham, Duke of, 150
Buriton, 105
Buxted, 58

Canada, 102
Canterbury, 27–32, 35, 57, 159
Carson, Lord and Lady Edward, 33–4
Catherine of Aragon, 129
Cernunnos (Celtic god), 203
Chalton, 104–5
Charles I, King, 154, 202
—— II, King, 126
Chartham, 32
Chatham, 17
Cheney, Sir John, 150–1
Chiddingfold, 157–9

Chilham White Horse, 24–5
Cockpole Green, Reading, 197–8
Cowfold Monastery, 51
Cranleigh, 171
Croydon, 166
Cuckfield, 57–8

Deal, 19, 180
Devizes, 146
Dickens, Charles, 19
Domesday Book, 129
Dorking, 160–2, 195
Droxford, 108
Dunsfold, 171–2

Ealing, 174
Eastbourne, 68–9
East Meon, 109–10
East Preston, 64
Eastwell, 40
Ecclesden Manor, Angmering, 61–2
Edward VI, King, 159
Elizabeth I, Queen, 169
Enborne, 188–90
Enfield, 176–8, 181

Farnham, 152–4
Finchampstead, 195–7
Fitzherbert, Mrs, 107
Fotheringhay, 57
Freshwater, 116, 119
Fyfield Manor, Pewsey, 126

Gatcombe, 122
George III, King, 203
—— IV, King, 107
Glastonbury, 145
Godalming 168–71
Godmersham 25
Golden Hill Fort, 117–8
Goudhurst, 9–10, 42–3
Graylingwell, 78
Great Chart, Kent, 14
Greenford, 172–3
Grey, Lady Jane, 129
Grove Airfield, Wantage, 185–6

211

Guildford, 154–7
Gwynne, Nell, 126

Hamilton, Emma, 78, 171
Hayling Island, 88–92
Henley, 198
Henry VIII, King, 30, 63, 129, 132
Herne the Hunter, 203
Hinton Ampner, 106
Hothfield Common, 12–14
Hounslow, 175
Huguenots, 127
Huntingdonshire, 24
Hurstpierpoint, 60–1

India, 82
Isle of Wight, 113–23
Isleworth, 172

James I, King, 169
John, King, 159–60
John of Gaunt, 201

Kemsley Mill, 16
Kendon, Lady Kate, 107
Kennet, River, 137
King's House, Salisbury, 150
Kintbury, 190–4
Kirlian Photography, 56, 179
Knights Hospitallers, 56
Knowl Hill, 202

Lamberhurst, 9
Lambourn, 184
Langrish, 111–2
Littlecote Manor, 132–3
Littlewick Green, 198
Loseley Hall, 169–71

Mackenzie, Alexander, 34
— —, Andrew, 206
Maidstone, 17
Mapledurham, 195
Marden, 10
Marlborough, 125–6
Mee, Arthur, 40
Meon Valley, 107–8
Midhurst, 81–2
Minster, Cleve Court, 33–4
Montague, Nell St. John, 196
More, Sir Thomas, 169, 172
Mountbatten, Lady Iris, 196
Moyle, Sir Thomas, 40

Needles, The, 121
Newbury, 186–7
Northney, 89

Oare, 127
Odin, 203
Oglethorpe, General J. E., 168
Oldbury Camp, 146
Old Sarum, 149
Oundle, 20, 55
Oxford English Dictionary, 206

Penshurst Place, 22–3
Petersfield, 104
Petworth, 82
Pevensey Castle, 79
Pewsey, 126–8
Pilgrimage of Grace, 63
Pluckley, 10–12
Poling, 56
Poltergeists, 76–7, 164, 181–2
Portsmouth, 101
Preshute, 137
Price, Harry, 196
Puttenham, 154–155
Pyscombe, 61

Quakers, 127
Quennells, 155

Reading, 195
Recurrent Spontaneous Psychokinesis, 33, 77
Remenham, 198
Richard I, King, 159
— — II, King, 203
— — III, King, 41, 150–1
Ridgeway, The, 124, 131
Ripley, 171
Robert the Wizard, 13–14
Rochester, 17–18
Romsey, 107
Romney Marsh, 79
Rother, River, 79
Rye, 79–81

St. Helen's (I.O.W.), 113
St. Osmund's Shrine, 149–50
Salisbury, 149–50
Savernake Forest, 129–32
Seymour family, 129, 132
Shearwater, 136
Sheppard, Colonel L. E., 89–90
Shottenden, 10
Silbury, 139, 144–6

Sidney, Sir Philip, 122–3
Silent Pool, 159–60
Simon of Sudbury, 30
Sittingbourne, 16
Smarden, 37–40
Society for Psychical Research, 34
Southampton, 88
South Harting, Sussex, 78
Southwold, Suffolk, 55
Staines, 178–9
Steyning, Sussex, 53
Stockbridge, 107
Stonehenge, 124

Tenterden, 10
Thames Valley, 197–204
Thomas à Becket, 25, 28–30
Thornton Heath, 164–7

Uppark, 78
Urchfont Manor, 134–6

Wansdyke, 130–1, 145
Wantage, 185
Wargrave, 198–202
Warminster, 134
Waterlooville, 90, 93
Waverley Abbey, 152
Weaver's House, Canterbury, 30, 32
Wecock, 101–4
Wells, H. G., 82
West Sea House, 120–22
Westwell, 13–14
Wiltshire, Kathleen, 142, 145
Winchester, 88, 106, 151
Windsor, 202–4
Wiston, 53
Wolfhall, 129–30
Worcester Park, 163–4
World War II, 44–45
Wyatt, James, 149

Yarmouth (I.O.W.), 120

213